To the Cloud

FUNDED BY

AANAPISI

Asian American Native American Pacific Islander Serving Institution

MISSION COLLEGE

D1018810

TO THE CLOUD

BIG DATA IN A TURBULENT WORLD

VINCENT MOSCO

Paradigm Publishers
Boulder • London

All rights reserved. No part of this publication may be transmitted or reproduced in any media or form, including electronic, mechanical, photocopy, recording, or informational storage and retrieval systems, without the express written consent of the publisher.

Copyright © 2014 by Paradigm Publishers

Published in the United States by Paradigm Publishers, 5589 Arapahoe Avenue, Boulder, Colorado 80303 USA.

Paradigm Publishers is the trade name of Birkenkamp & Company, LLC, Dean Birkenkamp, President and Publisher.

Library of Congress Cataloging-in-Publication Data

Mosco, Vincent.
  To the cloud : big data in a turbulent world / Vincent Mosco.
    pages cm
  Includes bibliographical references and index.
  ISBN 978-1-61205-615-9 (hardcover : alk. paper)
  ISBN 978-1-61205-616-6 (pbk. : alk. paper)
  ISBN 978-1-61205-618-0 (consumer e-book)
  ISBN 978-1-61205-617-3 (library e-book)
  1. Cloud computing—Social aspects. 2. Big data—Social aspects. 3. Privacy, Right of. I. Title.
  QA76.9.C66M663 2014
  004.67'82—dc 3
                                                              2013046088
Printed and bound in the United States of America on acid-free paper that meets the standards of the American National Standard for Permanence of Paper for Printed Library Materials.

Designed and Typeset by Straight Creek Bookmakers.

18 17 16 15 14   5 4 3 2 1

With thanks to Louise

CONTENTS

ACKNOWLEDGMENTS

As always, I am grateful for the ideas, criticism, and suggestions of Catherine McKercher, my partner in life and in research. She helped make this a better book in more ways than I can count. Most importantly, Cathy's unconditional support and love are a continuing source of inspiration. Dan Schiller has been a dear friend for thirty-five years. We have met all over the world to provide the best help a friend can offer: constructive but candid assessments of each other's work. Shortly before starting to write this book, I met up with Dan in Santa Fe, New Mexico, and, after patiently hearing what I had in mind, he advised that I write a chapter on marketing the cloud. I am not sure how he will find the execution of his recommendation in Chapter 3, but I am very grateful for his creative suggestion and for sharing research material that has strengthened the book. Thanks also to Derek Morton for accompanying me on my search for the cloud in New York's Metropolitan Museum of Art, where his photography helped me to reflect on Tomás Saraceno's *Cloud City* long after we left the exhibition. Derek was also kind to remember me when he came across material useful for the book. When a Microsoft advertisement for cloud computing seemed to vanish from the Internet, Madeline Mosco tracked it down for me. Thank you, Madeline.

I am always especially grateful when former students learn about a new book project and take the time to send me useful reports or just share their views. Thank you, Rick Emrich, Pat Mazepa, Ian Nagy, and Alex

Savulescu. Likewise for current students I meet when lecturing on a topic like cloud computing. In this case, special thanks to Adeel Khamisa of Carleton University, as well as Laima Janciute and Emma Agusita, whom I met at the University of Westminster, London.

Lecturing provides a great opportunity to try out ideas and encounter new ones. I am grateful to Daniel Paré, who hosted a talk on cloud computing at the University of Ottawa; to Christian Fuchs, who organized my lecture at London's University of Westminster; and to Aliaa Dakoury, who kindly invited me to deliver a keynote address to the annual conference of the Global Communication Association.

I would also like to thank the Canada Research Chairs Program and Queen's University for providing research funding. Finally, I am grateful to the many people who made their mark on my thinking over the past forty years of research and teaching on communication and information technology.

CHAPTER 1
THE CLOUD ATE MY HOMEWORK

> Like water or electricity, cloud computing should now be considered a key utility and therefore should be available to all. (Groucutt 2013)

The Internet had been around for a while when on July 5, 1993, the *New Yorker* magazine featured a cartoon that, in the minds of some, marked its *real* arrival. "On the Internet," says the dog at the computer screen to his canine friend, "nobody knows you're a dog." I knew it was time to write this book when I woke up one morning, downloaded my digital edition of the October 8, 2012, *New Yorker*, and came across a new version of a classic cartoon. A little boy looks up at his teacher and, with hope and trepidation, pleads his case: "The cloud ate my homework." Okay, perhaps not everyone got the joke, but most readers would have some conception of the cloud as the place where data lives until it is called up on the computer, tablet, or smart phone—or, in the case of a malfunction, the place where data goes to die. This book explains what little Johnny is talking about and why it is important. For better or for worse, the cloud has arrived.

The cloud that ate Johnny's homework is a key force in the changing international political economy. The global expansion of networked data centers controlled by a handful of companies continues a process of building a global information economy, once characterized by Bill

Gates (1995) as "friction-free capitalism." Companies that once housed an information-technology department with its craft tradition can now move most of its work to the cloud, where IT functions and its labor are centralized in an industrial mode of production, processing, storage, and distribution. Furthermore, the cloud takes the next step in a long process of creating a global culture of knowing, captured in the term *big data*, or what might better be called *digital positivism*. Here information production accelerates in networks that link data centers, devices, organizations, and individuals appearing to create, in the words of one guru, "a global superintelligence" (Wolf 2010). The cloud and big data are engines that power informational capitalism even as they enable an increasingly dominant way of knowing. These interlinked processes and the challenges to them comprise the major themes of *To the Cloud*.

I have been thinking about cloud computing since 2010, when it began to enter public consciousness, particularly after a couple of splashy Super Bowl ads aired during the 2011 game. Then Apple got into the act when it urged users to move their photos, music, mail, and files to its iCloud. Not wanting to give up control over my stash of family photos and worried about the security of my mail, I resisted doing anything more than uploading a few incidentals (although for some reason I did not mind sending my photos into the cloud known as Flickr). Like many people, I was aware that some of my things were finding their way from my computer to remote servers, but this left me feeling a bit uncomfortable. Stories about cloud security breaches, disappearing data, and environmental risks at cloud data centers were making people feel that not all clouds were bright and only a few were green. But the migration of organizational and personal data continued, as did the marketing.

I decided to take a closer look when references to clouds of all sorts began to appear, partly prompted by the arrival of cloud computing and partly owing to my growing cloud-consciousness. First it was media attention to an obscure medieval treatise, *The Cloud of Unknowing*, that led me to wonder about the philosophical assumptions embedded in cloud computing. Then there was David Mitchell's strangely titled novel *Cloud Atlas* and the announcement of a blockbuster film based on the book's mystical account of souls migrating like clouds across time and space. I began collecting images of cloud data centers as they continued to spring up around the world, and was struck by the clash between the banality of their form—low-rise, endlessly bland warehouses—and the sublimity of real clouds. There is nothing ethereal about these buildings. Moreover, my reading and conversations pointed to growing tensions in the political, economic, social, and aesthetic dimensions of cloud computing. But at this early stage of its development, most extended treatments remained limited to technical descriptions.

Although cloud computing did not make an appearance on my personal radar screen until 2010, I have been researching, writing, and speaking about computer communication for forty years, including working on and around predecessors to cloud computing. In the early 1970s, as a graduate student in sociology at Harvard, I handed over my punch cards to the central computer facility and hoped to receive a paper printout of research results using my professor's pioneering General Inquirer software that, remarkably for its time, analyzed the content of text. At that time, we were all in the cloud because the personal computer, with its built-in storage device, was years away. All that we could do was find time to enter data in a computer terminal, appropriately referred to as dumb, and wait for the mainframe to provide results. Ten years later I wrote about the cloud of its time, videotex, which promised, and in rudimentary ways delivered, text and images from central computers to enhanced screens (Mosco 1982). Moving to Canada in 1984, I tried out Telidon, which Canadian technologists and policy makers insisted was the most advanced of the new interactive telecommunications services. More importantly, I learned about the research of Canadian Douglas Parkhill, whose work, particularly *The Challenge of the Computer Utility* (1966), is widely recognized as a forerunner to cloud computing.

Over that time, in addition to addressing many of the issues that are now emerging in cloud computing, I began to understand the importance of recognizing problems that inevitably arise from new systems for storing, processing, and exchanging information. It is tempting to apply what appear to be the lessons of history to new technologies and, while it is certainly wise to situate new technologies in their historical context, it is also essential to recognize that changing technologies and a changing world also bring about disruptions, disjunctions, and, sometimes, revolutions in historical patterns.

There are now numerous technical guides and primers that offer useful overviews of the subject, and my book is certainly indebted to these (Erl,

Puttini, and Mahmood 2013). But my purpose is to promote the discussion of cloud computing beyond what these texts have to say by taking up its political, economic, social, and cultural significance. In order to do this, the book draws from the transdisciplinary contributions to be found in technology studies, sociology, cultural studies, and political economy. My aim is to unsettle traditional ways of thinking with a critical interrogation. Sending data into the cloud is a decision to engage with one or another data center, say Amazon's or Microsoft's. But it is also a choice that has implications that are economic (who pays for it?), political (who controls it?), social (how private is it?), environmental (what is its impact on the land and on energy use?), and cultural (what values does it embody?). A key goal of the book is to advance a conversation between the professionals who work in the field, those responsible for promoting it, and the researchers, policy makers, and activists who study cloud computing and think about its impact, implications, and challenges.

Why is it necessary to place cloud computing in the bigger picture of political economy, society, and culture? Is it not sufficient to simply describe what cloud computing has to offer a business and weigh its costs and benefits? I take up some of the practical problems involved in adopting and implementing cloud systems in the next chapter. However, limiting discussion to this point alone does not give sufficient credit to the cloud computing movement as a force in society. Notwithstanding the hyperbole that accompanies new communication technologies and systems, from the telegraph that would bring together nations in peaceful harmony to the promise of mass education on television, cloud computing is having an enormous impact across societies. This extends from companies that are moving their data and business-process software to the cloud, to the military that plans and executes battle strategies in the cloud, to schools and universities that are using the cloud to transform education, and to individuals who are storing the traces of their identities in the cloud. It also encompasses what some consider bottom-up versions of cloud computing, such as community grid projects that harness the combined power of personal computers to carry out public-interest research. The cloud is credited with catapulting companies like Apple into the corporate stratosphere. Amazon's cloud was one of the most important instruments behind Barack Obama's 2012 victory. While these are important developments, they are benign compared to the claim that the cloud can save capitalism by powering it to renewed heights of productivity, or the opposite expectation that it will open the door to carefully planned hacker attacks that will disrupt the world economy. Are China and Iran trying to bring America's financial system to the digital brink? Or, as China claims, is the United States becoming a major "hacking empire"?

Since exaggerated promises typically accompany the rise of new technical systems, it is easy to dismiss today's hype about cloud computing, but that would be wrong. This is not because the stories about a cloud-computing and big-data revolution, with their visions of boundless economic prosperity, are any more accurate than promises of world peace in the age of radio. Rather, the marketing hype supports myths that are taken seriously as storylines for our time. If successful, they become common sense, the bedrock of seemingly unchallengeable beliefs that influence not only how we think about cloud computing, but about technology in general and our relationship to it. The decision to give up your own or your organization's data to a cloud company is a significant one and companies promoting the technology would understandably have us focus on its benefits. Moreover, it is important to take the hype seriously as the mythic embodiment of what, in an earlier book, I called the digital sublime, the tendency of technology, in this case computer communication, to take on a transcendent role in the world beyond the banality of its role in everyday life (Mosco 2004). It is time to give cloud computing its due by starting a conversation about its place in society and culture.

Cloud computing is a significant development in its own right and a prism through which to view problems facing societies confronting the turbulent world of information technology. The cloud has deep historical roots and it is important to consider them, but it also has new features that require a close look at what makes cloud systems quantitatively and qualitatively different. Moreover, cloud computing serves as a prism that reflects and refracts every major issue in the field of information technology and society, including the fragile environment, ownership and control, security and privacy, work and labor, the struggles among nations for dominance in the global political economy, and how we make sense of this world in discourse and in cultural expression.

Chapter 2 tells the story of cloud computing, from its origins in the 1950s concept of the computer utility to the present-day giant data centers that fill vast open spaces everywhere in the world. Back in the 1950s, as even most casual histories of cloud computing describe, debates over the need for a "computer utility" anticipated today's debates about the cloud. At that time, people who were familiar with utilities that provided roads, water, and electricity wondered whether there was need for a public or regulated utility for computer communication. Was not information as essential a resource as roads, water, and power? With widespread agreement that it was both a resource and essential, some concluded that a handful of centralized computer facilities strategically located around the world and connected by telecommunications networks to keyboards and screens would satisfy the world's need for information. Today, there are far more than a handful of large data centers worldwide, but the principle of the utility is inscribed in cloud computing systems to the point that interest is returning to this venerable idea. Questions are also emerging about whether computer utilities should be government enterprises, or at least publicly regulated even if they remain commercial enterprises.

Chapter 2 examines a variety of the cloud's predecessors from when the computer utility was young. The Soviet Union staked much of its economic strategy in the 1950s on the ability to build large-scale "cybernetic" systems to carry out the work of a planned economy. In the 1970s the Chilean government experimented on a democratic version of such a strategy, with workers on the ground contributing to the economic-planning process through computer systems. The 1980s saw the development of government and commercial systems for providing information on demand through what were called teletext and videotex systems. Their full potential was not realized until the Internet appeared on desktop computers and in *New Yorker* cartoons in the 1990s.

Chapter 2 proceeds to define cloud computing and take up its diverse forms and characteristics. Cloud computing has been defined in many ways, but most would agree that it is a powerful system for producing, storing, analyzing, and distributing data, information, applications, and services to organizations and individuals. If you communicate with Gmail, download music from iCloud, buy Kindle books from Amazon, or if your company uses Salesforce to manage its customer database, then you know about and use the cloud. Among its major characteristics, cloud computing enables on-demand self-service access to information and services delivered over global networks—including, but not limited to, the public networks of the Internet. Information and applications can be pooled to meet user needs, provided and withdrawn on demand, and paid through measured service billing. The chapter describes the range of cloud computing forms from the simple provision of an infrastructure, such as a data storage center, to services that include applications, software, and analytics that add value to data. It also considers types of cloud computing from public clouds that are available to all paying customers, a rather limited meaning of the term "public," to private clouds that sell storage and services only to a select set of customers who prefer their data gated and secure, and hybrid clouds that offer combinations of the two.

The chapter examines the leading cloud companies, including the well-known firms that grew up in the Internet era, helped to create social media, and are now serving companies and individuals in the cloud. Amazon is arguably the leading cloud-computing provider, but the list of familiar names also includes Microsoft, Google, Apple, and Facebook. In addition, legacy firms such as IBM, Oracle, and Cisco are trying to make the transition to the cloud after years of success servicing corporate and government IT departments. Then there are the companies born in cloud, such as Rackspace, Salesforce, and VMware, that provide general and specialized cloud-computing and big-data services. Chapter 2 covers the battles among key competitors and the growing concentration of power at the top of the industry. Private firms dominate the cloud, but the U.S. government is helping to shape its expansion primarily through partnerships with leading companies, mainly in the military and intelligence sectors but also in education, including the humanities. This is leading some to wonder about the rise of a military information complex that promotes the power of a handful of companies and the expansion of the surveillance state, best typified by the National Security Agency. The U.S. cloud industry is powerful, but it is increasingly challenged by foreign competitors—especially China, which is constructing entire cloud cities to close the gap with the United States.

There is a massive, worldwide movement to promote cloud computing, and Chapter 3 examines its many forms. The campaign includes advertising, blogs, the reports of corporate research and consulting firms, international economic-policy organizations, lobbying campaigns, conferences, and trade fairs. Having begun in the banality of a technical diagram and in the hazy visions of computer pioneers, the image of the cloud has taken on a richer aesthetic in the hands of today's Mad Men, the advertising gurus marketing the next new thing. In this respect, the materiality of the cloud is not limited to buildings, computers, software, and data. It is also embodied in campaigns to remake the prosaic stuff of engineering into the compelling image of the cloud. There was no magic in how this happened. To bring the cloud into widespread awareness it took marketing campaigns that developed from Salesforce's two very expensive advertisements featured in the 2011 Super Bowl game; they highlighted the singer Will.i.am of the Black Eyed Peas and the animated character Chatty "the magical cloud." Laying the groundwork for this big splash was IBM's foray into cloud marketing with its 2010 "smart cloud" campaign pitched to corporate decision makers, and Microsoft's "To the Cloud" advertisements aimed at small business and consumers. Apple joined the chorus in a big way by changing the name of its online service, which began as ".mac," shifted to the personal (and, some would say, self-absorbed) ".me," and then settled on iCloud.

Commercial advertising is important to reach both institutional and individual customers. However, it is only one part of a circuit of promotion that also includes blogs, newsletters, and social-media sites that provide information about the industry with an emphasis on how to sell cloud computing by countering its critics and advancing its benefits. One of their most important functions is to serve as a transmission belt for the findings of more legitimate outlets like the reports of private research and consulting firms, including Gartner, McKinsey, Deloitte, and Forrester. Each of these leaders in the field has produced one or more reports on cloud computing and big data. With the exception of one, which appeared early (and was nullified by a later report by the same company), they are all massively optimistic in their forecasts about the cloud. The message is simple: move to the cloud. Although their reports are expensive, the essential findings and the enthusiasm, as Chapter 3 demonstrates, circulate through the hundreds of blogs and newsletters that share the enthusiasm. The circuit of promotion expands internationally with reports that bring together global players in business and government to promote the cloud. Chapter 3 concentrates on a report produced by the World Economic Forum, best known for the annual Davos conference, that documents the unassailable significance of information technology, cloud computing, and big-data analytics. With the stamp of global legitimacy and the blessing of national and international government agencies, as well as corporate participants, the World Economic Forum adds to the legitimacy of the cloud as the leading-edge force for the expansion of the world economy. The chapter concludes by examining two more vital elements in this circuit of promotion, lobbying, and trade shows. For most of its history, especially since the development of the Internet, the information-technology industry has not invested significant resources to lobby Washington. In recent years, but especially with the growth of social media and the cloud, all of that has changed, and Chapter 3 demonstrates the importance of lobbying at the local, national, and international levels of power. Finally, trade shows and conferences bring the major cloud and big-data players together to promote their products, the industry, and the myth of the cloud as a transcendent force to solve the world's problems. This section draws from my participation in the largest annual cloud-computing conference and sales event, Cloud Computing Expo 2013 in New York City.

Chapter 4 explains why a massive promotional effort is essential. Cloud computing faces serious problems because it puts great stress on the environment, requires significant power supplies, threatens privacy, is difficult to secure, and challenges the future of IT work. These problems, understandably, receive little attention in the promotional accounts addressed in Chapter 3. When discussed, they are typically dismissed out of hand or framed in the context of how to counter arguments against moving to the cloud because of these problems. Chapter 4 demonstrates why, contrary to the claims made in the promotional culture, it is important to give them careful attention.

Cloud companies promise, and their customers expect, that data centers will operate with no down time. This alone makes enormous demands on the electrical grid, but the demand increases substantially because servers require a constant source of cooling to avoid overheating. Moreover, 24/7 operation makes it necessary to build backup power sources like diesel generators and chemical batteries that create significant environmental problems for the communities that host data centers. Moving to the cloud is far from entering the ethereal, weightless, and green environment that the image of the physical cloud and the mythology of cloud computing suggest. The next dark cloud to appear, in Chapter 4, is the threat to privacy and security. After examining a range of ways to think about privacy and security, it takes up three major problems, starting with the multiplication of hacking attacks against cloud computing systems emanating from within and outside the borders of companies offering cloud services. Cyber-attacks have become an instrument of government policy. Furthermore, privacy and security are challenged by the nature of what I call *surveillance capitalism*. A significant source of revenue in the cloud and big data is the opportunity to market information about subscribers and customers to advertisers. For example, Facebook could not survive as a commercial enterprise without the ability to exercise close surveillance on its 1.3 billion users. Alongside surveillance capitalism is the *surveillance state*, which, as the revelations about the National Security Agency revealed, has almost complete access to data stored in the cloud and delivered over the Internet and other electronic networks. It is no wonder that institutions of all sorts, as well as individual consumers, are increasingly worried about the security implications of moving to the cloud, whether the data centers are located in China, Europe, or the United States.

One of the primary reasons for moving to the cloud is to streamline, if not entirely eliminate, an organization's IT department, amounting to an emerging dark cloud for professional labor. But the issue is not limited to IT. Specialized cloud companies like Salesforce can take over the management of customer relations, thereby freeing firms to cut back on their in-house sales and marketing activities. Moreover, since the preponderance of knowledge labor increasingly involves IT work, whether in education, journalism, or health care, this dark cloud now hovers over a large segment of the occupational world. Chapter 4 documents these developments and situates them within a dynamic international division of labor in the information-technology industries where chains of accumulation meet chains of resistance, from Foxconn in Shenzhen to Apple in Cupertino. As more organizations and individuals decide to enter the cloud, will the global system that supports it remain intact? What happens if it ruptures?

Chapter 5 concludes the book by shifting to the cultural significance of cloud computing. It is guided by the view that culture resists essentialisms of all types, including the tendency in the digital world, now embodied in cloud computing, to reduce the cloud to an information repository and the foundation for the digital positivism of big-data analysis. It starts to pursue this theme by considering what we can learn from the movement to use the cloud for large-scale data analysis—what has been called big data. The chapter assesses the assumptions and components of big data, including a reliance on quantitative, correlational analysis, free from theoretical considerations and aiming to predict events. Many of big data's proponents fervently believe that the data will speak for itself, enabling researchers to eschew qualitative data (or try to render it in quantities) and end reliance on causality, theory, and history, the traditional bedrock of social scientific analysis. Concluding that a technical critique, however useful, is insufficient to address the philosophical grounding of what is primarily a digital positivism, the chapter draws from the culture of clouds to take up the specific way of knowing that underlies big-data analysis. This matters because every technology contains an aesthetic, a way of seeing and feeling, that is drawn from the machine's design—as well as from its discursive associations. Cloud computing is no exception. The simple schematic diagram of a network of clouds that gave rise to the term presents a well-ordered, natural, and benign way to think about it that is challenged by the culture of clouds, a subterranean stream of thought that provides a powerful counterweight to digital positivism.

From the early days of the Internet, supporters were not shy about dressing it up in the language of philosophy and even mysticism. For example, many big names, including such luminaries as Al Gore and Tom Wolfe, praised the Jesuit priest Pierre Teilhard de Chardin (who was also a philosopher, paleontologist, and poet) as a cyberspace visionary. He never used a computer and died in 1955, but *Wired* magazine exclaimed, "Teilhard saw the Net coming more than half a century before it arrived" (Kreisberg 1995). Although he predicted nothing about computers and wrote in the impenetrable language of a mystic, the Jesuit priest appealed to cyber-gurus and others because he saw information as the leading force in cosmic evolution. For Teilhard, the growth of information literally produced an atmosphere of thought, what he called the *noosphere*, which encircled the globe, putting increasing pressure on the planet. Eventually, the pressure of information would create a massive explosion, taking humankind into the next phase of cosmic evolution. However bizarre the image and however it clashes with everything we know about physics, there are few more dramatic ways to mythologize the burgeoning digital world than with a *cloud of knowing* pointing the way to progress.

However, other voices in the culture of clouds answer, "not so fast." There is more to the metaphor of the cloud than capturing the sublimity of cloud computing. In its rich history, that metaphor contains a critique that challenges utopian visions finding transcendence, if not the divine, in new technology. Considering its ubiquitous presence and persistence throughout time, it is no surprise to find the cloud in many expressions of the human imagination. The written word, music, and the visual arts would be much poorer without the metaphorical cloud. From the broad sweep of the cloud in culture, I have chosen three exemplars from vastly different periods in Western society to document contrasts between the metaphor and the information technology that would adopt it.

It begins with *The Clouds*, a comedy written by Aristophanes that satirized intellectual life in fifth-century-BC Greece. It raises a clear, and humorous, challenge to the adamantly rational model of thought that the cloud and big data embody, and questions the inherent superiority of the seemingly apolitical philosopher-technician. Its chorus of clouds reminds audiences to this day that even the most seemingly objective of intellectuals, in this case the great philosopher Socrates, is embedded in a political world where practical experience often trumps technical knowledge. For the Greek playwright, the way of knowing established 2,500 years ago comes not in the form of the intellectual living a life of contemplation in the clouds of abstraction. That was little more than a Platonic aspiration. Rather it is the philosopher-trickster, the intellectual spin doctor, who dominates with rhetoric and propaganda seasoned with just enough information. In the Western way of knowing, there is no pure truth stored and processed in the cloud—just the ongoing struggle between reason and rhetoric. It is a message that today's philosopher kings, the computer gurus and data scientists that live in our new cloud, would benefit from hearing.

Next, we move ahead to the last half of the fourteenth century AD and *The Cloud of Unknowing*, the work of an English monk who advises a young monk on how to live a good, moral life. Although written in the Middle English of the time, it is not an obscure work today. There are numerous contemporary translations and it has received attention from such literary giants as Don DeLillo, who uses it in his magisterial novel *Underworld*. What makes this book most interesting is its use of the cloud as a symbol of what gets in the way and blocks people from knowing themselves and realizing their destiny. As one would expect, *The Cloud of Unknowing* is written in a religious idiom. For the unknown writer of this spiritual guide, the goal is to come as close as possible to god. But just as one does not have to accept Teilhard's god, the god of perfect information, we do not have to believe in the monk's god in order to appreciate the point that the cloud of information that increasingly saturates our world can get in the way of fulfillment, spiritual or otherwise. Writing in strong yet conversational language, the elder monk advises the neophyte to empty himself of information in order to grow as a person. The cloud that appears so attractive is actually a deterrent to wisdom, a cloud of unknowing.

The Cloud of Unknowing bears the imprint of Eastern philosophy, making it all the more remarkable that it comes from the work of a medieval English monk whose world had been shaken by the Black Plague. The view that we need to empty ourselves of what passes for knowledge in order to achieve true wisdom and fulfillment is increasingly popular in the West, where people appear to be overwhelmed by data, even as they work to figure out the latest device that promises instant connection to the digital world. My reason for analyzing it in the final section of this book is to address the conflicted nature of our thinking and feeling about the cloud. Cloud culture is a contested terrain featuring different views about epistemology (what it means to know), metaphysics (what it means to be), and moral philosophy (what it means to live ethically).

One of the most interesting cultural expressions of uncertainty is contained in David Mitchell's novel *Cloud Atlas*, which became a feature film directed by the team responsible for the *Matrix* trilogy. The title itself presents a jarring clash because the traditional atlas is meant to chart fixed geographical forms such as oceans and landmasses, not the constantly changing mists of water vapor. The cloud is anything but a fixed entity and defies conventional mapping, something that is borne out in the plot of *Cloud Atlas* as we follow the six separate stories that take both book and film over several centuries. For Mitchell and the film's trio of producers, the cloud represents neither the certainty of information nor the barrier to perfection, but the wispy and vaporous connections that link people over generations. The variety of structured and random actions that propel people through life touches those who come after them, so here mapping the cloud becomes telling the stories of their connections not in the network diagram of cloud computing, but in the much looser but no-less-powerful image of the material cloud. This atlas of clouds rethinks the conventional atlas by mapping connections in time and not just in space. For these reasons, *Cloud Atlas* offers one alternative for how to think about cloud culture that does not simply require a choice between the cloud of knowing and of unknowing.

This book concludes by taking up artistic manifestations of these ideas in cloud culture, one of whose icons is René Magritte's *The Empire of Light*, a painting that features the bright blue of a daytime sky filled with puffy white clouds that oversee a row of houses in nighttime darkness. Something is awry in the clouds and on the ground. Taking a different perspective is a contemporary work, Tomás Saraceno's remarkable installation *Cloud City*, an assemblage of large, interconnected modules built with transparent and reflective materials that occupied the roof garden of the Metropolitan Museum of Art for six months in 2012. We call on Magritte to question the seeming harmony of cloud networks and on Saraceno to see ourselves in the reflecting glass of his cloud. Where are we in cloud computing? Some artists are beginning to address this issue directly by producing work about cloud computing. For that we consider Tamiko Thiel, whose installation *Clouding Green* depicts differently colored clouds that hover over eight major Silicon Valley cloud-computing providers to describe their environmental record. These surreal representations draw from and add aesthetic power to a 2012 Greenpeace environmental assessment, "How Clean Is Your Cloud?"

To the Cloud recognizes that it is time to move beyond technical descriptions of cloud computing by producing a critical assessment. To begin the process, the next chapter explores the origins of cloud computing in visions of the computer utility. It proceeds to examine the principles that distinguish cloud computing, describes what cloud computing actually does, and maps the state of the cloud-computing industry.

CHAPTER 2
FROM THE COMPUTER UTILITY
TO CLOUD COMPUTING

We are on a shift that is as momentous and as fundamental as
the shift to the electrical grid. It's happening a lot faster than
any of us thought.
—Arthur R. Jassy, head of Amazon
Web Services (Hardy 2012a)

Most general accounts of cloud computing attribute the use of the cloud
image to its appearance in diagrams that identify key elements in a telecommunications network. The term *cloud computing* emerged in 1996
when technology leaders with Compaq, then a major desktop-computer
company, met to discuss the future of computing and especially the Internet. Specifically, they hoped that "cloud computing–enabled applications"
would boost sales. Although not entirely clear about this, they concluded
that online consumer file storage would likely be among the successful
applications. Their prescience was rewarding for the company because it
contributed to Compaq's decision to start selling servers to Internet service
providers, which became a $2 billion annual business for the company.
However beneficial for Compaq, which HP bought in 2002, the server
decision was not as successful for one of the meeting's participants, Sean

O'Sullivan, who went on to start a less than successful firm selling file storage and video-on-demand to individual customers. It was just too early for this cloud to rain dollars, even on innovators with foresight. The genuine growth of the cloud awaited the expansion in computer processing power and in telecommunications networks, as well as a general economic recovery following the dot-com collapse of the early 2000s. It was not until 2006 that the term cloud computing came into more general use as companies, led by Google, Dell, and Amazon, started using the term to describe a new system for accessing files, software, and computer power over the Internet instead of from a computer's own hard drive or some other portable storage mechanism (Regalado 2011).

Defining Cloud Computing

There are those who believe that the first use of the term in the twenty-first century was by Eric Schmidt, Google's CEO, when he described the cloud at an August 9, 2006, industry conference: "What's interesting [now] is that there is an emergent new model. I don't think people have really understood how big this opportunity really is. It starts with the premise that the data services and architecture should be on servers. We call it cloud computing—they should be in a 'cloud somewhere.'" The PC maker Dell saw marketing value in the term, and in 2008 the company tried to secure a trademark for "cloud computing." That attempt, which upset many in the industry, ultimately failed. As a result, anyone was free to use the term and many companies decided that the cloud was a great way to capture the next stage in the development of online services (Regalado 2011).

There is no generally accepted definition of cloud computing. Indeed, one overview suggests that twenty-five cloud pundits would likely define it in twenty-five different ways (McFedries 2012). An entrepreneur who teaches programmers how to use the cloud describes it as "a metaphor for the Internet. It's a rebranding of the Internet. That is why there is a raging debate. By virtue of being a metaphor, it's open to different interpretations." But the debate continues because "it's worth money" (Regalado 2011). Most cloud analysts do not equate the Internet with cloud computing. Although cloud systems use the network of networks we know as the

FROM THE COMPUTER UTILITY TO CLOUD COMPUTING 17

Internet to transmit data and applications, they also make use of private networks that may be linked to the Internet but are separate from it and accessible to only a fraction of users. Moreover, since cloud computing also involves the customized provision of applications and services, it is generally considered to be more than a network of networks. Although the cloud as a defining concept may eventually withdraw into the powerful banality of technologies like electricity, most agree that it has not yet reached the sweet spot of generic universality (Linthicum 2013e).

As of 2013, years after cloud computing began to circulate in public discourse and well after the first mass advertising, including two commercials that aired during the 2011 Super Bowl, Americans remained unclear about what it means. A survey of 1,000 adults carried out in August 2012 suggested that few people had even a rough idea of what cloud computing means. Nevertheless, most indicated that they expect to be working "in the cloud" in the future and, when they had it explained, demonstrated savvy in understanding its potential problems—primarily price, security, and privacy (*Forbes* 2012).

When the U.S. government decided that cloud computing might be a cost-effective way to deliver services, it pushed departments to consider a move to the cloud. However, when department heads expressed little knowledge of cloud computing, the government's chief information officer asked the National Institute of Standards and Technology (NIST) to come up with a definition and description (Regalado 2011). So the closest we have to a generally accepted formal definition is, in the words of a NIST report, "a model for enabling ubiquitous, convenient, on demand network access to a shared pool of configurable computing resources (e.g., networks, servers, storage, applications, and services) that can be rapidly provisioned and released with minimal management effort or service provider interaction" (Mell and Grance 2011). To put it in plainer language, cloud computing involves the storage, processing, and distribution of data, applications, and services for individuals and organizations. It is generally viewed as the fastest-growing, or near the fastest-growing, segment of the IT sector, even though in 2012 it represented only 3 percent of all IT spending (Butler 2012b). NIST's definition of cloud computing has been widely accepted throughout the industry as an objective description of the service. But it is important to understand that cloud-computing descriptions, however objective in appearance, are typically conflated with promotion. Whether it is the federal government's chief information officer, NIST, or the National Science Foundation, which in 2012 announced its own commitment to fund cloud-computing research, the goal is to promote the cloud and not just to understand it. So along with the clear definition, NIST proclaims, "The Cloud Computing model offers the promise of massive cost savings combined with increased IT agility. It is considered critical that government and industry begin adoption of this technology in response to difficult economic constraints" (NIST 2013).

The Early Cloud: The Computer Utility and Videotex

To deepen understanding of what cloud computing means, it is useful to consider how it is both an extension of earlier forms of computer communication and, at least in scale, a new development in the use of information technology. In the 1950s, the computer scientist Herb Grosch forecast a world that would share computing resources so that no more than fifteen data centers would be needed to meet the world's information needs. In the 1960s, the concept of the computer utility emerged when Stanford IT expert John McCarthy imagined "computation as a public utility" (C. Ross 2012). This was formalized in 1966 with the publication of Douglas Parkhill's widely read book *The Challenge of the Computer Utility*. Why is it useful to think of cloud computing as a utility? In part it is because some specialists see the cloud as little more than an extension of the computer-utility concept, once referred to as "time-sharing," because usage time on a central computer was shared by multiple users. For example, according to Linthicum, "If you think you've seen this movie before, you are right. Cloud computing is based on the time-sharing model we leveraged years ago before we could afford our own computers. The idea is to share computing power among many companies and people, thereby reducing the cost of that computing power to those who leverage it. The value of time share and the core value of cloud computing are pretty much the same, only the resources these days are much better and more cost effective" (cited in McKendrick 2013a).

Most people are familiar with public utilities for resources like roads, water, and electricity, which provide services to the public over an infrastructure that utilities manage and operate. They can be owned by government or by private enterprise but when it is the latter, utilities are typically subject to some form of local (city, community) or regional (state, county, province) regulation. Without entering the dense thicket of debate over whether they provide a net public benefit over a competitive market arrangement or whether the government-owned or private utility is best, it is sufficient to state that the utility arrangement is typically chosen because it is expensive to build the infrastructure for water and power. When governments conclude that duplicating infrastructure so numerous competitors can enter the market will likely waste resources, they declare a "natural monopoly" and establish a public utility.

As the concepts associated with computer technology, among them cybernetics, information processing, and communication flows, attracted the attention of a wider circle of scholars and policy makers in the 1950s and '60s, some began to think of information as a resource not unlike water and power. The shift from analog to digital methods of processing information provided a tangible or material output that made it easier to think of information in resource terms. The mathematicians Claude Shannon and Warren Weaver (1949) built a widely accepted model of communication flows that emphasized the materiality of communication over the abstract senders and receivers through which communication flowed. They were less concerned with the social forces that made some people senders and some receivers than they were with identifying communication as a tangible flow. When the economists Dallas Smythe and Herbert Schiller began to turn their attention to communication in the 1950s and '60s, they drew connections between their new field of study and the resources, like agriculture and oil, that had occupied economists for many years (Mosco 2009, 82–89). Around this time the computer scientist turned public-policy analyst Anthony Oettinger developed a general resource theory that linked energy and materials to information, and it became the conceptual foundation for the Harvard University Program on Information Resources Policy, which Oettinger chaired for several decades. When the communication scholar Marc Uri Porat (1977) published his influential map of the shift to an economy powered by information workers, it became time to think about an information economy.

These developments gave renewed force to a view that had been debated since the emergence of postal communication and extended to electronic communication technologies, starting with the telegraph and repeated with the telephone, radio, and television. Is it appropriate and useful to employ the concept of a resource to identify the product of these devices and, if so, should this resource be organized in the form of a utility? Over the years, different constellations of political forces produced different policy responses to these questions. But with the foundation of thinking, for example, about the provision of telephone service as a "natural monopoly," experts examining the output of computer technology began to wonder whether the resources propelling the information economy were creating the need for a new utility.

Advancing this discussion of how to organize information resources, Douglas Parkhill wrote about the challenges facing what he foresaw as the coming computer utility. From the start Parkhill recognized that the idea of organizing computer systems as a utility was in the air: "Even now the subject of computer utilities is very much in the public eye, as evidenced by many articles in both the popular and technical press, prognostications by leading industrial and scientific figures and growing signs of interest on the part of governments everywhere" (1966, v). Parkhill took this popular idea and gave it the clear definition and specificity required to move it forward. For him, there were five key components to the computer or information utility:

1. Essentially simultaneous use of the system by many remote users
2. Concurrent running of multiple programs
3. Availability of at least the same range of facilities and capabilities at the remote stations as the user would expect from a private computer
4. A system of pricing based upon a flat service charge and a variable charge based on usage
5. Capacity for indefinite growth, so that as the customer load increases, the system can be expanded without limit by various means

Parkhill envisioned the computer utility to be a public service in the sense that it would make available to anyone, wherever located, a wide range of information resources and services in an online form. With that said, he did not make a commitment to any specific management form, but rather addressed the merits of public, private, and mixed systems because "it is necessary to consider each application of computer utility separately on its merits and balance off in each case the gains and losses resulting from the adoption of the utility concept" (1966, 125). Elements changed as yesterday's computer utility became today's cloud-computing system, but it is worthwhile to reflect on how much of Parkhill's thought is repeated in today's discussions of cloud services. We are now more likely to ask if a system is scalable rather than if it has the "capacity for infinite growth," but new terms should not mask the striking conceptual similarities. Parker would go on to play an important role in implementing his vision of the computer utility through the creation of what bore the discernible yet odd name of *videotex*. This was a computer-based service that delivered information from a central facility to users at terminals in their homes, in public places, and, to a lesser degree, in businesses. Users were able to interact with the service by making specific information requests. Parker helped bring about the most advanced of these systems in a Canadian government-sponsored project named Telidon. Because its use of color images and its processing demands outstripped the capacity of the existing telecommunications network, the system did not advance far out of the starting gate. Nevertheless, simpler systems featuring more manageable services were widely distributed. The best known of these, France's Minitel service, brought terminals to libraries, post offices, and other public places, providing users with basic information like the telephone directory, train schedules, information on government services, stock quotes, and the opportunity to chat with fellow users and have messages delivered to a "mail box." The service provided millions of connections each month and was not retired until 2012 (Sayare 2012). Videotex held great promise as report after report predicted major transformations in every aspect of life, with comparisons made to the automobile and the television (Tydeman et al. 1982).

Videotex was only one of many cloudlike services that emerged in the pre-Internet decades. In fact, what is very interesting to observe, and often lost in the linear histories that see the past as simple precursor to the present, are the vast arrays of different applications that arose under the resource/utility umbrella. Consider the atlas of clouds represented by the Soviet Union's cybernetic systems of the 1960s, Chile's experiment to bring about computerized workplace democracy and economic planning in the 1970s, and the Pentagon's development of a research computer network that helped to create the Internet from the 1970s to the early 1990s.

Cybernetics in the Soviet Union

In spite of World War II's devastating impact, the Soviet Union produced leaders in the burgeoning field of cybernetics, formally the science of communication and control in machines and animals. In the West, the computer scientist Norbert Wiener led the field of luminaries, with a stellar group that in 1953 included John von Neumann, Claude Shannon, William Ross Ashby, Gregory Bateson, and Roman Jakobson, who met regularly under the auspices of the Macy Foundation from 1946 to 1953. Rebelling against established approaches to theory and applied science, they transformed established disciplines and helped to create new ones. Little was left untouched in fields as diverse as biology, communication studies, computer science, linguistics, and psychology. It might only be the gentlest of overstatements to conclude that cybernetics became a Holy Grail of general theory that many believed would revolutionize human thought (Parkman 1972).

These ideas slowly simmered in Soviet science, permitting quiet questioning of rigid theory enshrined in the work of Trofim Lysenko in biology and Ivan Pavlov in psychology while Joseph Stalin retained his iron grip on power. But when Nikita Krushchev consolidated his control as Premier in 1958, change accelerated and the cybernetics that had been officially denounced as "not only an ideological weapon of imperialist reaction but also a tool for accomplishing its aggressive military plans" was by 1961 hailed as the primary technical means to realize the Communist ideal (Gerovitch 2010). In that year the Soviet Academy of Sciences published *Cybernetics in the Service of Communism*, a detailed examination of how cybernetics would transform practically every field of knowledge and application, but especially, to the pleasure of the representatives meeting that year in the Twenty-Second Congress of the Communist Party, the modern Soviet economy.

For its supporters, economic cybernetics would demonstrate the superiority of the Soviet system by applying the new science to the new technology of powerful computers to precisely plan for the production and distribution of goods and services throughout the Soviet Union. In 1962 the chairman of the U.S.S.R.'s Academy Council on Cybernetics made the importance of the marriage between cybernetics and economic planning absolutely clear when he declared that "However unusual this may sound to some conservatives who do not wish to comprehend elementary truths, *we will be building communism on the basis of the most broad use of electronic machines*, capable of processing enormous amounts of technological, economic, and biological information in the shortest time. These machines, *aptly called 'cybernetic machines', will solve the problem of continuous optimal planning and control*" (ibid.). In effect, these words announced the birth of the Soviet computer utility. A network of computer centers would be built across the vast expanse of the U.S.S.R., through which a continuous stream of data would flow from shops, factories, and offices. Planners would use the data to assess the success or failure of policies and to plan, in the most minute detail, future economic activity. Regional computer centers would link up in a nationwide network under the auspices of the Central Economic Mathematical Institute, giving the country "a single automated system of control of the national economy" (ibid.; Spufford 2010). This was a plan for state-directed cloud computing in the service of central economic planning, and U.S. intelligence services—already worried about the growth of Soviet military might—feared what might result.

The CIA responded in 1962 by setting up a special unit to study the threat posed by the Soviet cybernetics initiative. One of the most remarkable conclusions drawn from the spy agency's investigation was the expectation, and consequent unease with the idea, that the Soviet plan would actually succeed. According to its task force report, "tremendous increments in economic productivity as the result of cybernetization of production may permit disruption of world markets" (Gerovitch 2010). The CIA concluded that economic success would bring an additional threat: "The creation of a model society and the socio-economic demoralization of the West will be the added ideological weapon" (ibid.). So concerned was the intelligence agency that it continued to discuss the issue with Kennedy administration officials in the period leading up to and throughout the 1962 Cuban Missile Crisis. The president's people were equally worried. In a memo to Attorney General Robert Kennedy, Arthur Schlesinger Jr., historian and special assistant to the president, concluded that the "all-out Soviet commitment to cybernetics" would give the Soviets "a tremendous advantage" and that "by 1970 the USSR may have a radically new production technology, involving total enterprises or complexes of industries, managed by closed-loop, feedback control employing self-teaching computers." Pulling no punches, he concluded that if the United States continued to neglect cybernetics, "we are finished" (ibid.).

Even discounting for the hyperbole that often accompanies the effort to convince those in power to take action, Schlesinger's statement and those of the CIA amount to a declaration that the Soviets' early version of the cloud, with its central planning through cybernetics, would work and might very well defeat the United States. The furor continued as President Kennedy set up a task force to examine the threat of Soviet cybernetics and the CIA continued to sound the alarm. The U.S. military got into the act, too, with the commander of the Air Force Foreign Technology division alarmed that "the system could be imposed upon us from an authoritarian, centralized, cybernated, world-powerful command and control center in Moscow" (ibid.).

As with many U.S. assessments of the Soviet threat, these fears proved exaggerated. Only a small fraction of the Soviet program was implemented because the government diverted available resources to the military, which steadfastly refused to share them with what top commanders believed was the useless project of the economic cyberneticians. This cloud did not vaporize overnight, however. The Soviet Union's cybernetics team was able to patch together a semblance of a computer system for planning and allocating resources, producing less than a robust network, more mist than cloud. Moreover, it took a national network of human "fixers" whose job it was to use whatever means necessary to keep chains of production and distribution working, or, at least, keep them from seizing up entirely, so that the façade of central planning through cybernetics and what Francis Spufford (2010) called the belief in "Red Plenty" could be maintained.

The Soviet Union's dalliance with an early version of cloud computing demonstrated both the potential and the pitfalls of using it for national economic planning. Most analysts have understandably focused on negative lessons, including some combination of the inherent difficulty of developing a cloud model for a massively complex economy, the structural problems built into the Soviet system, and the recognition that computers were not nearly advanced enough to carry the load. Scholars are just beginning to assess the actual potential of the Soviet cybernetics program to meet the government's economic goals (Dyer-Witheford 2013). It would also be interesting to consider the impact of the cybernetics program on the ultimate opening of Soviet life. We know that it permitted scientists and intellectuals to consider alternatives to Stalinist absolutes. Perhaps if more than one generation had continued to work on the program, cybernetic planning might have nudged open more doors in the Soviet Union. We do know that one alternative early computer utility or cloud experiment, Chile's Project Cybersyn, was influenced by the Soviet cybernetics project, but it departed from the Soviet project in significant ways as well.

The Computer Utility Comes to Chile (Almost)

After the people of Chile elected Salvador Allende to the presidency in 1970, he proceeded to carry out social democratic reforms that included increasing the minimum wage and expanding education, public housing, and food programs for the poor. More controversial was the government's decision to nationalize Chile's lucrative copper industry, which had been largely under the control of U.S.-based multinational corporations. In 1973, with the assent and support of the United States, the Chilean military overthrew Allende in a coup resulting in thousands of deaths and imprisonments. The military ruled for the next fifteen years.

During Allende's presidency and with the assistance of an American computer expert Stafford Beer, Chile experimented with computer-assisted economic planning. Arguably the first of the cyberneticians to achieve business success, Beer was dubbed by none other than Norbert Wiener himself as "the father of management cybernetics" (Miller 2002, 3). Soon after Allende's election, Beer accepted the invitation of Fernando Flores, an engineer working in the Chilean State Development Corporation, to establish Project Cybersyn (Proyecto Synco in Spanish), a program to build a computer communications network that would help run the Chilean economy. Like the Soviet system, it would process, organize, and display information on economic activity in real time. But unlike the U.S.S.R.'s system, Cybersyn would use the information to enable workers and local managers to participate by providing information and making decisions. Specifically, the project's developers planned to have workers participate in the development of production models, in the design and implementation of technology, and in economic management at the local and national levels (Medina 2011).

In the 1970s the concept of worker democracy was popular as a means of tapping into the tacit knowledge of skilled workers; as one way to combat what was viewed as pervasive workplace alienation, especially among young workers; and as a means of extending participation from the electoral arena into the modern workplace. Experiments in workplace democracy and worker control were taking place at the time in numerous locations, including prominently in the United States, Israel, and in what was then Yugoslavia (Hunnius, Garson, and Case 1973). With worker democracy in the air, experts in the new technology of computer communication thought about how to apply their technical skills to what was becoming a global movement. As Beer said in 1972, "In Chile, I know that I am making the maximum effort towards the devolution of power. The government made their revolution about it; I find it good cybernetics" (Medina 2011, 3). Allende and his government agreed that cybernetics would enable them to build a computer system that would help "to create a new political and technological reality ... , one that broke with the strategic ambitions of both the United States and the Soviet Union" (ibid., 3).

Limited computer resources and the short life span of the Allende government did not permit implementation of Project Cybersyn, but it remains important in the history of cloud computing for several reasons. It demonstrated that the history of the cloud contains an important chapter from outside the United States, the Soviet Union, and other centers of world power. Audacious as it was, Project Cybersyn was proposed and designed primarily by engineers and planners in what was then called a third-world country—in the minds of some, a backward nation that should have been concentrating on mining copper for transnational corporations instead of experimenting with computer-assisted planning. Moreover, Cybersyn was consciously designed as an alternative to standard models of economic development on offer from the United States and the Soviet Union. Beer sought a balance between centralized and decentralized control, and between the overall needs of a firm and the autonomy of its component parts. His work tapped into a line of thinking that has found its way into discussions of the cloud. How can we create computer systems that bring about efficiencies through centralization without sacrificing local autonomy? Will big data in the cloud facilitate democracy or overwhelm it? Beer's thinking lined up well with the Popular Unity government's interest in promoting national development without sacrificing civil liberties, a free and open media, and individual autonomy. Finally, the proposal for the Chilean version of a computer utility demonstrates the need to consider the social relations of technology in any discussion of cloud computing. For Chile, the Cybersyn network was important because it would advance national development, but also because it would promote public participation in the political and economic life of the nation. Too valuable to be kept under private control, it would serve society as a whole.

It is easy to question whether Allende's government moved too fast to nationalize resource industries and promote workplace democracy with new information technology. Or perhaps it proceeded too slowly, because the government refused to arm supporters under militant attack from U.S.-backed sectors of the society. It is also easy to brand Beer as an eccentric who got in over his head in a place he did not understand. But before doing so, it is worthwhile to compare Chile's ambitious plans to use a new technology to bring about a thorough democratization of society with two examples from the political uses of today's cloud. The first is generally viewed as an unalloyed success because it is widely seen as a major contributor to returning Barack Obama to the White House. I am referring to his campaign's use of cloud computing and big-data analysis provided by Amazon Web Services (AWS), a division of the online retail giant, to identify potential voters and successfully deliver enough of them to the polls to exceed many pundits' expectations. The campaign built more than 200 apps that ran in AWS, making such heavy use that the company's chief technology officer tweeted his personal congratulations to his counterpart in the Obama campaign once victory was certain. The campaign utilized the Amazon cloud in many ways, but the skilled deployment of databases in modeling, analytics, and integration was key. Specifically, "This array of databases allowed campaign workers to target and segment prospective voters, shift marketing resources based on near real-time feedback on the effectiveness of certain ads, and drive a donation system that collected over one billion dollars (making it the 30th largest ecommerce site in the world)" (Cohen 2012). Another key was a set of tools that helped the campaign determine the most efficient television advertising buys (dubbed the Optimizer) and targeted messages to Twitter and Facebook users (called blasters) (Hoover 2012).

There is nothing especially unusual about these and other strategies in the Obama campaign's partnership with Amazon. It appears that the campaign simply made better use of its data-management resources than did the opposition. What is striking, however, is how little this has to do with practicing democracy, with civic participation, or with activism at any level. In place of democracy, including anything envisioned in the Cybersyn project, we have population management and control.

The second example comes from Great Britain, where Prime Minister David Cameron, a big fan of the iPad and especially the game Fruit Ninja, ordered the creation of an app that would enable him and his inner circle to monitor the British economy. Dubbed No. 10 Dashboard, according to the website of the government's cabinet office, it provides a summary view of national and international information, including housing and employment data and stock prices, as well as data on the performance of government departments. In addition, there is "political context" data drawn from polls, commentary, and a sampling from Twitter. Proud of the app, the prime minister showed it off to newly reelected President Obama at a G8 summit meeting.

It would be easy to draw the conclusion that with Obama's use of the largest cloud-computing company and Cameron's No. 10 Dashboard, we are now light years ahead of Chile's Cybersyn. After all, rooms full of 1970s equipment and software can now fit on a handheld device. But on closer inspection, something substantial has also been lost. The fruits of Cybersyn were to be shared with the entire nation in a transparent process of data production, modeling, display, and distribution. The goal was to advance the Chilean national economy even as it promoted democracy in the workplace and in society. Cameron's app, like Obama's use of AWS, is intended to better manage a population. Neither has much to do with public participation in political decision making. Responding to just this type of criticism, the data director of Obama's campaign felt compelled to declare, "I am not Big Brother." He insisted that "campaigns don't know any more about your online behavior than any retailer, news outlet or savvy blogger" (Roeder 2012). Although it is more than a bit disingenuous to compare a campaign organization that spent over $11 million on technology services with the resources of a savvy blogger, it is accurate to compare what both campaigns knew about online and offline behavior with what Walmart, Target, or any other large, global retailer knows (Gallagher 2012). But what kind of defense is it to maintain that a presidential campaign is no worse than a giant retailer like Walmart when it comes to surveillance? Obama's data director may not be Big Brother, but does this justify the conclusion that "new technologies and an abundance of data may rattle the senses, but they are also bringing a fresh appreciation of the value of the individual to American politics" (Roeder 2012)? What would we think if this came from the data director of Target only with "the American economy" replacing "American politics"? The same holds for No. 10 Dashboard. Indeed, as one commentator noted, Cameron's "app could … be an apt metaphor for politicians reduced to spectators by the surges and shocks of the globalized world" (Wiles 2012). It does not really empower the inner circle of people for whom it was made. In that respect, it is not dissimilar from a special-purpose iPad app made for the team responsible for restructuring Greece's debt. But this conclusion misses a more important point. Politicians who build apps that take a snapshot of the economy may or may not be powerless to do anything. But there is little, if any, consideration for how such data might empower citizens, nor for how citizens might participate in its creation as workers, voters, or customers. That is why it is important to revisit the precursors of cloud computing, like Project Cybersyn, whatever their outcomes. Moreover, we need to do more than marvel at the advance in technology over the decades because history suggests that technological progress does not necessarily bring about advances in the practice of democracy, and sometimes can result in genuine regression.

The Pentagon and the Internet

Although they left behind important legacies and lessons, videotex, Soviet cybernetics, and Project Cybersyn are no longer around. The work of the Defense Advanced Research Projects Agency (DARPA), on the other hand, is not only important for understanding where cloud computing comes from; it is a significant participant in current military cloud-computing projects. When the Soviet Union successfully placed *Sputnik*, the first operational satellite, into orbit around the earth in 1957, it caught the U.S. government by such surprise that President Eisenhower created an agency within the Pentagon whose job it was to keep these surprises from happening again.

Starting in 1958 the agency, then known as ARPA, was responsible for carrying out research and development on projects at the cutting edge of science and technology. While these typically dealt with national security–related matters, the agency never felt bound by military projects alone. One outcome of this view was significant work on general information technology and computer systems, starting with pioneering research on what was called time-sharing. The first computers worked on a one user–one system principle, but because individuals use computers intermittently, this wasted resources. Research on batch processing helped to make computers more efficient because it permitted jobs to queue up over time and thereby shrunk nonusage time. Time-sharing expanded this by enabling multiple users to work on the same system at the same time. DARPA kick-started time-sharing with a grant to fund an MIT-based project that, under the leadership of J. C. R. Licklider, brought together people from Bell Labs, General Electric, and MIT (Waldrop 2002). With time-sharing was born the principle of one system serving multiple users, one of the foundations of cloud computing. The thirty or so companies that sold access to time-sharing computers, including such big names as IBM and General Electric, thrived in the 1960s and 1970s. The primary operating system for time-sharing was Multics (for Multiplexed Information and Computing Service), which was designed to operate as a computer utility modeled after telephone and electrical utilities. Specifically, hardware and software were organized in modules so that the system could grow by adding more of each required resource, such as core memory and disk storage. This model for what we now call scalability would return in a far more sophisticated form with the birth of the cloud-computing concept in the 1990s, and then with the arrival of cloud systems in the next decade. One of the key similarities, albeit at a more primitive level, between time-sharing systems and cloud computing is that they both offer complete operating environments to users. Time-sharing systems typically included several programming-language processors, software packages, bulk printing, and storage for files on- and offline. Users typically rented terminals and paid fees for connect time, for CPU (central processing unit) time, and for disk storage. The growth of the microprocessor and then the personal computer led to the end of time-sharing as a profitable business because these devices increasingly substituted, far more conveniently, for the work performed by companies that sold access to mainframe computers.

DARPA is even better known for the creation of the Advanced Research Projects Agency Network—ARPANET—the first wide-area network using packet-switching technology. Packet switching breaks up data into blocks or packets, which seek the most efficient network routing. The blocks are reassembled at the end point and, unless there are major network problems, appear to an end user as a unified data, voice, or video transmission. The network was created to link secure military installations and major research facilities and became a direct precursor of today's Internet. In fact, some date the birth of the Internet to January 1, 1983, when for one day ARPANET completely shut off service to the 400 hosts the system served in order to replace the NCP protocol with the TCP/IP network protocol that has defined the Internet ever since (Kerner 2013). The growth of the Internet released the brake on cloud computing that the expansion of the first microcomputers and then personal computers had applied. In addition to requiring significant expansion of distribution capacity in wireline, wireless, and switching capabilities, the Internet's accelerating demand for data storage and processing hastened the arrival of cloud systems.

The precursors of cloud computing demonstrate that what we now call the cloud came from various places that used computing for different goals. Videotex systems aimed to link terminals and television receivers to remote computers that, in practice, provided basic information to people in a handful of nations. The Soviet Union applied its leading role in cybernetics to develop a national system of economic planning. Notwithstanding strong fears in the Kennedy administration, including the CIA, that the program would enable the Soviet economy to overtake its competitors in the West, it was at best a partial success. It fell victim to the limited capacity of computer systems and to the power of the Soviet military, which resisted investing technology resources to build the domestic economy. Chile's Cybersyn sought to bring about a social-democratic version of national development planning by connecting central computers to terminals throughout the country, primarily to establish an interactive system of economic decision making. The short-lived rule of the Popular Unity government of Salvador Allende meant that Cybersyn never made it out of the planning phase. Nevertheless, it demonstrated that cloud computing has historical links to the Global South, where democratic values existed side-by-side with technical visions. Finally, DARPA made use of big military budgets during the Cold War to help bring about time-sharing and the Internet. Perhaps most importantly, unlike the Soviet military, which was hostile to civilian-sector participation, DARPA worked with corporations that developed business applications that eventually led to cloud computing. DARPA continues to be very active in the development of a military cloud.

Anatomy of the Cloud

Today's cloud computing deepens and extends key tendencies established by these and other predecessors. The rise of data centers controlled by a handful of companies continues a process of creating global networks of informational capitalism (Schiller 2014). Companies that once contained an IT department, with its craft tradition, can now move to the cloud, where IT and its labor are centralized and streamlined in an industrial mode of production, processing, distribution, and storage. Furthermore, the cloud takes one more step in a long process of building a global culture of knowing in which information production accelerates through networks that connect data centers, devices, organizations, and individuals. The cloud makes up both a new industrial infrastructure and a culture of knowing, based on digital positivism.

It is easy to lose sight of the significance of cloud computing for informational capitalism and for building a culture of knowing because time and time again in the early years of a technology, there is a tendency to concentrate on those flashy utopian or dystopian visions that make up what has been called the technological sublime (Nye 1994). This is understandable. Just as it was hard to resist the feeling of magic the first time a web page scrolled down a home computer screen, so too was it magical when, for the first time, street lights brightened the night with electricity's illumination and voices emanated from the musical box that came to be called radio. Cloud computing currently resides in this magical sublime phase where transcendent visions of ending space, time, and social divisions tend to dilute our appreciation of the more grounded, long-term, but banal consequences of implementing cloud systems. The experience with electricity is especially relevant because its early days were focused on the capacity to bring light and power, an admittedly significant, if not revolutionary, development. But electricity's sublime allure wore off when people got used to universal lighting, especially when the promised end to crime on the streets did not pan out. The sublime became banal. But the genuine revolutionary power of electricity awaited its withdrawal into the woodwork of banality. It was not until electrical generation was organized into utilities and sent out to power industrial and household applications (yesterday's apps) that one could safely conclude that electrification was a principal participant in an economic and social transformation. From powering automobile assembly lines to turning on vacuum cleaners, electricity's many applications were not terribly sublime, but certainly were transformative (Nye 1990). Indeed, some economists argue that electrification, including centralized power generation and near universal distribution, has been the most significant technological force for economic growth in the modern era (Gordon 2000).

Cloud computing is moving from the sublime stage of infinite promises to what may amount to a similar banality. In this respect, the cloud is a gathering of utilities, certainly not the same as the electrical-power generators that enabled a leap in the industrial revolution, but not so different that it is inappropriate to consider a similar process at work. The sublime cloud is entering a banal phase where there is less focus on it as a discrete entity and more on the transformative applications that it is enabling. As one analyst puts it, "In the mid 19th Century, centralised generation allowed electricity to be provided as a utility, meaning that consumers only had to pay for what they used. Consumption could be scaled up or down to meet demand without the need for capital expenditure. A century and a half on, this is precisely the emancipating effect that cloud computing is now having on the enterprise. Organizations no longer need to build, maintain and renew cumbersome IT infrastructure in order to consume as much, or as little computing resource as they need" (John 2013).

Cloud computing builds on its predecessors, but there are sufficiently significant differences that mark its departure from earlier models. It is useful to consider some of these differences, beginning with the extraordinary growth in the sheer size and scale of cloud facilities. It is no overstatement to argue that cloud centers require a major stretch in our conceptual vision to begin to understand their enormity. Consider the plans for the largest data center (in cost, size, and processing power) now under construction. In September 2012 China's major social-networking firm Baidu, a Chinese version of Google and Facebook combined, announced that it would spend $1.6 billion to build a new cloud center in Yangquan, Shanxi Province, covering 120,000 square meters (about thirty acres), roughly the size of the U.S. Pentagon, one of the largest standalone buildings in the world. The Yangquan facility will contain the capacity to store 4,000 petabytes (PB) of data (1 PB equals 1 million gigabytes; see the following table). When completed in 2016, it will deploy 700,000 central processing units. Drawing comparisons and making estimates is always perilous, but it has been estimated that digitizing the entire collection of print, audio, and video stored in the collection of the Library of Congress would amount to roughly 15 terabytes of data. The storage capacity of the Baidu cloud center would therefore enable it to house the data equivalent of 268,000 Libraries of Congress.

From Megabytes to Zettabytes

1,000 megabytes = 1 gigabyte (GB)

1,000 GB = 1 Terabyte (TB)

1,000 TB = 1 Petabyte (PB)

1,000 PB = 1 Exabyte (EB)

1,000 EB = 1 Zettabyte

When it opens in 2016, the Baidu center will set a new standard for data facilities, but those operating now are far from small. As of December 2013, the largest existing cloud data center was a 400,000-square-foot structure, part of a 2.2-million-square-foot interconnected collection of data centers operated by the Switch corporation in Las Vegas, where the absence of natural disasters provides a margin of safety. Admittedly, data centers of this size are at the outer edge of typical cloud data centers, but the trend is to build ever-larger ones because size provides efficiencies that are needed as data storage and processing demand continues to grow. In fact, China, in a joint venture with IBM, is in the process of building its own "cloud city" in Langfang, an old industrial district near Beijing, that will cover over 6 million square feet of facilities, including a giant data center and offices to house IT development companies (Zhu 2013).

The corporation Cisco, a major participant in the cloud industry, has put together an index of global data-center traffic. These are estimates, but they provide a general sense of the growth in the sheer amount of data in the cloud, and once again require a stretch of the imagination. Cisco estimates that by the end of 2017, 69 percent of all Internet protocol (IP) traffic will be processed in the cloud as opposed to in facilities operated by a specific organization, like a corporation or government unit, or by individual consumers. Annual global cloud IP traffic is forecast to reach 5.3 zettabytes (ZB) (a single zettabyte is equal to one billion terabytes or, in more concrete terms, 250 billion standard DVDs or 36 million years of HD video) by the end of 2017. Global cloud traffic is expected to grow sixfold by that year (Cisco 2013). This has led some to worry about a cloud "plumbing problem" because the amount of data stored is growing much faster than the bandwidth of network connections needed to process and analyze data (Wegener 2013).

Statistics on the industry are not easily obtained because cloud data centers are either under private control or operated by governments not inclined to share information. Estimates vary, but one census produced a total of 509,000 data centers worldwide at the end of 2011, occupying close to 300 million square feet. Cloud centers are located everywhere in the world but tend to be concentrated in places where land is plentiful but not far from communication and power facilities. This includes what was once agriculture land on the outskirts of population centers, where companies can benefit from low labor costs. These considerations have led Apple to locate its cloud data centers in rural North Carolina and in Oregon. The North Carolina location is especially interesting for both Apple and Google because low labor costs are matched with low energy costs—30 percent lower in North Carolina than the national average. Moreover, North Carolina possesses an increasingly valuable commodity that one would not naturally associate with cloud computing: pig manure, or, as it is referred to more euphemistically, black gold. The state holds 14 percent of the swine population in the United States and pig manure can produce methane gas energy to help meet the massive power-consumption needs of data centers. Apple and Google are not only competing for clicks and customers; they are in a race to determine who can best exploit this unlikely North Carolina resource (Wolonick 2012).

Security is a growing concern, especially as the size and therefore the value of facilities and data have grown. This has led some cloud companies to locate their facilities in mountainous regions that, while quite far from urban areas, offer added protection. Increasingly, the propensity for earthquakes and severe climate events is taken into account in the choice of location. Energy costs for a 24/7 operation are a key consideration and this is leading some cloud companies to explore the novel solution of burying facilities inside mountains close to supplies of cool water to lessen the requirement for air conditioning. For example, Norway's Green Mountain Data Centre is located on the shores of the island of Rennesøy, close to a large fjord. The center itself is contained in concrete buildings within caves built into the mountain. Racks of servers fill halls once used to store ammunition for NATO forces, but what makes the location especially attractive is proximity to a fjord that provides a constant supply of cool water to keep sensitive systems from overheating. Locations like Rennesøy provide both enhanced security and lower energy costs.

It is interesting to observe, and not a little bit ironic, that a technology promising freedom from locational constraints is itself constrained by the need to maximize the ability to house enormous amounts of data and guarantee system reliability. Companies increasingly aim for the sweet spot: cold climate, access to low-cost power, abundant water supply, high-bandwidth Internet connections, political stability, and financial incentives. Several countries meet the requirements, but none more so than Canada, which is increasingly a data-center destination of choice (Perkins 2013). Facilities in Canada take advantage of a technology known as "free cooling" that reduces energy requirements by about half through the use of a cooling circuit that draws on outdoor air to supplement a data center's energy-intensive needs. A specialized heat exchanger uses outdoor air to cool water and glycol that circulate to the server racks, thereby reducing the load on compressors and pumps, which are the big energy hogs in data centers. IBM opened a $90 million data center in a small Ontario community partly because the company can cool the facility for 210 days a year without running energy-consuming chillers. While exotic locations like mountains and fjords attract attention, Canada works for many companies because practically the entire country is in a cold climate, which means there are numerous locations near power and water supplies and close to large cities. According to the head of one IT research company, "The advantage Canada has is it's far cheaper and easier to bring data to power sources, and vice versa. It's much cheaper to stick your data next to a hydro dam" (Stoller 2012). The town of Barrie, Ontario, which houses the aforementioned IBM facility as well as facilities of major banks, has abundant, reliable, and inexpensive supplies of water and power, and benefits from proximity to Toronto, which provides it with excellent Internet connections. Canadian cloud-data-center companies have also pioneered the use of energy-saving systems. OVH.com, a Quebec-based company, uses a unique heat-dissipation and cooling system that has completely eliminated the need for air-conditioning servers in its Canadian locations, and reduced it by 98 percent in its worldwide locations.

Canada, like the Scandinavian nations with which it vies for data-center business, also benefits from political stability and strong data security. Additionally, Canada benefits from proximity to the United States and the additional incentive that data located in Canada is not subject to the USA PATRIOT Act, which permits the U.S. government to intercept and analyze data stored within its borders without a search warrant. In addition to Canadian and Scandinavian locations, Switzerland, with its long-standing political neutrality, is an increasingly favored choice for data centers, but it is expensive. All the discussion of size and proximity to resources makes clear that cloud computing is a very material industry with locational requirements that belie the image of an ephemeral cloud. Cloud-computing data centers are the communication version of those industrial transportation hubs of the past where, for example, the city of Chicago played a large role in America's industrial expansion. It should not be surprising that, until recently, the largest cloud data center in the world was located in that city. Of course, data centers are not rail yards, but just as transportation centers were key nodes in the global industrial grid, cloud data centers are material hubs for global information and communication traffic. Images of invisible data moving through clouds help convey a sense of what the sociologist Zygmunt Bauman (2000) describes as our era's "liquid modernity." Today's iconic products are data, information, and messages, which flow around the world through thin wires or just through the air. But they are rooted in physical structures that make significant material demands on resources and that call to mind the factories of an earlier era. Understanding cloud computing absolutely requires an appreciation of its materiality, of its substantial physicality and its extraordinary demands on the environment.

There are many other ways to describe this dance of petabytes and zettabytes, and we will certainly explore some of these, but suffice it to say that nothing in the history of communication and information processing approximates in scale the levels of storage, processing, and distribution that the cloud makes possible. With that said, it is important to give attention to something missing from cloud computing, but in order to do so we need to address more of its characteristics.

On-demand self-service. Cloud computing allows users to choose their storage requirements and server time automatically without requiring human interaction with the provider of each service.

Broad network access. Users can access the cloud in standardized ways through any platform, such as a tablet, smartphone, or personal computer.

Resource pooling. Resources like storage, processing, memory, bandwidth, network, and virtual machines can be brought together by the provider to serve multiple users with different physical and virtual resources assigned and rapidly redeployed to meet user demand. This enables the provider to engage users without regard to location, unless users demand that the provider specify a location by nation, region, or data center. For example, users in the United States may not want to be served by a data center in China whose "Great Firewall" of censorship limits access to the online world. Or, fearing the application of the PATRIOT Act, users in Europe or Canada may not want to be served from the United States.

Rapid elasticity. Cloud resources can be expanded and contracted quickly based on customer needs. Users are not locked into IT investments, but can make use of just what they need. However, it also means that they must rely on a provider that is typically not as familiar as an internal IT department with the history and culture of the organization. Since moving to the cloud increases the likelihood that an organization will shrink its IT department, that leaves the organization with less inside technical expertise or tacit knowledge to help determine its information-technology requirements.

Measured service. Cloud companies can provide and control services efficiently by employing a measurement based on one or more specific services, such as amount of data stored, bandwidth used, or quantity of processing. If the provider is using a metric that reasonably reflects the service provided, then there is transparency for both provider and user.

Types of Cloud Computing

In addition to these characteristics of cloud services, one can identify three different types of cloud service models that focus on infrastructure, platform, and software, with each model providing the customer with different levels of control. These are not inviolate categories but, in spite of large gray areas at the margins, they are nevertheless useful in adding a sense of what different types of cloud models aim to accomplish, from simply providing a storage service to offering additional applications and software for customers to use.

IaaS: Infrastructure as a Service. With this model, the cloud-service provider manages a storage infrastructure for customer data, leaving the customer to deploy its own software, including operating systems and applications. Furthermore, under this model customers can control certain network components, like firewalls. It is ideal for repetitive uses that require elasticity or the capacity to expand or contract quickly depending on use. Examples include online gaming sites, online advertising networks, video-sharing sites, and social-media applications.

PaaS: Platform as a Service. Here, in addition to offering storage facilities, the cloud provider deploys onto the cloud infrastructure applications that the customer has created or acquired using programming languages and tools that the provider supports. Once again, the customer does not manage the infrastructure; all of that is left to the cloud provider. Rather, the customer gets to control the deployed applications. For example, the city of Edmonton, Alberta, contracted with a cloud provider to create its own tool, called Open Data Catalogue, which made information about city services accessible to the public. The U.S. Department of Defense (DOD) used a cloud provider when it needed to emulate battlefield conditions. In the latter case, DOD technical staff developed an application on the Microsoft Azure platform.

SaaS: Software as a Service. Under this model, cloud companies offer their own applications for customers to use on the cloud infrastructure. Customers typically access these applications through what is called a *thin client interface,* such as a web browser that might provide the customer with document processing or web-based email. The customer leaves to the provider control over such infrastructure items as operating systems, networks, server storage, and application capabilities. For example, instead of buying a copy of Microsoft Word, a customer rents the use of the word-processing software for a fixed charge per month or pays a per-use fee. To use the software, the customer logs into the cloud company's system. Similarly, a small business might rent a sophisticated sales database from a cloud company like Salesforce because it would not make economic sense to purchase such a database. Success depends on the quality of the rented software and the reliability of the cloud provider, especially when the software involves multiple tools responsible for running several different units of a business (sales, accounting, administration, and so on). A primary benefit of SaaS is that it minimizes or entirely eliminates the requirement for in-house IT professionals. Companies selling software through the cloud gain from a regular flow of income, especially when they are able to shift popular software from a purchase to a monthly subscription model, as Adobe did with its popular Photoshop (Pogue 2013).

It is also important to distinguish among different models of deploying cloud systems, including private, public, hybrid, and community clouds.

Private cloud. Under this model, the cloud is customized and deployed for a single organization. It may exist on or off the organization's premises, but when it is off premises, the private cloud is protected by the organization's firewall. Private clouds tend to be chosen by organizations, like banks, that have security and regulatory concerns prohibiting them from using cloud services that are widely available to the general public. In essence, the private cloud is a gated community set aside for those willing to pay for an extra degree of security. In this respect, it is a manifestation of a trend, troubling to some, that would dissolve the Internet into a set of privately run networks (Moses 2012). This model is tempting because private clouds can serve as vaults to secure data from snooping eyes, the essence of the business model of companies like Reputation.com (Singer 2012).

Public cloud. This model is typically provided by large cloud-services businesses, such as Amazon Web Services, and offers software, platforms, and infrastructure to the general public or to an industry association. In essence the public cloud is available to anyone who can pay for it and it is expected to grow five times faster than overall IT-industry expansion through 2016 (Lee 2013b). Public cloud SaaS configurations are the most widely known because they include familiar services like Google's Gmail, Apple's iCloud, and the marketing services provided by Salesforce. Organizations that require the greater control but prefer to stay in the public cloud might opt for a PaaS system like Microsoft's Azure or Google's App Engine. Those needing still more control turn to IaaS public-cloud services like those provided by Amazon and Terremark.

Hybrid cloud. When the cloud infrastructure is composed of both public and private clouds that remain unique entities but are linked by technology that allows for data and application portability, we refer to a hybrid cloud service. Many organizations have divided requirements that might lead them to seek out the public cloud for most of their needs and a private cloud configuration to maintain the security of sensitive data. Hybrid-cloud providers who share ownership and management with their customer organizations enable them to enjoy the benefits of both types of deployments. While hybrid clouds appear to be an excellent choice because they can be all things to their customers, they also require careful management to balance the component cloud formations. The company Rackspace has become a leader in the hybrid model.

Community cloud. This model brings together several organizations that have common interests, such as a similar organizational mission, similar set of regulatory requirements, security needs, compliance expectations, or policies. One or more of these organizations might manage the cloud or, what is more frequently the case, they may together hire a third party who runs the cloud in the data center of one of the organizations or houses it off-site. For example, a group of airlines might build a community cloud to house a common reservation system. Community clouds are chosen because they can be customized to meet the specific needs of an organizational group, such as a collection of media firms interested in sharing file-based digital media content. Community clouds are also interesting because they have kept alive the early cloud-computing discussion of building systems that are not primarily under vendor control and operate in a more environmentally sustainable fashion (Briscoe and Marinos 2009).

What's Missing?

Although the words *public* and *community* are used in cloud computing, every cloud model is presumed to be a private service operated by a business with the goal of maximizing profit. Government systems, which often use private provisioning (even the CIA will be using Amazon Web Services for $600 million worth of cloud projects), are primarily employed for management, control, and surveillance (Babcock 2013a). In the context of cloud computing, "public" simply means that vendors will sell to the general public rather than to a single preferred customer, and "community" refers to the common commercial interests shared by users of that cloud model—for instance, they are all airlines. These are very narrow uses, if not outright distortions, of the terms public and community. The public traditionally refers to citizens who participate in the decisions that affect their lives, and a community is a collection of active citizens with common interests. The history of computing has included extensive debates about public and community participation in the construction of networks and in the provision of services. Unless a cloud system is specifically set up to provide information to a public or to a community of citizens, then the vast majority of people do not participate in the cloud as citizens, but rather as consumers who are valued not for their participation in decision making about the cloud, but rather for their propensity to purchase services and to provide information to companies about their consumption patterns.

In addition to being an extraordinary leap in processing and storage power over early cloud-like systems, cloud computing, unlike computer systems that preceded it, is a singularly market-driven project with little consideration of alternatives to the model of management and control that governs it. Where are the debates about using the cloud to expand economic or political democracy? How about worker participation in corporate decision making or greater citizen participation in national or community life? What about public participation in decisions about cloud data centers or cloud systems? Unlike earlier communication systems that, whatever the outcome, sparked vigorous encounters about their potential to expand citizenship and democracy, the cloud is essentially silent on these issues. There appears to be an enormous gap between the prodigious sublimity of the cloud's power to process, store, and distribute information and the banality of its current applications, however practical and profitable.

While almost all cloud systems operate according to a commercial model, there are a few exceptions. For example, grid computing is a means of creating a cloud from below by harnessing the combined power of millions of personal computers to carry out projects. But even these are typically organized by commercial enterprises. Since 2004, IBM has sponsored the World Community Grid, which takes the principle of using the available space on mainly household PCs to address a variety of public-health and environmental research projects. Specifically, it makes this combined computer power available to public and not-for-profit organizations for use in humanitarian research. All results are in the public domain open to the global research community. Research projects cover clean water and energy; the development of drugs to combat malaria and dengue fever; as well as research on muscular dystrophy, cancer in the young, and AIDS. For example, advanced computational methods help to identify candidate drugs that have the right shape and chemical characteristics to block HIV development. Commercial projects are beginning to take advantage of this distributed processing model, including harnessing idle PCs in homes (Novet 2013). These open a door to an alternative form of large-scale computing that does not require a top-down cloud computer model.

Cloud computing therefore distinguishes itself from earlier models in two fundamental ways. First, receiving the most attention is the capacity to store, process, and distribute data beyond anything that preceded it. What were once the exceptional "supercomputers" are now standard in the half million or so data centers worldwide. Second, even as it has exceeded its predecessors, cloud computing operates from a diminished vision that is almost entirely driven by the twin goals of profit and control. There is little interest in using the cloud to bring democracy, citizen-driven design and implementation, worker control, or even worker involvement in decision making. While all of these ideas have been raised in the course of computing's history, they are not part of debates about today's or tomorrow's cloud computing.

Is the Cloud a Utility?

This may change before long because there is a contradiction at the center of cloud computing that will likely heat up the debate. Put simply, some forecasts for computing are coming to fruition and the cloud is taking on more of the characteristics of a genuine utility (Clark 2012a). It is not just the academic and policy communities that are beginning to think of today's IT environment in public-utility language. When asked what his two companies, Twitter and the e-payment firm Square, have in common, Jack Dorsey answers, "They're both utilities." Moreover, Facebook head Mark Zuckerberg has spent years referring to his company not as a social network, but as a social utility. However, when asked if his utility should be regulated, the Facebook founder backed off: "Something that's cool can fade. But something that's useful won't. That's what I meant by *utility*." Of course, most of the cool things we think of that will last are not referred to as utilities. But whatever the definition or the reaction, the concept of the utility is increasingly part of the ongoing debate about the developing structure of the computer universe (Fox 2013). Cloud computing has made it a more frequently used concept.

Taking into consideration the experience of earlier utilities, such as water, gas, and electricity, one energy expert defines the requirements of a utility market as comprising the following:

- A source of energy generation
- A transportation network
- A transmission and distribution capability
- A metering capability
- A pricing mechanism
- A regulator to ensure adherence to rules
- A customer (James Constant, cited in Clark 2012a)

This configuration of characteristics can be debated, but most would agree that they are among the major ones defining a utility. According to Clark, cloud computing meets most of these criteria. It is a source of energy generation in its ability to compute and store data. The Internet and the telecommunications systems connected to it form the transportation network. Data centers handle the transmission and distribution capability because they house the storage and processing capabilities. Cloud services, especially "public" ones, can meter precisely how much storage and processing are being used at any particular time, albeit with different providers applying different pricing methods. Pricing is determined by the cost to receive, process, and respond to a request for storage, processing, and distribution. Although a wide range of factors is involved, cloud providers directly control the costs of hardware and software because they engineer their own systems, and the costs of other factors, such as facilities, staffing, and electricity, depend on the particular market within which they operate. Finally, there is no shortage of customers. Indeed the market most likely will grow to one in which a handful of providers serve practically everyone, just as, for example, water and energy markets do. As Clark concludes, "All that's lacking is a regulator. Whether the cloud computing industry should be regulated is a complex issue that will undoubtedly become a major debate before too long" (Clark 2012a; M. O'Connor 2013).

One can debate whether a government regulator will ever become essential to the cloud computing industry. What cannot be debated is whether cloud computing will be subject to governance; that is, to the need for general management, coordination, and oversight. This can be accomplished by agencies of government, as has been the case historically for most utilities, or it can be accomplished by those with market power. These are both governance structures, notwithstanding the mythology of the market's "invisible hand." The myth tends to focus on the magic of invisible coordination more than on the hand, which, in reality, is quite visible. It is apparent to most observers of cloud computing that, however they might feel about government regulation, there is a growing concentration of power among a handful of cloud providers, most of which are also key players in the production and distribution of software and content. Utility markets often become government regulated because one or a few producers, who use their position to exercise significant power over services and pricing, come to dominate.[1] Historically, this has been the case throughout the history of communication media that was marked in the United States, for example, by Western Union's control over telegraphy, AT&T's over telephony, and the broadcasting networks' domination over radio and then television. In each case regulation was called on to temper the threats of monopoly or oligopoly control. This pattern was followed in other nations, but some of these also turned to public ownership to guarantee widespread, if not universal, access to an essential service. So it is not very surprising that along with the term *utility*, the concept of regulation has entered public debate in today's computer and social-media world (Marshall 2013). The demise of specific cloud services, such as Google Reader, because companies cannot recover fixed costs from their provision, has led some economists to wonder whether government ownership or regulation through public utility status is inevitable for essential but unprofitable services like search (Kaminska 2013). Even as businesses in the less developed world begin to embrace the cloud, they fear that it might do more harm than good without the stability provided by government regulation (Hanna 2013).

One of the key reasons why expert attention is returning to the concept of the utility in cloud computing is that the industry is rapidly becoming dominated by a handful of companies. The power of Amazon, Apple, Google, Facebook, and Microsoft is troubling enough to lead some to doubt that the "invisible hand" will prove adequate to restrain their ability to dominate cloud markets (McKendrick 2013b). Consequently, they maintain, we should begin to think about broader national or even international oversight by elected representatives. As one concerned analyst put it, "The Internet has taken the place of the telephone as the world's basic, general-purpose, two-way communication medium. All Americans need high-speed access, just as they need clean water, clean air, and electricity. But they have allowed a naive belief in the power and beneficence of the free market to cloud their vision. As things stand, the U.S. has the worst of both worlds: no competition and no regulation" (Crawford 2012). According to Crawford, when it comes to the Internet, the United States should follow the historical example of other utilities. When, for example, electricity came under the control of a handful of firms that provided service only to those who paid top dollar, public pressure led to the creation of regulated utilities and public corporations. Opponents of this view argue that the Internet and the cloud are fundamentally different from roads, water, and electricity and that government regulation would stifle the incentive to risk-taking innovation. In 2013, the divide between cloud computing and electrical utilities blurred when research found that a growing number of cloud companies were making significant profits by reselling electricity to customers in addition to providing space to house data. This practice, what has been dubbed the creation of "wildcat electrical utilities," has led to more calls for government regulation of the cloud (Glanz 2013).

In addition to these concerns, there is the issue of data preservation. Absent some form of regulation or mutual agreement within the IT industry, and specifically among those who are major cloud-services providers, there is no requirement to preserve the photos, email, videos, postings, data, and files that individuals and organizations believe are securely stored in data centers around the world. As a result, much of the digital evidence from the daily lives of individuals and the decisions and activities of organizations will vaporize, irrespective of how many cloud data centers fill the world. As one concerned tech writer argued, "We're really good at making things faster, smaller, and cheaper. And every step along the way makes for great headlines. But we're not nearly so good at migrating our digital stuff from one generation of tech to the next. And we're horrible at coming up with business models that assure its longevity and continuity" (Udell 2012). Another person who has been active in the online world for years, hosting numerous sites and archives, worried, "Not to be dramatic or anything, but no more than forty days after I die, and probably much sooner, all the content I am hosting will disappear" (Winer, quoted in ibid.). To date, the only reason most of this material has been preserved is due to the heroic efforts of individuals who personally port archives when technology and standards change. Referring to several archives dating from the turn of this century, Udell commented in a *Wired* column, "If I hadn't migrated them, they'd already be gone. Not because somebody died, it's just that businesses turned over or lost interest and the bits fell off the web. Getting published, it turns out, is a lousy way to stay published. With all due respect to wired.com, I'll be amazed if this column survives to 2022 without my intervention" (ibid.). There are some efforts, primarily by governments, to archive and preserve files. The most notable of these may be at the U.S. Library of Congress, which, among other things, is archiving the massive database of Twitter postings. These are all important activities, but they are isolated and much more data disappears than is preserved. Of course, one can argue, there is a great deal of digital content that is not worth paying to preserve. Society has survived in the past without carrying forward from generation to generation the entire weight of the historical record. Nevertheless, since most of that record is now digital, is it not worthwhile to develop strategies to preserve at least some of it in a systematic fashion?

Now it is important to turn to an overview of major participants in the cloud marketplace, starting with the five companies generally considered dominant on the Internet and in the cloud.

Mapping the Cloud Industry: Leaders and Challengers

Arguably the leading force in the U.S. cloud computing industry, and a global giant as well, Amazon began by applying computer power to transform publishing and then the general retail industry. As prodigious as this accomplishment has been, one commentator concluded that these achievements "may be footnotes to the company's larger and more secretive goal: giving anyone on the planet access to an almost unimaginable amount of computing power" (Hardy 2012a). By 2013, according to most accounts, its subdivision, Amazon Web Services, was the leader in U.S. cloud computing. As an analyst for the consulting firm Forrester described it, "Almost every major consultancy supports Amazon; almost every advertising agency runs on Amazon; if I need to hire 10 people tomorrow to help me build my application, it's super easy to find people who have Amazon experience" (Miller and Hardy 2013). While Amazon does not break out revenue for cloud computing, 2012 estimates range from $800 million to as much as $2.4 billion (ibid.; Mims 2013). The company operates its cloud services through the aforementioned AWS, which achieved widespread public attention in 2012 because the Obama presidential campaign used AWS to organize its successful voter analysis and voter-turnout drive. By the middle of 2013, one typically modest industry observer concluded, following the company's thirty-seventh cut of its cloud prices, which sent tremors through the industry, "The proof is in: Amazon fully controls the cloud" (Linthicum 2013c). This conclusion may be premature and a tad overstated, but it does correctly identify Amazon as an increasingly dominant force in the cloud business.

AWS was created in 2004 with about forty employees, and was the first company to rent its data storage and computing power to other companies. Although it is highly secretive about most of its operation, by 2012 Amazon was regularly listing more than 600 job openings on the company's website. It operates several large data centers in the United States, each of which contains multiple buildings with thousands of servers. It also runs data centers outside the United States and has several under construction. AWS is not the largest cloud provider in the United States by quantitative measures such as size of data centers or total number of servers, but it is arguably the most powerful because it is part of the Amazon corporate empire and the relationship marks one of the few times when the often-used buzzword "synergy" is an understatement. AWS benefits from the sheer size of its parent's computing power. For example, while the parent Amazon does not reveal the size of its operations, an executive who knows Amazon well maintains that just one of the company's data facilities in the eastern half of the United States contains more servers dedicated to cloud computing than does the entire operation of one of the major hybrid-cloud companies, Rackspace, which in 2013 served 200,000 clients, mainly business customers, with about 100,000 servers in nine data centers. AWS also benefits from the data that Amazon gathers on its millions of customers whose purchases of books, homeware, clothing, and so on provide information that AWS uses to forecast consumer behavior, a boost for both the parent and the firms that purchase AWS's services. Among its major customers are popular media firms like Netflix, Pinterest, Shazam, and Spotify. Amazon has been so successful in the cloud that company management expects it to become the leading revenue producer for Amazon, topping even its renowned retail division, with sustained growth estimated at 45 percent per year through 2017 (Finkle 2012).

Market power gives Amazon considerable leverage over its competition, large and small. As the head of AWS put it when asked about a stepped-up challenge from Google, "We've always been very good at making everything as low-cost as possible, then we lower it some more" (Miller and Hardy 2013). The company is able to price its services, particularly the storage and data-analysis capacity of its servers, so inexpensively that neither many established nor start-up companies any longer bother investing in their own. Instagram, for example, the highly successful web photo company, which is now a part of Facebook, did not bother investing in its own computers. The start-up Cue, which admits to spending $100,000 a month on AWS services, uses them to scan millions of emails, Facebook postings, and corporate records to provide enhanced data that subscribers can use in all of their online activity. Over 185 federal government agencies also run some part of their services through AWS and Amazon has won a $600 million contract to provide cloud services for the CIA (Babcock 2013a). The company is active internationally; in addition to having data centers located in Asia, Europe, and Latin America, it hosts numerous corporate and government clients outside the United States. For example, a German company used AWS to make digital copies of 20,000 television shows, a job that cost the firm less than it would have spent on the electricity alone if it had done the work in house. AWS servers located in California and Ireland provide people in Africa with the ability to comparison-shop cars using smartphones connected to AWS. There is no gainsaying Amazon's rich database of customer searches and purchases, which adds value to AWS's offerings. As one customer commented, "You can now test a product against millions of users for just a few thousand dollars, or start a company with just one or two people" (Hardy 2012a).

To multiply these success stories, Amazon has to successfully deal with two major challenges: providing continuous reliable service and fending off the competition. AWS has been a generally reliable cloud provider, but a handful of notable outages have damaged the company's reputation. One of the most significant took place over the Christmas holidays in 2012, when Netflix customers lost access for the better part of Christmas Eve and Amazon itself lost service for its own customers on Christmas Day. In 2013 Netflix relied on Amazon for 95 percent of its data-center needs and, in the highly competitive video-streaming marketplace, the company cannot tolerate significant downtime. As one independent analyst concluded, "Netflix and other organizations which rely on AWS will have to reexamine how they configure their services and allocate their service requirements across multiple providers to mitigate over-dependency and risks" (Finkle 2012). Amazon is not alone in experiencing outages. They affect the entire industry, are primarily caused by power problems, and, on average, last for 7.5 hours (Talbot 2013). They also lead to unanticipated consequences and hidden costs (Franck 2013).

Reliability also requires guarantees of security, another problem for public cloud companies, and Amazon is no exception. In 2013, a single security researcher managed to uncover 126 billion files that were left open to the public. From a sample of 40,000 files, he found exposed data belonging to a medium-sized social-media service, the sales records of a car dealership, employee spread sheets, and video game source code from a mobile-games developer. The shockingly exposed files also included unsecured passwords. Amazon took measures to secure the data and warn customers, but this one event left its clients understandably worried that public-cloud data was far more exposed than anyone thought (Brian 2013).

Amazon also needs to overcome competitive pressures, especially from a handful of companies that can also leverage their leadership in new-media hardware, software, and media services. Some of these, like Microsoft, IBM, and Oracle, have more experience than Amazon in the market for large corporate clients. One way for AWS to succeed is by heavily discounting cloud services, then, once the competition is driven out of the market, raising prices once more, a tactic that proved successful in Amazon's retail book-selling operation (Streitfeld 2013). It is not an exaggeration to say that even in this early stage of development, the struggle for competitive dominance in cloud computing, just as across the Internet, is narrowing to a handful of corporations that can marshal a similar degree of leverage (McChesney 2013). These include familiar names: Apple, Google, and Microsoft. Of these leaders, Microsoft is probably the most committed to providing general cloud services, especially to businesses, which have helped the company maintain its elevated position even as the others have successfully challenged its consumer-services market. Businesses and government agencies have long been committed to Microsoft software and the company now aims to move these and new customers from reliance on physical programs to online services for a fee. So far it has been reasonably successful, with over 100,000 businesses using the company's cloud services. It is important to emphasize this point because much of the day-to-day attention in the popular press goes to the others, primarily because Google is the major gateway to search, Apple to music, and Facebook to social media. Even Twitter, a much smaller company, garners more notice than Microsoft. But the company Bill Gates started in 1975 has a very strong foundation in business software and, with software migrating to the cloud, Microsoft has invested heavily in cloud platforms. Over the last few years, the company has quietly built up its Server and Tools division and it now generates $18 billion a year in revenues, with six of its subdivisions topping the $1 billion mark.

Microsoft is counting on the cloud platform offering its Azure service to enable customers to develop applications and otherwise make profitable use of their own information. Azure provides both Platform and

Infrastructure as a Service and once again demonstrates the value of proximity to services and systems within a large company like Microsoft, which developed Azure by using some of the elements of its successful web browser Bing (Wilhelm 2012). In recent years Microsoft has not been as successful in consumer services, but it is also making a big push to take individuals and families, as its advertising slogan repeats, "to the cloud." These include Windows Live, a suite of cloud services that includes file storage, image, video, email, messaging, the Bing search engine (now the second most popular in the United States), and Xbox Live. Finally, Microsoft expects that the cloud version of its very popular suite of word-processing, spreadsheet, and related programs will succeed in the cloud, as what it calls Office 365 begins to deliver them on a subscription basis.

Google's concentration on consumer services pioneered in its search engine has led the company to focus on that side of the cloud market. It has expanded the company's consumer cloud beyond search with document storage (Google Drive), word processing (Google Docs), and entertainment (Google Music) applications. Furthermore, however much it worries tech observers, the company also sells its own devices that are entirely dependent on the cloud for data storage and applications (Gilmoor 2013). These include the familiar Chromebooks as well as Google Glass, which Google hopes to use to sell pay-per-gaze, for which it holds a patent, to advertisers (Bilton and Miller 2013). But with competitive threats from AWS and Microsoft, Google has begun a major push into the business market with Google Compute Engine (GCE), its IaaS unit. Again, as with Amazon, built-in leverage matters a great deal. In this case, Google runs its IaaS on the same technology that powers Google search, which leads the company to claim greater reliability than AWS, especially because of the notable outages the latter experienced in 2012 (Chen 2012). In 2013, Google tied GCE to the Google App Engine and its global network of app developers in the hope of beating the competition by providing customers with a cloud service that includes privileged access to the largest set of apps in cyberspace (Hardy 2013d). This is why Google is not reluctant to boast: "For the most part, GCE is positioned as a way for customers to benefit from years and years of infrastructure investments, which span everything from our datacenter design to our operational practices, our hardware design and software design, [and] includes the software stack"

(Clark 2012b). Reassurances aside, breakdowns lead users to worry that they are not keeping a close enough eye on their own data. Indeed, one of the key challenges for companies like Amazon and Google is to balance the costs of meeting worried companies' demands for geographical proximity to data, even as they make use of a global network of data centers to ensure sufficient network redundancy to support their claims of protection against outages.

Like its rival giants in the industry, Google is comfortable moving into new territory, in this case the business applications market, long dominated by Microsoft. Indeed Google has been so committed to innovative product development that it has been dubbed the General Electric of the twenty-first century (Gapper 2013b). For years, Google Apps was pitched mainly to small firms and start-ups because Microsoft dominated the market for large businesses. But Google has begun to cut into this lucrative segment with major private-sector clients like the pharmaceutical giant Hoffmann-La Roche, where 80,000 employees use the package, and public-sector clients such as the U.S. Department of the Interior, where 90,000 use Google Apps as their staple business-productivity software. Borrowing a page from Amazon's playbook, Google relies on consistent low pricing that Microsoft has difficulty matching (Hardy 2012b). Microsoft fights back, but does not appear to take Google very seriously as a contender in this market. Some might consider this a mistake, but Microsoft is clear that Google is not a threat in the business cloud market because, according to the general manager of Microsoft's business division, Google "has not yet shown they are truly serious" about enterprise applications. "From the outside, they are an advertising company" (Kerr 2012). There is some substance to this view. After all, in 2011 only 4 percent of Google revenue came from its business services, whereas 96 percent came from advertising. Microsoft's cloud-based Office 365 is intended to keep Google's business market share from growing, but Microsoft has yet to demonstrate widespread uptake of the service because businesses, worried about security and outages, still prefer Microsoft's more familiar Office software (ibid.). Early in 2013 Google accelerated a push to challenge Amazon and Microsoft in cloud services. It doubled the size of its office space in the Seattle area, near the headquarters of both rivals, and began large-scale hiring of cloud-computing experts. In addition to opening another in the many revenue streams that Google enjoys, the company expects it will have the multiplier effect of luring app developers and other companies to use Google products and to launch from the Google platform.

It is hard to contend with the view that Apple has succeeded in creating a successful consumer cloud. With iCloud and iTunes Match, Apple has the largest share of the consumer cloud-services market in the United States, substantially ahead of Dropbox, Amazon Cloud Drive, and Google Drive. Moreover, the sheer size of Apple's data centers in the United States (its North Carolina facility alone is one of the largest in the world) and its seemingly constant process of expansion demonstrate the company's continuing popularity. So do the sales of its line of computers, tablets, and smartphones (Fingas 2013). Much of this success can be traced to the vision of its founder Steve Jobs, who recognized the importance of the cloud in 2008 and committed to it in 2011 when, although ill with the cancer that would soon take his life, he announced to a Worldwide Developers Conference the company's "next big insight": "We are going to demote the PC and the Mac to be just a device and we are going to move the digital hub into the cloud" (Isaacson 2011, 533). While Google, Facebook, and Twitter garner attention as media disrupters, Apple has become one of the world's largest media companies by creating cloud versions of traditional media. Apple's iTunes Store and App Store, through which people purchase music, video, and e-publications, earn more money than the combined revenue of the *New York Times*, the Simon & Schuster publishing company (which put out the best-selling biography of Apple's founder), Warner Bros. film studios, and Time Inc. (the largest magazine publisher in the United States). For the fiscal year ending September 2012 Apple's media cloud services earned about $8.5 billion, or $300 million more than the combined revenues of the others (Lee 2012). Because Apple does not clearly break out its pure media sales from those, for example, of its nonmedia apps, not all of its iTunes earnings come solely from media. Furthermore, Apple's content division is still dwarfed by conglomerates like News Corp. and Disney. Nevertheless, Apple's cloud media is increasing at a 35 percent annual rate, making it the fastest-growing commercial media operation in the world.

As successful as it has been in consumer services, Apple has barely made a dent in the business market for cloud services. When it has tried—for example, with iWeb, a website-publishing service—the company has failed to win over customers from its business-services competition. As

Apple backed off from iWeb, its customers needing applications to design websites and a host to serve them were left out of the cloud and in the cold. Unlike that of Amazon, Google, and Microsoft, Apple's business presence is felt only in hardware sales. These are admittedly substantial, but there has been little crossover from hardware into platforms, applications, and services. As one review maintained, "While iCloud, again, is awesome for personal use, businesses will find themselves better served by a terminal server parked in a secure data center, VPN [virtual private network] access to a corporate server, or another cloud-based file sharing solution that ensures only authorized users securely access corporate data" (Eckel 2012). In other words, customers will continue to shop the cloud at AWS, Google, Microsoft, or one of the other cloud business-service companies like Rackspace.

Facebook is also a major player in the cloud computing industry but, like Apple, it uses the cloud to service the gargantuan needs of its own site, which includes about 1.3 billion users. The company learned about cloud computing the hard way when in 2006 its computers came close to literally melting down. At that time Facebook was renting a small space in Santa Clara, California, and filled it with the racks of servers needed to store and process activity on its members' accounts. When electricity powering the growing system overheated critical components, the chief engineer and a few staff headed to a local pharmacy and bought every electric fan in the store. The fans worked, the servers were saved, and the rest, as they say, is history. The company had 10 million subscribers at the time and would not have reached anything close to the billion-plus members who upload 300 million photos a day if it failed to master the cloud (Glanz 2012b). Today, all those photos amount to 7 petabytes of data each month, and a cloud server system that calibrates storage conditions, including temperature, by calculating the likelihood that members will access information and photos. For example, colder storage slows retrieval time, but that works fine for the billion photos a day uploaded around Halloween that members are unlikely to want to retrieve after the costumes are put away for another year. These issues are challenging, but Facebook benefits from keeping all of its data needs in house. As a result, the key pressures facing any cloud provider or user, such as sharing, securing, and syncing, are more easily addressed by Facebook than by companies that are in the business of serving thousands of different businesses.

Amazon, Microsoft, and, to a lesser degree, Google, demonstrate their market dominance to cloud customers through ongoing price cuts that benefit the general user and drive smaller competitors out of business. It is certainly a problem for older companies like Oracle, HP, and IBM, which have significant costs associated with legacy systems that are not as scalable as the latest technology. As a result, these firms are starting to change, either by joining in partnerships with cloud companies or by acquiring promising smaller firms, as all three did in mid-2013 (Hardy 2013b, 2013e, 2013h; Kolakowski 2013). Moreover, IBM, which operates twenty-six data centers around the world, has begun to transform itself into a company that resembles marketing giants like WPP, Omnicom, and Publicis (Waters 2013c). All of this is taking place even as these same advertising firms are transforming themselves into ones driven by the use of big data in the cloud. The merger of Omnicom and Publicis to form the largest advertising business in the world is grounded in the need to take on the new competition from integrated cloud-based information-technology companies (Vega 2013).

Price cuts would appear to be an unqualified benefit to the cloud computing industry and especially to its users, who are increasingly dependent on the service. However, when carried out by industry leaders like Amazon or Google, they are also classic strategies to concentrate power over a market. This has been demonstrated throughout economic history, including in the communication industry from Western Union in telegraphy to AT&T in telephony. For years, AT&T initiated price cuts in telecommunications at the mere whiff of a competitive threat, only to raise them again when the competition was erased. That the company was able to accomplish this even under the regulatory nose of the Federal Communications Commission is evidence of its power and of the continuing failure of government to carry out regulatory responsibilities. It was not until the largest corporate users of telecommunication services organized collectively to fight back that AT&T's grip on the market was broken. Today, analysts wonder if cloud computing will go down that same path. According to one analyst, "There is a race to the bottom when it comes to cloud pricing, as the larger providers try to capture as much share as they can of this exploding market. The downside is that the smaller providers without huge war chests of cash, but with impatient investors, won't be able to make money at the prices that the larger names charge. Many of them will struggle to hang in through the days of low or no cloud computing profits—and many of them will have to toss in the towel or have the towel tossed in for them."[2] The only long-term upside is for the largest providers: "Once the smaller providers are pushed out, you can begin to raise your prices. Hmm, it sounds suspiciously like a page from the big-box stores' playbook—and a warning for cloud adopters not to count on low, low prices as the norm" (Linthicum 2012).

One of the keys to creating and maintaining market control is to exercise power up and down the chain of production. A handful of companies are doing this in one direction through price cuts and in another direction through their relationships with key IT producers—particularly the giant in this market, Intel, the world's largest and most highly valued semiconductor producer. Intel worries that the hardware world it dominated, led by the venerable PC, is in decline. According to one analyst, "Intel still has a lot of dough, but their old world is cracking" (Hardy 2013f). As a result, the company is especially concerned with pleasing what it refers to as the Big Four: Google, Microsoft, Amazon, and Facebook (Apple purchases its chips mainly from Samsung) not only because of their size but also because they lead a critical and growing market. Intel has been losing revenue in the personal-computer market that made it a historic leader. The $25.8 billion it earned from its PC client group in 2012 remains enormous, but that figure represents a decline of 2.25 percent from the first three quarters of the previous year, largely because of the shift to tablets and smartphones from standard personal computers and laptops. On the other hand, the company's revenue shot up by 6.7 percent in its data-center business, where it earned $7.9 billion. That has triggered a serious makeover at the company, which now views itself as more of a cloud-computing company than a client-server business (Hardy 2013f, 2013g).

The head of Intel's data-center group realizes that the company has to change direction, but believes that if it does so successfully, it could boost data-center revenues to $20 billion by 2016. But in order to accomplish this, Intel needs to listen and at times take direction from large, influential companies, something it is not used to doing. As Intel's data-center director described the situation, "The Big Four operate at a very different beat rate, and they are very tech savvy, so they don't want a lot of input. They all get a dedicated salesperson, the same as the others in our Top 40 customers, but there is a lot more direct innovation from them, and a lot of sharing of ideas" (Hardy 2012c). The Big Four are now active in engineering, innovating, and testing new semiconductors, including one Intel installed in September 2011 but did not introduce to the general public until March 2012. Intel admits that its willingness to absorb the potential production problems associated with a new chip that has not yet been released to the general public in order to have the latest semiconductor "was a new thing" for the company (ibid.). Meanwhile Apple, which has been dependent on Samsung for the bulk of its chips, is seriously contemplating manufacturing more of its own, partly because of the Korean manufacturer's announcement in November 2012 that it would boost chip prices sold to Apple by 20 percent. But this is also because Apple simply wants to control more of the production process (Whittaker 2012). Patent battles with Samsung are certainly an issue, but the need for control and the ability to carry it out are even bigger.

Large cloud companies are challenging firms at all points in the chain of production, from small cloud competitors to chip manufacturers. They are also going after companies that manufacture computers. Amazon, Apple, Google, Microsoft, and Facebook all now build their own and challenge companies like Intel and HP to meet or exceed performance specifications. Perhaps the most surprising for its activity in this area is Facebook, because it has not been among those identified with devices. The company has joined with both HP and Intel in the public announcement of a new chip. Google has even developed its own semiconductor but has not patented it because the company is concerned that doing so might reveal too much about its plans (Hardy 2012c). Amazon is building a global computer system including its own customized computers, data storage systems, networking systems, and power stations (Hardy 2013a).

These examples demonstrate some of the ways that large cloud companies are expanding to control the market. They are integrating internally to rationalize production from hardware to software, applications, and pricing. These moves enable companies to extend their control over cloud computing markets and, from there, establish key positions in the development of informational capitalism. One way to look at this process is to see it as a series of steps on the way to the computer utility. That would be accurate but, as was noted earlier, with no regulatory apparatus in place or on the horizon, it is also reasonable to see them as steps on the way to a global cartel, different from but also similar to the oil cartel that influenced global energy-resource markets for many years. Before long, it may be time to think seriously about the implications of a global cartel in information resources. As in oil, such a cartel would provide for the needs of organizations and individuals, using control over various stages in the production and distribution process that powers global capitalism to expand profit and control. Just as in oil or other global commodity markets, there will be small- and medium-sized producers who, from time to time, disrupt the system. Geopolitical upheavals and technological change will also have an impact. In short, cloud computing is rapidly becoming a powerful force in the world because of the quantitative and qualitative leap in information production, processing, storage, and distribution, *and* because of the way the cloud is evolving into a global, private oligopoly, well on the way to becoming a global cartel. It is also interesting to observe the ways that some of the companies making up what might become a cartel are beginning to internalize the appropriate identity for this new role. Consider Google, whose founder, Eric Schmidt, now talks about the need for the company and its competitors to start thinking of themselves as nations, especially when it comes to dispute resolution: "The adult way to run a business is to run it more like a country. They have disputes, yet they've actually been able to have huge trade with each other. They're not sending bombs at each other.... I think both Tim [Cook, Apple's CEO] and Larry [Page, Google's CEO], the sort of successors to Steve [Jobs] and me if you will, have an understanding of this state model" (Lessin 2012).

Schmidt may take this view more seriously than people think. In January 2013 he came under some pretty harsh criticism from the U.S. State Department for traveling to North Korea to meet with its leadership in a round of private diplomacy unsanctioned by the U.S. government. Citing U.S. concerns about a North Korean rocket launch one month earlier, a State Department spokesperson commented, "Frankly, we don't think the timing of this is particularly helpful." Moreover, "They are traveling in an unofficial capacity. They are not going to be accompanied by any U.S. officials. They are not carrying any messages from us. They are private citizens and they are making their own decisions." Coming from the agency responsible for American diplomacy, these are pretty strong words about a prominent U.S. citizen (Gordon 2013; see also Schmidt and Cohen 2013).

Developments like these lead some to wonder whether we are soon to face the problem of monopoly market domination that once led the government to intervene against the power of Standard Oil, IBM, and AT&T. Some have maintained that it was government pressure on IBM, even as it dropped the thirteen-year-old case in 1982, that led the company to unbundle its software from the hardware portion of the business and thereby advance the massive growth of the U.S. information-technology industry. Furthermore, it was likely that the breakup of AT&T around that same time helped make the Internet possible. In addition, the government's 1990s case against Microsoft, which had suffocated innovative companies like Netscape, made it considerably easier for Google and Facebook to appear (Fox 2013).

Not everyone agrees with the view that an oligopoly or a cartel is about to be born. Some maintain that, even with continuous price cuts, Amazon will face stiff competition from within and outside the major cloud providers, including from small innovative companies. There are also concerns about Apple's ability to enjoy elite status in the cloud. Analysts point to the difficulty the company has experienced in making its bedrock iTunes service meet the promise of seamless integration and synchronicity across platforms. Moreover, the company has not expanded its services with offerings that have earned Google and Microsoft the reputation of general cloud-server companies. Also, while everyone agrees that Microsoft has succeeded in building on its success in business services as it has moved to the cloud, doubters wonder whether Windows 8 and SkyDrive will succeed in creating a major cloud-computing presence in the consumer market (*Cloud Tweaks* 2012). Some also insist that many companies, seemingly beaten by the new Big Four (or Five, if you include Apple), have the capacity to fight back and are beginning to do so. These include big broadcasters who have seen their audiences diminish in the expansion of digital social media. According to one analyst, "But as more and more Internet-connected smart televisions find their ways into people's homes, broadcasters see a new opportunity to remain at the center of the global ad industry" (Steel 2012b). They can do so partly because the new wave of Internet-connected televisions permits broadcasters like CBS to sell new forms of advertising to direct marketers who do not typically purchase commercial advertising because they focus on coupons, search ads, and direct marketing. Internet-enabled television receivers permit broadcasters to add web advertisers to the brand advertising that built the industry. Broadcasters now capture only $10 billion of the $60 billion spent annually on direct marketing. But the shift to Internet television has the potential to enable broadcasters to expand that share and enter new markets. So while it is likely that there is some hyperbole in the statement by a CBS researcher that this will usher in "a new golden age of network television," it does indicate that "legacy" companies like NBC, CBS, and ABC will have something to say about the emerging consumer cloud cartel (ibid.).

Three of the most important challengers to Amazon and other major players in the cloud should be familiar to anyone who has purchased a computer or printer over the last twenty years: IBM, HP, and Dell. These companies hope to profit by building on their established base in data processing and storage to provide services to cloud customers and by serving other cloud-computing companies. It should come as no surprise that IBM is involved in the cloud; the company has had its fingerprints on just about every device associated with the history of computing. In addition to the standard business of hosting providers offering applications over the Internet, IBM is well on its way to, in the words of one analyst, "becoming a sort of arms provider for the cloud, selling customized hardware and software that helps governments, large and mid-sized companies, or Web developers" (Ante 2012). The company is involved in every facet of cloud services, but in 2012 it made a major move to promote its cloud to mid-sized businesses, which meant taking on market leaders AWS and Salesforce. The company was initially successful, posting double-digit gains in its cloud business. However, as with other firms whose history of providing software and other IT services preceded the development of cloud computing, success in the cloud may come at the expense of its core business. This major risk was captured in continuing revenue declines in IBM's Global Services unit and in software sales. The problem for companies like IBM, as well as for HP, Dell, and Microsoft, is that cloud services can cannibalize their own key businesses, including selling software and offering consulting services to help companies run their own IT-linked supply chains. With more and more of IT bumped to the cloud, companies are less likely to require software and services that maintain their own individual IT silos. According to one investment analyst, "We could be seeing the tip of the iceberg on an important deflationary force for traditional packaged applications services" (Ante 2012). That just happens to represent the majority of IBM's global-services business. Compounding the problem is that as long as cloud services live up to their promise of lowered IT costs for companies, and so far they have, cloud revenue for firms with a long history cannot possibly keep up with what they enjoyed in the past when they sold software and services to a host of individual businesses. This is not a problem for companies like Amazon (with its AWS offering), which does not have a legacy business to protect. How IBM, HP, Dell, Microsoft, and now Apple handle this classic case of the "innovator's dilemma" will go a long way to determining whether they have a future of any consequence in or outside the cloud (Bradshaw 2012).[3]

Rackspace represents a set of cloud companies that, unlike IBM, does not have either the advantages or disadvantages of legacy systems to worry about and has moved full bore into providing cloud services. The company, which began in 1998 as a small Internet service provider in founder Richard Yoo's garage, quickly grew to become an established host for customized applications, providing private, public, and hybrid cloud services. Widely recognized as one of the leading cloud companies and with more than 4,000 employees, Rackspace relies on what is called the OpenStack, software that is universally available based on open source principles.[4] In 2012 it approached 200,000 customers using close to 100,000 servers in about 250,000 square feet of data-center space around the world. Demonstrating that it can play with the heavyweights, the company's annual revenues surpassed $1.5 billion. Nevertheless, with long-established firms pouring money into cloud offerings, Rackspace faces an uncertain future. Consider that Dell alone invested $1 billion into its cloud in 2012. How does a firm that takes in not much more in annual revenues keep pace? Additionally, Rackspace benefited from complicated pricing for companies unsure of the technology and the market and unable to gauge pricing well. Now, as the cloud approaches commoditized utility status, with standardized pricing based on hourly use for all customers, Rackspace will have a more difficult time distinguishing itself from large firms like Dell and AWS.

Unlike Rackspace, which has grown to become a leader in general cloud services, companies like Salesforce, which uses the cloud for managing customers, and VMware, which provides cloud services through virtualized servers, are leaders among the specialists.[5] The general public became acquainted with Salesforce when it ran two ads costing $3 million during the 2011 Super Bowl. Marc Benioff founded the company in 1999 as one of the first to offer Software as a Service, and the company has since added Platform as a Service to its offerings. Its specialty is customer-relationship management (CRM), a system for managing interactions with clients and prospective clients, primarily to expand sales but also to manage customer service and technical support. CRM has been in use for two decades and is now expanding into the cloud. It operates through software that enables companies to manage their sales and customer-service processes and assess successes and failures. Rather than house CRM internally, companies contract with Salesforce, which provides software and services from its cloud servers. These include storage for all data associated with marketing and sales for a specific company and access to 20 million or so files on business contacts. Companies can also work with Salesforce to develop their own applications and tools in the Salesforce cloud. In April 2012, the company employed close to 8,000 people and generated $2.25 billion in annual revenues. In 2013 it joined a wave of merger and acquisition activity in the industry by spending $2.5 billion on ExactTarget, a company that specializes in managing sales campaigns. As cloud leaders like AWS bulk up with takeover activity, Salesforce felt the need to keep pace. The upside of specialization is that it enables a company to concentrate resources and expertise, but the downside is vulnerability. The company faced this in 2007 when it fell victim to a phishing attack that enabled hackers to lure an employee into revealing credentials that were used to gather customer contact data. The attackers went on to send further attacks to customers through fake Salesforce invoices. Some customers fell for the scam and coughed up more information. For a company specializing in the secure management of customer relations, this was an especially difficult and almost company-destroying failure. Larger firms like Amazon have faced similar challenges, but highly diversified companies like Amazon are better able to weather such storms.

The other challenge for a specialist company is facing genuine competition from one of the giants that can bankroll a major initiative and keep it going in the absence of an immediate boost in profit. Such a challenge came from Microsoft, which moved into CRM after Salesforce but has begun to catch up in customers, markets, and offerings. More importantly,

Microsoft Dynamics CRM can draw from users' familiarity with Microsoft products like Office and Outlook to make them feel more secure about taking the leap into cloud-based CRM. Furthermore, because Microsoft has years of experience in servicing on-premises IT departments, it can offer clients a mix of cloud and on-premises data-center services. The key point here is that challenges to leading cloud companies like AWS and Microsoft do come from the diverse set of firms in the cloud marketplace, but big players can also respond powerfully to even substantial inroads from specialist firms (CRM Software Blog Editors 2011). Undaunted, management at Salesforce is rethinking its future by preparing for what it calls Cloud 2, or use of the cloud in social media, especially in mobile communication. In 2012 it took a step in this direction with the $212 million purchase of Heroku, a leading Platform as a Service provider that helps companies develop cloud-based applications.

It is hard to determine whether Salesforce can withstand the competitive push from one of the giants and move into new lines of business. The outcome will also depend on how well Salesforce fends off pressure from other companies making software cloud services a key part of their business. One of the firms to contend with is Oracle, a major business-software provider that until 2012 eschewed the cloud in favor of selling software directly to its business clientele. In fact, its CEO, Larry Ellison, is known to have dismissed cloud computing as a fad. The success of Salesforce and similar companies has changed this view and, after years of foot dragging, the company went on a buying spree that added eleven new companies to the Oracle stable, all but one of which sells software applications through the cloud.[6] In 2013 the company extended its reach into the cloud by launching a set of partnerships, including deals with Microsoft and with Salesforce. These drew a lot of attention, especially among those concerned about growing concentration in the cloud industry (Hardy 2013h). Another challenger to Salesforce, the German software company SAP, has been even more aggressive than Oracle, spending $8 billion on cloud software companies. SAP and Oracle are especially concerned that the cloud will disrupt their traditional model of providing software to business clients (Waters 2013d). All of this amounts to both intense competitive pressure in the growing market to sell software through the cloud and growing consolidation in the cloud software marketplace. Although a number of small firms remain, most are facing amalgamation by choice or necessity. As one industry expert explained, "a wave of deals is likely to leave only a small handful of bigger and more diversified companies standing" (Waters 2012).

Telecommunications Companies Take to the Cloud

For several reasons, telecommunications companies have an enormous stake in cloud computing and they are well positioned to battle the leaders in the industry (Babcock 2013b). It is important to understand that these businesses, especially large companies like AT&T and Verizon, are not just conduits for other firms' data. Through their subsidiaries, they are well integrated into the entire digital economy, including content provision. Consequently, the cloud challenges the entire telecommunications industry because it provides new ways to offer services that have been part of the telecommunications industry for years. The challenge deepens as a handful of integrated conglomerates, the digital giants Google, Apple, Amazon, Facebook, and Microsoft, solidify their hold on cloud services. As these firms build towering silos of their own, once-dominant telecommunications companies are wondering about their place in the cloud economy. Rather than sit back and wait for the industry to settle, firms like AT&T and Verizon have moved quickly to secure a stake. Verizon, in particular, has become a major leader among cloud-telecommunications firms by employing a strategy that has been used over and over again in the industry's history: when the next new thing comes along, buy it. Verizon did so in 2011 by spending $1.4 billion on the major cloud company Terremark, and by acquiring the cloud-application firm CloudSwitch to make the total of the company's cloud investments for the year more than $2 billion. These deals took Verizon to the top of a growing field of telecommunications companies that have moved into the cloud and, in the words of one industry analyst "are prepping Verizon for massive future growth" (Hickey 2012). As important as it was to purchase these assets, Verizon's more important challenge was to integrate them into its other lines of business, especially wireless and FIOS, its bundled Internet access, telephone, and cable service delivered by fiber-optic cable.

For Verizon, the cloud is a key component of a media, telecommunication, and information convergence strategy that will allow the company to control practically all key nodes in the networks that produce, store, process, and distribute services to individual and organizational customers. Moreover, Terremark gives Verizon a significant international presence, something that the company has lacked, particularly in Latin America. It is uncertain whether Verizon can make this strategy work. Many companies, with AOL Time-Warner the most celebrated, have run aground with "can't miss" convergence deals. The outcome will go a long way to determining whether Verizon can join the leaders in the cloud-based communications industry. Complicating matters for Verizon is the expansion of competitive pressures that threaten its comfortable duopoly with AT&T in the United States. The acquisitions of Sprint and of Clearwire have made SoftBank, in the words of one analyst, "a better-funded number three with the spectrum to launch low-priced wireless data products." Moreover, the T-Mobile–Metro PCS merger created a fourth big player in the U.S. market and the ability of the spectrum-rich Dish Network promises to further disrupt the comfortable control of the market that Verizon has enjoyed (*Globe Investor* 2012; Taylor 2013b).

The U.S. Government: Trusting the Cloud and Commercial Providers

Not all cloud computing is controlled by private organizations. But it is interesting to observe the extent to which the U.S. government depends on the private sector for its cloud computing needs, including relationships based on no-bid, sole-supplier contracts with the largest cloud providers. This is significant for several reasons, not the least of which is the amount of money involved. According to one report, the government spends $80 billion annually on information technology and plans to move about 25 percent of its IT budget to the cloud. An example of the movement to cloud services provided on a single-source, no-bid basis is the Naval Supply Systems Command's plan to use Amazon Web Services to store and distribute digital photography and video. The Navy's argument is that AWS offers a single, integrated package that is more reliable and less prone to attack than other cloud services (Foley 2012). Furthermore, NASA, which helped to develop OpenStack, the open source standard that IBM uses for its cloud, also contracted with AWS (Thibodeau 2013). Even the

CIA planned to tender AWS a $600 million contract until IBM blew the whistle, raising questions about how the federal government handles cloud contracts, and a review of the agreement with AWS (Woodall 2013). While waiting to learn whether its bid for the CIA's cloud business would succeed, IBM won the largest government cloud-computing contract, worth $1 billion, from the Interior Department (Miller and Strohm 2013). That helped cushion the blow for IBM when Amazon was officially awarded the CIA contract (Babcock 2013a).

These moves are not very surprising, particularly in light of the history of the U.S. government's relationship to large communication companies (Mazzucato 2013). For years, government agencies, including the Department of Defense, had a very close relationship with IBM for computing and an even closer one with AT&T for telecommunications services. Even as business consumers lined up to support breaking up AT&T and deregulating the telecommunications industry in order to lower prices, the DOD argued that national security required the end-to-end service that AT&T provided. It was not until the Pentagon was assured that security needs would be met that it dropped its opposition to breaking up the telecommunications giant (Schiller 1981). Given this preference for large, stable companies, it is not surprising that the government would turn to AWS to meet some of its cloud-computing needs.

The U.S. government's current move to the cloud is propelled by the belief that cloud computing must become a central means of meeting its information-technology needs. In December 2010 the federal Chief Information Officers Council released a plan to reform government information technology, which included requiring agencies to adopt a "cloud-first" policy for new IT deployments. According to the plan, cloud-first is driven by three interrelated forces. First, large data centers provide economies of scale that are necessary to meet the growing needs of the federal government's "computation infrastructure." For federal IT planners, it is less expensive to centralize data in a few large centers than to retain it in local offices. Second, cloud systems are able to provide almost any type of computation on demand. It is difficult to predict the type and speed of processing and analysis that will be needed and the planners side with those who believe that cloud systems are agile enough to meet their needs, including those they cannot now anticipate. Finally, the cloud unleashes unprecedented analytics capability on large data collections. It is clear from this view that federal IT planners rank big data among the major attractions of cloud computing. Data centers are intended to be not only storage warehouses that agencies can call on when they need data, but also active producers of information that draw on stored data sets (Page 2011). In 2011 NIST released its report defining cloud computing and carefully describing the cloud's specific characteristics to enable managers and staff operating within agencies to have a better idea or, in some cases, their first clear idea of what it was they were being ordered to implement. In 2012 the National Science Foundation (NSF 2012) produced a short report supporting NIST's conclusions and committing the government to fund research into cloud computing. The combination of strong affirmations from the federal government's CIO, from NIST, and from the NSF provided the grounding for strong state support for the cloud.

There are also major implications in a number of government demonstration projects in education and research. One of the most significant is a program operated out of the National Endowment for the Humanities Office of Digital Humanities. It demonstrates how government's use of the cloud and big data is contributing to the restructuring of education, and not just in the areas where we would expect change, such as computer science and the disciplines associated with the sciences. It is also reaching into the social sciences and even the humanities. One can learn a lot about the direction of change from the size of a force creating it, but one can also learn a great deal from its reach, as when government projects extend to fields traditionally kept outside the scope of computerization. Chapter 5 examines the digital humanities in the context of assessing big data in the cloud. Suffice it to say here that the digital humanities project represents an important initiative that is often lost in the understandable focus on larger military and civilian projects. Its significance for the future of education and research far outweighs the size of its budget (Gold 2012).

In spite of the enthusiasm for the cloud in government, there remain several issues that have the military and intelligence sectors especially concerned about moving data to corporate-owned cloud systems. Arguably the most important is security. At the very least, there is concern about moving classified data and computer power essential for combat missions to off-site locations. Formal concerns have already been raised with respect to the security of data in NASA's cloud systems (Kerr 2013). Furthermore, the size and complexity of government and especially military computer systems make the prospect of moving to the cloud very expensive. It would not be a matter of simply relying solely on available technologies because many government departments, and especially the military and intelligence sectors, require customized systems that are integrated within and across units. Finally, government, and especially defense, requires a very high level of support and, while some of the major providers have developed excellent backup for their customers, it is uncertain whether the necessary support is available in the current cloud industry (Gangireddy 2012).

Even in the face of these worries, the government is showing a level of faith in private cloud companies that has surprised some experts. This extends to using private cloud firms to provide security for the government's systems. For example, the Naval War College awarded a single-source contract to the SaaS vendor CloudLock to safeguard the implementation of online tools like Google Docs and Google Drive. Given the concern with security, one analyst responds to this use of the cloud to protect the cloud with the conclusion that "it's remarkable that agencies are defying conventional wisdom in this way" (Foley 2012). In a more significant step, intelligence agencies are beginning to make use of commercial cloud computing, including the public cloud, which serves all customers. Furthermore, according to one IT leader in the intelligence community, agencies now have enough confidence in the public cloud "to bring some commercial cloud capabilities inside our fence lines" (ibid.).

The alternative to this use of commercial cloud services is to retain IT activity on-site or to develop a government, military, or intelligence-agency cloud capability. This is certainly taking place too. In 2011, Los Alamos National Lab began providing IaaS services from its own data center and has joined with the National Nuclear Security Administration to develop a community cloud that extends to the entire Department of Energy (ibid.). Of greater strategic significance is the Department of Defense decision to create a military cloud as a means to fend off cyber-attacks that have been proliferating in recent years. These include the April 2010 attack emanating from China that redirected 15 percent of Internet traffic through China's networks for eighteen minutes and the 2011 virus attack on U.S. drone weapons. The latter used malware to record keystrokes and required continuous deletion and rebuilding of hard drives. To avoid these attacks, DARPA set up Cloud to the Edge (COE) in 2011, which began by opening a set of hotspots for secure communication. According to one analyst, COE looks a lot like Google's suite of online services, minus the search engine (Tanaka 2012). It is hosted on a secure system of servers by the Defense Information Systems Agency, which has itself given out a $45 million sole-source contract to the Alliance Technology Group for a data-storage facility to provide four exabytes of storage capacity (Hoover 2013). To back up its cloud initiative, the Department of Defense committed another $5 million to advance its cyber-battleground project, with the auspicious title of Plan X, that would allow the agency "to rehearse and manage what officials call 'cyberwarfare in real-time, large-scale, and dynamic network environments'" (Nextgov 2013).[7] To implement its plan the Pentagon will hire and deploy 4,000 military and civilian technology specialists to the U.S. Cyber Command, but that is not likely to be enough (Brannen 2013). This prompts some to anticipate a near-term shortfall in cloud experts (Weisinger 2013).

It is not just security that prompts interest in the cloud. The DOD also wants to better manage its IT budget and hopes the turn to cloud computing will go a long way to saving 30 percent by 2016. Already engaged in the consolidation and modernization of data centers, the DOD has eliminated many and cut the number of technical support desks in half. Overall, it would like to reduce the number of networks, data centers, and help desks by 80 percent (Tanaka 2012). Storing everything from unclassified to top-secret information, the military cloud began with a test case led by the National Security Agency, which gathers, stores, processes, and analyzes huge amounts of data. Typically sheltered from the public attention that is more typically directed at the CIA and the FBI, the NSA, which is three times the size of the CIA and has one-third of total U.S. intelligence spending, burst onto the front pages of newspapers worldwide in the spring of 2013. A series of leaks and newspaper accounts revealed that, contrary to previous claims, the agency worked closely with U.S. telecommunications providers and the largest Internet companies to gather data on Americans and foreigners by scooping up and analyzing telephone conversations, emails, social-media postings, and other electronic communication. With the $20 million Prism program that included major Silicon Valley and telecommunications companies that shared information on users with the NSA, the spy agency hoped to better target threats to the United States by analyzing metadata—that is, who was contacting whom, as well as content whose keywords big-data analysts could use to root out suspected terrorists (Luckerson 2013). Nevertheless, many critics took issue with what appeared to be an unprecedented and, until the leaks, secretive attack on the privacy of users (Wilson and Wilson 2013). Controversies aside, government policy makers hope that cloud computing will enable the NSA to meet its goals with greater security and at lower cost, thereby demonstrating the value of moving other government agencies to the cloud. Nevertheless, experts worry that concentrating military information in one large cloud system, however well secured, provides an inviting target for cyber-attackers around the world. One expert worries that the move to the cloud is the equivalent of "painting a cyber bulls-eye" on the NSA and the military: "Cloud computing, in military terms, fosters a target-rich environment because the very things that make the cloud appealing also make it a tempting mark. Because of this and the high probability that a vast amount of data will be stored on a cloud, attackers only need to be lucky once as compared to having to be lucky multiple times when attacking a legacy system. With this in mind, a more appropriate question for the NSA would be 'what kind of information would your organization refuse to place on a Cloud?'" (Tanaka 2012)

It is not as if military planners are unaware of the security problems of cloud computing. According to DARPA, "Cloud computing infrastructures, in particular, tightly integrate large numbers of hosts using high speed interconnection fabrics that can serve to propagate attacks even more rapidly than conventional networked systems. Today's hosts, of course, are highly vulnerable, but even if the hosts within a cloud are reasonably secure, any residual vulnerability in the hosts will be amplified dramatically" (ibid.). Nevertheless, like many other agencies, it is convinced that, with appropriate security measures, the military benefits of cloud systems outweigh the risks because "clouds and distributed computing environments can: provide redundant hosts, correlate attack information from across the ensemble, and provide for diversity across the network" (ibid.). What matters for the military is whether it can develop what it calls "mission-oriented resilient clouds" that can be deployed effectively in combat.

Clouds over China

Cloud computing systems have a firm foothold in the United States, where about 40 percent of the world's data centers are located, but they are also spreading internationally. Outside the United States, Scandinavia has become a major data-center venue and the cloud is no stranger to the Middle East, but China has made the most significant progress in the overall development of cloud computing (Horn 2011; Glover 2013). By the end of 2012 China represented about 3 percent of the global cloud marketplace, but it is expected to grow at a 40 percent annual rate, reaching $18.6 billion in annual revenue by the end of 2013. Led by China, the Asia region is expected to lead the world in cloud traffic and workloads by 2016 (Ong 2012). China's burgeoning cloud industry benefits from minimal competition with the major U.S. providers. Amazon is not there and Microsoft has just begun to introduce its Azure cloud service in China. This has left lots of room for the development of indigenous cloud services, including the Alibaba Group, which provides both cloud infrastructure and services to a variety of national and multinational clients over its Aliyun network. In addition, Baidu, known in the West as the "Google of China" for its prowess in search services, has invested heavily in cloud storage and processing, evidenced in a 2012 investment of $1.6 billion in a new data center and a deal to offer free personal cloud storage on Android phones. Baidu's major competitive challenge comes from Tencent, an instant-messaging and online-gaming company with 400 million users, making it one of the largest consumer-application cloud companies in the world, with a valuation in 2012 of $60 billion. In 2013 Tencent took a major leap in the cloud marketplace when it announced that it would be the first to build a center in the western China city of Chongqing, where planners expect significant new growth in the cloud (*People's Daily Online* 2013). In 2012, the world's leader in telecommunications equipment production, Huawei, also moved into cloud computing and storage, a decision that led to a significant growth in company profit (Reuters 2013a). China's cloud development is helped by the presence of Asian firms like Pacnet that benefit from having developed network and data-center services in the Asian region, including Hong Kong, Singapore, and Australia (Powell 2013).

In 2013, Baidu demonstrated that it does far more than provide service to China when it signed a deal with France Telecom to offer its mobile browser throughout Africa and the Middle East on the French company's smartphones (Thomas 2013). In addition to these network-driven cloud providers, companies have emerged that provide storage services. A leader in this area is MeePo, a storage service similar to Dropbox. The company has experienced remarkable growth, with capacity in 2012 reliably estimated at 50 terabytes (Chou 2012).

One of the most ambitious cloud projects in the world is China's commitment to build cloud cities. The goal is to construct giant data centers connected to firms that provide value-added services, as well as research and development for domestic and international markets. Some of these involve working with major international partners who provide capital and expertise, even as local companies control the project. For example, China-based Range Technology is teaming up with IBM to construct a 6.6-million-square-foot cloud-computing center in Langfang, near Beijing. It will provide cloud services to government and private-sector organizations, as well as host cloud systems and mobile devices (Bundy and Haley 2012). In addition to linking up computer-service providers like Baidu and computer companies like Lenovo, cloud centers also welcome the involvement of China's large telecommunications companies. For example, in 2011 China Telecom formed a partnership with the global cloud-services company SAP to offer cloud services to small and medium-size businesses in China. In 2012 the country's three giant telecommunications firms, China Telecom, China Mobile, and China Unicom, agreed to invest $47 billion to develop data centers, including one of the world's largest, to help create an economic hub in Chengdu, a city in China's southwestern province of Sichuan. Chengdu already builds one-fifth of the world's computers and the plan is to expand the Tianfu Software Park around the cloud data centers. In this way Chengdu will move up the value ladder from computer manufacturing to data storage, processing, and transmission, on the way to becoming a center for research and development (Evans-Pritchard 2012). With fifty-one universities graduating 200,000 scientists and engineers each year, Chengdu has the foundation to take these steps to higher-value production.

China certainly appears to be poised to become a world leader in cloud computing. It is building enormous cloud data centers, including some of the world's largest, at a feverish pace. Not satisfied with the construction of cloud facilities, it is creating entire cloud cities. Of equal significance, China is carrying out a detailed cloud-computing strategy that is most significant for integrating all the major participants, including hardware manufacturers who are becoming leaders in server production for the global marketplace, software designers, application developers, business-service providers, and telecommunications companies. But there is another side to this success story. China faces technical challenges, including connectivity problems and the absence of certification programs for cloud companies and their staff, something that has been institutionalized among leading companies like Amazon. Moreover, as Chapter 4 describes, cloud computing faces numerous environmental, social, and labor challenges. These are all greatly heightened by the size and speed of cloud development in China, as well as by the unsettled nature of its political and legal infrastructure (Qian 2013).

Cloud computing creates significant environmental problems associated with its massive energy requirements and, secondarily, with construction and disposal of materials and equipment. These are all exacerbated in China because the country is already plagued by widespread air pollution as energy needs have spiked across the country, and reliance on coal-fired power plants deepens the problem. Building the world's largest cloud facilities, including entire cloud cities, will only add to an already critical problem. The same holds for security, surveillance, and privacy issues. These pose challenges everywhere, but nowhere more prominently than in China, where there is no guarantee that if they build it, the world will come. China has long been mired in controversies about the security of personal and organizational data. Will Western companies and governments that have complained about the theft of data store their information in China's data centers? A society that practices massive surveillance of its own citizens and routinely censors information can hardly be surprised to find very low trust in the security of its cloud systems. It is not only foreign businesses that worry about surveillance issues. A 2013 Forrester Research report documented concerns among Chinese entrepreneurs who are reluctant to take to the cloud. Some of this results from the lack of experience with outsourcing or externally managed services. With little to prepare them for the cloud, companies are understandably cautious. But security worries loom large and this accounts for a distinct preference for private-cloud services as the less risky cloud option (Qing 2013). Finally, China's hyper-accelerated industrialization has created massive labor problems that include but extend well beyond the notorious practices of the electronics manufacturer Foxconn. Annually producing 200,000 scientists and engineers in one city alone is an outstanding achievement, but managing them and the millions of new workers who constitute China's army of knowledge workers is an entirely different challenge. From construction to operation, from maintenance to support, cloud computing makes enormous demands on labor markets and workplace practices. To add these demands to a society already in the throes of labor upheavals across the country will certainly tax China's leadership for years to come.

This overview of cloud computing has covered key features of its genealogy, defining elements, key characteristics, and major exemplars. The next chapter builds on this foundation by examining how cloud computing is promoted in marketing and myth, and describes why it is important for supporters to fashion this complex, but nonetheless banal, technology into the technological sublime.

CHAPTER 3
SELLING THE CLOUD SUBLIME

Windows gives me the family nature never could.
—Television commercial for
the Microsoft cloud

How does a massive data factory give rise to the image of a cloud? Although the metaphor of the cloud came up from time to time in early discussions of computing at a distance, the immediate reason can be found in most technical primers on the subject: the image of a cloud was used in diagrams to describe the interconnected elements of a computer communications network. With its start in the banality of a technical diagram, the image of the cloud has grown to take on a richer aesthetic that corporate marketing has taken the lead in building. To appreciate the significance of cloud computing, it is important to go beyond what the many technical books describe to understand how it is being constructed in discourse and sold to business, government, and individual consumers because these too help to shape what cloud computing means. The materiality of the cloud is not limited to data centers, computers, software, applications, and data. It is also embodied in campaigns to remake the prosaic stuff of engineering into the compelling aesthetic of the cloud. Just as it was important to describe the technical, political, and economic dimensions of cloud computing in the last chapter, it is also essential to examine how it is being sold in advertising, social media, private-think-tank reports, intergovernmental reports, lobbying, and trade shows. Discourse, myth, and magic have a large role to play in creating the cloud.

It does sometimes feel as if technologies appear like magic, not *deus ex machina* but more like *machina ex deo*, as machines emerging from the genius of inventors (preferably working in their parents' garages). Even well-regarded biographies like Walter Isaacson's (2011) on Steve Jobs cannot help but build a shrine, even as they tell a good story. Indeed, when it comes to technology, the shrine appears to be an essential part of the story. Myths celebrate this magic and it is important to take this process seriously because it helps us to understand how we think and feel about the cloud. But it is also important to draw back the curtain on this version of "the great and glorious Oz" and reveal the process that gives life to the magic. As Chapter 2 described, cloud computing is made up of data centers, servers, software, applications, and data, all of which are designed, built, and operated by thousands of workers, ranging from highly skilled engineers to unskilled laborers. These provide the familiar foundations for successful cloud systems. But the cloud is also made up of words, starting with the name *cloud*, as well as the images and discourses that give shape and form to how we think about cloud computing. Put another way, technology is not only composed of the material that enters its creation; it is also defined by the *labor* of those who design, build, and operate it and by the *language* we use to describe and imagine it. More formally, technology results from the mutual constitution of objects, labor, and language. This chapter focuses on how cloud computing is created in language and discourse by constructing, with an eye to selling, the cloud sublime.

Assessing the effort to sell cloud computing is important because companies in the cloud business have a steep cliff to climb if they are to convince companies, government agencies, and individual consumers to sign up. That is because selling the cloud means convincing a potential client to give up its data on employees, customers, products, services, and competitors and trust that it will be available when needed. This raises questions about data security, the privacy of transactions, system reliability, and the future of the client's IT unit. Businesses and government agencies know that when a cloud company tries to sell them on the idea of ending dependence on separate data silos, they are not just talking about cost savings and efficiency. It also means a fundamental change in how the business or agency works, how it is organized, and how power flows throughout its structure.

There is also nothing simple about winning over individual consumers to use the cloud for anything more than the most basic tasks like Gmail. Why store files, audio, and video in an unknown location when you can leave it all on your own device or back it up to a portable external drive? Aside from the fees charged for cloud storage, people wonder about the wisdom of giving a company, even one with a good reputation, photographs of your family, your treasured music collection, personal email, and sensitive files. Companies may promise that your files will be secure and available the instant you want them, but just how secure are they, how reliable is the service, how private are your communications, and what will your cloud provider do when a government agency demands to access your files? What happens to your data if the cloud company you deal with goes out of business? The decision to enter the cloud, for businesses as well as for individuals, is far from automatic and certainly not simple, and so it has to be promoted vigorously.

Advertising the Cloud

On February 6, 2011, a worldwide audience in the hundreds of millions, including 111 million Americans watching on Fox, to that date the largest audience in U.S. television history, settled in for the annual spectacle of the Super Bowl. In addition to the many keen to see whether the Pittsburgh Steelers or the Green Bay Packers would win the Lombardi Trophy that goes to the annual winner, there were many whose primary interest was watching and assessing the commercials. Given the size of the audience and the intensity of the spectacle, sponsors save their best ads for the big event. Among the recognized best that year were a Volkswagen commercial featuring a young Darth Vader practicing the Force, an ad for the Chevy Camaro about the demure but dangerous Miss Evelyn, and a plug for Coca-Cola that brought together a desert border guard and a dragon. Given the price of buying the attention of all those viewers, it is not surprising that big companies dominate the ads, paying $3 million for a spot.

Sandwiched among these tall trees was a lesser-known company that sold something many Americans used but knew very little about. For it was at Super Bowl XLV that the cloud-computing company Salesforce debuted two advertisements for its Chatter service. Both commercials were slick animations meant to introduce the audience to a free private network for businesses that could use the cloud to help internal communication and collaboration, as well as expand their reach. The ads features Will.i.am, lead singer of the musical group Black Eyed Peas, who poses the question, "What do you think of the cloud?" which leads to a tour of Chatter. The spot focuses on Chatty the Cloud, who helps keep the band "in line … and on the same page," with band members communicating about tour updates, "fly shoe designs," and new DJ gigs. All of this is done in complete privacy and safety. The slogan that ends the spot, "Do impossible things as a team," marks the difference the cloud makes (Chatter .com 2011a). The second spot features Will and the Peas demonstrating some of those impossible things, including getting a job, turning an old factory into a Silicon Valley workplace palace, and finding great clothes. It ends on the most impossible note of all, as Chatty brings together the warring Republican Party elephant and the Democratic Party donkey in a conciliatory embrace (Chatter.com 2011b). Each ad pointed to a website that provided more details about the Salesforce cloud.

These ads were unusual because they promoted a specialized business product, as opposed to the more typical consumer goods and services aired during most mass-audience events. Chatty the Cloud was not the stuff of hot cars and beer, nor even of GoDaddy, whose ads approach—and some say cross—the boundary of permissible sexual content. Nor was Chatty a critical success. Most analysts did not relegate the commercials to the trash bin of Super Bowl failures, but the lack of punch did not make them memorable. If anything, the Salesforce ads succeeded in letting the audience know that there was this new thing called the cloud, which mattered enough that well-known pop musicians gave it a ride.

Arguably the ad's most important point, which occupies the critical last frames, is the proclamation "Do impossible things as a team," because it turns cloud computing into a myth. In this case a myth does not refer to something that can be judged by whether it is true or false.[1] After all, doing the impossible is by definition a false proposition. Rather, myths are judged by their resonance: not by their truthfulness, but by whether they are alive or dead in the popular imagination. They are the stories we tell each other to help deal with life's unanswerable questions, and when it comes to technology, they help raise our latest "next new thing" to the realm of the transcendent. Myths provide ballast for the sublime but fleeting visions contained in the promise of universal knowledge, virtual worlds, and unlimited communication that were once embodied in religion and nature but are now more likely supported by digital technologies. The assertion that cloud computing enables a group to do the impossible is similar to the claim that the telegraph would bring world peace or that lighting up the streets with electricity would end crime (Nye 1994). It is not an exaggeration to suggest that we make myths whenever we make new technologies, and furthermore that technology, especially communication technology, has become, like religion and the natural world before it, a source of the sublime. Today, many people have become cloud worshipers (Lohr 2013c).

Specifically, technology becomes sublime when we attribute to it superhuman powers, either heavenly or hellish, that were once reserved for religion and the supernatural, or for treasured natural wonders. Prior to the development of the technologies that propelled the modern age, such as the railroad, the telegraph, and electrification, the sublime was associated with images of transcendence located in religion and in nature. First, only the gods or god could achieve the level of transcendence that transported people beyond all language and certainly beyond the banality of everyday life. The very name Yahweh, according to one commentator, "also bespeaks the utter transcendence of God. In Himself, God is beyond all 'predications' or attributes of language: He is the Source and Foundation of all possibility of utterance and thus is beyond all definite descriptions" (Parsons 2013). The "unutterable name" conjures both the rapturous awe and the terrifying shock of the sublime. For many, the religious sublime increasingly came to be met by the natural sublime as wonders of nature like the Grand Canyon, natural eruptions like earthquakes and volcanoes, or the celestial magic of a solar eclipse conjured some of the same awe-inspiring and fearsome feelings. While certainly not eclipsing the religious sublime, which remains a powerful force around the world, the natural sublime has grown in significance and may continue to do so as the terrifying results of climate change leave more and more people speechless. But as Rebecca Solnit (2010) has described in her remarkable book about how people respond to unspeakable disasters, there is considerable evidence that, just as an extraordinarily resilient community arose in the time of Yahweh, we observe sublime acts of community-building in an age of natural disasters.

It is difficult to capture the sublime in words, so we refer to images like the locomotive ripping through a prairie field in the 1870s that terrified onlookers into a sublime stupor, or the Grand Canyon resplendent in the morning light that renders sublime its seemingly infinite layers of contrasting color. Some of the great modernist writers could create a sublime riff through a stream of consciousness such as the one described by Virginia Woolf in the character of Clarissa Dalloway, who transcends time and space in a morning walk through London. Indeed one of *Mrs. Dalloway*'s most sublime scenes involves what has to be one of the first acts of cloud creation, as a sky-writing airplane lifts the eyes and then the hearts of observers on the ground until the airplane reveals a commercial purpose in a banal advertisement for candy. Echoes of this cloud return in the work of photographer Sergio de la Torre, whose 2003 digitally constructed skywriting cloud exclaims against an azure sky, "Thinking About Expansion." Today, great popular filmmakers like Steven Spielberg conjure the sublime in what has been described as his signature visual technique, what the film writer Matt Patches dubs "the Spielberg face" (think of the young Dakota Fanning gazing back through the rear window of her dad's car as the carnage erupts in the film *War of the Worlds*), and is best described in a video essay by Kevin B. Lee: "Eyes open, staring in wordless wonder in a moment where time stands still. But above all, a childlike surrender in the act of watching" (Scott 2012).

Yes, doing the impossible is a marketing exaggeration—some would say a marketing convention. But it is also the foundation for a myth that asserts superhuman or sublime prowess. The historian of culture Leo Marx put it best when he asserted that "the rhetoric of the technological sublime" involves hymns to progress that rise "like froth on a tide of exuberant self-regard sweeping over all misgivings, problems, and contradictions" (1964, 207; see also Mosco 2004). No longer locked into what Edmund Burke 250 years ago called the "stale, unaffecting familiarity" of the banal (Burke 1998, 79), the sublime technology becomes transcendent.

The Salesforce ads had the widest reach of any cloud-computing spots, but that company was not the only one to hitch its wagon to the National

Football League's (NFL's) star. In fact, strange as this may sound, one of its major competitors, SAP, paid for the right to be the "official cloud solutions software sponsor" of the NFL. Nor was Salesforce the first to try to sell the cloud to a mass audience. In earlier ads Microsoft sought to reach its business and consumer audiences separately. The software giant's campaign reflects one of the chief marketing challenges that cloud companies face: how to sell a service aimed at both corporate and individual consumers. Microsoft's answer was separate tracks, both of which attempt to advance the myth of the all-powerful cloud but, as with most campaigns that try to sell technology, with more magic in the sales pitch to consumers. In 2010 with the unveiling of its new business cloud services, Microsoft developed commercials around "cloud power." The typical one features managers and IT professionals boasting about all that they can do with the new force of the cloud:

I can change how everyone works ... without changing how everyone works.

I can turn a spike in demand into a joy ride.

I can expand overseas, overnight.

I can take apps live in fifteen minutes.

I am master and commander of my own private cloud.

I am the champion of a corporate culture of yes.

I have cloud power. I have cloud power. I have cloud power.

The most comprehensive solutions for the cloud, on earth. Microsoft.

The ad is simple, with the sublimity restrained by winking references to bringing about change without the unsettling experience that change often involves. The emphasis is on pleasure. The equally unsettling spike in demand is no longer an IT nightmare; it is a joy ride. Global expansion takes place overnight and software that would inevitably bring bug-infested turmoil goes out in just fifteen minutes. Executives are now (Jedi?) masters and the boss whose workday is typically filled with painful repetitions of "no" can now say "yes" over and over again. These promises are the stuff of corporate myth, but not so utopian as to undermine a sales pitch to knowing executives. They remain within the realm of the real, the heavenly cloud on earth, delivered by Microsoft. The products themselves—Windows Azure, Microsoft Office 365, and Windows Hyper-V Server—make the briefest of appearances, with the emphasis placed on the value of the company providing the service. Microsoft itself is mythologized in the faces of the presenters, whose nationalities and speech describe a company that covers the entire globe, from the British executive who turns change into a joy ride to the Indian businessman who can go global overnight. It may be the cloud on earth, but the earth is well covered by Microsoft (Warren 2010).

A bit later Microsoft released a very different advertisement that, understandably, aroused controversy. This campaign directs individual consumers who learn that the solution to problems involves a trip "To the Cloud." The ad features a Mom carefully examining the family photo she wants to preserve. And what an unruly family it is! With a frustrated look on her face, Mom complains because her daughter is texting, her son is sticking an action figure in his brother's ear, and Dad is trying to remove it (the action figure, not the ear). The solution is found in taking a trip "To the Cloud," where Mom "can take all these unruly shots and swap in some smiles." This means downloading from the cloud images of each member of her family in happy repose and placing them in the appropriate spots to perfect her family photo. Mom is thrilled because, thanks to the cloud, "finally a photo I can share without ridicule." As if this were not enough, Mom turns to her "real" family, which is looking bored, except for Dad, who appears depressingly sad, as he bows his head in shame. The spot ends with Mom's thankful conclusion: "Windows gives me the family nature never could."[2]

This ad stirred some controversy for a couple of reasons—primarily because it features a mom who appears to prefer a digitally altered version of her family to her "unruly" real one. Who needs the family nature provided when the cloud can send you a better one, or at least one free from the all-too-human propensity to act autonomously? Added to this is the admittedly geeky concern that Mom has not really gone to the cloud at all. Both concerns are captured in the comments of one apparent cloud enthusiast: "Wrong, bad and misleading. This has nothing whatsoever to do with Cloud Services. A touch screen PC and Windows 7 running Live Essentials LOCALLY to mash up a family picture. Where's the 'Cloud' in that? The only on-line experience is pushing the resulting piece of fakery to Facebook. These adverts are the worst piece of Cloudwashing around at the moment."[3] It is hard to know what is more phony, Mom's new Windows family or Microsoft's claim that she has taken to the cloud. One might reasonably argue that the charge of cloudwashing, the term applied to identifying as a cloud service what is really something else, is a quibble. Mom appears to be going to a cloud service to find more appropriate portraits of her family. One might also make the case that the cloud does expand Mom's options. She could use the "unruly" photo or the one that the cloud makes possible. What makes this advertisement particularly interesting is that it explicitly represents the triumph of the technological over the natural sublime.

It would be easy to overinterpret this ad. After all, it's just a commercial and, like so many that came before, it uses provocation, simplification, and exaggeration to send a message, keep it in the viewer's head, and sell a product. But it is also safe to say that this particular spot is doing more than just selling viewers on the benefits of cloud computing. It also reflects and advances a stream of thought generally described as post-humanism, a philosophical perspective that questions the human-centered values that emerged in the Renaissance and became foundational in Enlightenment thought (Hayles 1999). The humanist would find it beyond the pale for anyone, let alone a mother, to replace a flesh-and-blood family with a technological substitute. For the post-humanist, it is nothing more than accepting the reality of our time and using it to human advantage. Rather than feeling guilt for appearing antihuman, Mom is justified in demonstrating the pride of accomplishment for accepting what technology has to offer. Post-humanist thought has helped to shape how many people, and not just professional philosophers, think about technology, whether it has to do with biological or informational systems. Some have taken serious issue with the position, arguing that it is little more than surrendering progressive values to a wealth machine masquerading as a new philosophy of technology (Winner 2004). The debate around post-humanism has illuminated many issues that are far more serious than the ethics of image substitutes. These include using technology to extend life or end it, to begin life or to terminate life before it emerges. They also address robotics, automation, and the opportunities and threats posed by thinking and feeling machines. The "Mom's Family" spot *is* just an ad, but it also provides cloud computing, and Microsoft, with the opportunity to take sides in a growing debate. Clearly they choose the technological over the natural sublime and, in doing so, advance an increasingly powerful myth or story line in global culture: the superiority of technology over humanity as an instrument of transcendence.

Microsoft chose to pursue both business and the home consumer in its cloud-computing marketing campaign. Two other IT giants chose a different strategy, with IBM focusing on business customers and Apple concentrating on the individual consumer market. They are both significant for understanding the discursive construction of the cloud. From its first commercials in 2009, IBM has had the longest run among major corporations of advertising cloud computing. Despite a simple message and a reliance on talking heads, IBM's ads are among the most lavishly produced. The 2012 ad "All in the Clouds" used thirty-two animators, designers, illustrators, and modelers to bring to life an imaginary world that exists only in the cloud (IBM 2012a). According to the company, "Everything in the spot was painted by hand and then mapped onto 3D wireframes to create the completely bespoke look. Each character has a backstory, which sparked the animators' imaginations. Every 'location' was extensively researched to make sure the transformed world looked like the real one" (Marshall 2012). The commercial begins with a voiceover welcoming viewers "to business as usual," thanks to "the IBM smart cloud." As we see, however, business as usual is anything but. The first animation swoops down on a small laboratory in Berlin that uses cloud computing to fight cancer. The second lands in China, where the cloud is making it possible for an industrial city to become a high-tech hub in less than four years. Then it's back to the West, where Britain is building a smart grid to help cut emissions by up to 80 percent. Finally, we return to Asia, where "even an independent studio in Malaysia can produce big-time blockbusters." Then we see the one nonanimated human in the commercial, a woman who, behind studious-looking eyeglasses, announces, "Transforming business through the cloud. That's what I'm working on. I'm an IBMer. Let's build a smarter planet."

Smart is the operative word in these IBM commercials and, even though the visuals have gotten more sophisticated and expensive, the message remains what it has been since the series began in 2009: computers, including the cloud, will construct a smarter planet. IBM departs from most cloud companies, which have been reluctant to advertise widely for their business services. Indeed, one industry observer has chided cloud executives who "think their *totally awesome* solution can market itself. Once people try it and see how great it is, they'll be sure to tell their business associates—right? Well, actually . . . no" (Shaw 2013). IBM has certainly not been among the reluctant and, in a step unusual for most of today's advertisers, whatever the business, it has deployed a major print advertising campaign around the cloud. This includes a print campaign, which proclaims, in case you forgot the operative term, "Smarter Technology for a Smarter Planet." Like most of the company's ads, it does not shy away from clever hyperbole: "For a technology that's built to be invisible, cloud computing is making sweeping changes everywhere you look." It then demonstrates this with examples from "the mainstream" to "the revenue stream" (IBM 2012b).

For IBM, by 2012 the cloud, or more specifically, the IBM SmartCloud, had already made it into the mainstream, bringing "a change in the atmosphere." Companies can now sell seafood "fresh off the hook," engineers can create new medicines from genomics, and tennis tournaments can serve "dynamic tension outside the venue." While these do appear to be far from the examples that conclusively demonstrate "how businesses are reinventing themselves with IBM SmartCloud," IBM appears to be more interested in demonstrating how companies are beginning to move from these mainstream examples to the "revenue stream." This represents for IBM a kind of cloud 2.0 whereby companies move from a cloud "taken at face value"—that is, as "a conduit for increasing flexibility and reducing complexity." Now, "forward-looking businesses are rethinking the cloud" by taking profitable advantage of new mobile, social, and big-data analytical capabilities. IBM promises that its customers will be able to change models for how to do business, disrupt whole industries, and speed up the process of getting products and services to market. While some might mourn the demise of the IT department, the SmartCloud enables conversations that were once limited to the tech experts to take place across the company. The ad is short on specifics, singling out only one company, 3M, which uses the cloud to analyze eye movement so that graphic designers can more effectively "grab viewers' attention." One might think that improving the delivery of eyeballs is not the most spectacular example to lure people to the company's Smarter Planet strategy. Nevertheless, it is clear from the ad that the purpose of the cloud is to make everyone, everywhere, smarter.

Perhaps because it is directed at the business customer, IBM's campaign never reaches the drama of Microsoft's "To the Cloud." Yes, the hyperbole is inescapable, with phrases like "sweeping changes" and "perfect storm" and words like "reinvention" and "transformation" used again and again. But the object is to sell intelligence and rationality rather than to create the family that nature never could. Yet the message is just as profound. IBM's cloud is not about emotion or empathy; rather, its SmartCloud is about knowledge and rationality. IBM's is clearly a cloud of knowing and other large cloud providers, like Verizon with its 2013 "Powerful Answers" campaign, have followed IBM's lead (Verizon Wireless 2013). We will consider the deeper importance of this view in Chapter 5 when we contrast it with "the cloud of unknowing," a stream of influential thought derived in part from a late fourteenth-century book with that title.

Advertising is about many things, but one of the most important is a specific form of perfection. For Microsoft business customers, it is perfect power; for consumers, it is the perfect family. For IBM, it is perfect knowledge and for Apple perfection takes the form of synchronized harmony. Like IBM, Apple pitches mainly to one side of the business/consumer divide—to the individual customer. Apple customers have been in the cloud for some time now, but it was not until October 12, 2011, that the company formally invited its customers to join iCloud. Prior to that time, Apple subscribers could enter the cloud with an iTools account, which launched a primitive cloud service in 2000. Improvements led to the 2004 creation of .mac and that gave way to MobileMe in 2008. Many of us who used the early Apple cloud found MobileMe, with the ".me" suffix attached to everything, a bit hard to accept. After all, Apple had a reputation for narcissism and what more mirror-gazing service can you think of than one celebrating *me*. Perhaps more importantly, MobileMe was plagued with glitches that prompted even Steve Jobs to wonder aloud whether people would ever trust Apple cloud services. According to the company's founder, people were justified in saying, "Why should I believe them? They're the ones that brought me MobileMe!" (Sutter 2011). One of the service's biggest problems was synchronizing customer files, music, videos, mail, contacts, and calendars across multiple devices. The source of many complaints, the world of MobileMe was anything but harmonious. That is probably why, when the cloud symbol became the icon for the company's online services, Apple was keen to focus on harmony.

The first iCloud ads predated the launch and provided a simple explanation of the service that demonstrates its capacity to seamlessly integrate customer devices. After the frame featuring the image of a cloud, the voiceover explains, "With iCloud, when you buy a song on one device, it instantly downloads to all of your others. Take a picture here, it shows up there. Start a project in one place and pick up right where you left off in another. Capture the moment here, and it's waiting for you there. Make a change on this, and it updates on that. And with iCloud it all works instantly and wirelessly. So you always have the things you want, exactly where you want them" (Apple 2011). Having educated its users in iCloud basics, later advertising came with no voiceover at all (Apple 2012). The ads were composed of purely visual images of music, photos, books, and apps downloaded from and uploaded to the cloud and instantly synchronized across iPhones, iPads, and laptop computers. No voiceover, and one frame of script: "Automatic, Everywhere, iCloud," a description of pure harmony.

With or without a voiceover, Apple ads are distinctive because the discourse on perfection is embodied in the commercial aesthetic. The participants start perfect and raise the level of perfection through the cloud. There is no dramatic tension, just a new level of sublime harmony. This differs sharply from the Microsoft ads, which, whether directed at business or consumers, acknowledge the world's imperfections and demonstrate how to use technology to correct them. The source of difference is uncertain, but it is clear from interviews with the founders of these companies, Steve Jobs and Bill Gates, that the former was a perfectionist whose goal was to control the entire experience. Gates is a supporter of open systems that risk flaws in order to expand the number of users, a position that Google has followed with its Android-based devices (Isaacson 2011, 534).

Commercials like Apple's for iCloud help to construct the discourse around cloud computing. The examples we have explored are particularly significant for their attempt to surround the cloud with visions of perfection amounting to variations on the technological sublime. They differ only in how perfection is imagined. For Salesforce, the sublime is rendered in businesses enabled by the cloud to do the impossible. In Microsoft ads directed at a business audience, perfection means technological change without negative disruptions. In a different form of perfection, Microsoft's cloud brings to consumers the technological key to creating the perfect family. For IBM, progress comes from building a smarter planet through a culture of knowing that extends rational thought and practices to all areas of social life. Finally, there is Apple, deepening and extending the perfection already present in life through harmonious synchronization of all the devices that fill our lives.

There are no guarantees that the discourse embedded in advertisements is the same as what viewers, readers, and listeners take away. After all, a quick review of comments reveals that some people were offended by Microsoft's perfect-family ad and some thought the company had no business claiming that the ads revealed anything about the real meaning of the cloud. It is hard to imagine anyone convinced by the company announcing without irony or satire, "To the Cloud." But the point is not about assessing the extent of an ad's influence. That is much too difficult to accomplish with any scientific rigor. After all, there are many other variables to consider. Does someone's adoption of iCloud or some business's decision to join the IBM SmartCloud have any direct relationship to an advertising campaign? Advertising may or may not have some small or large impact. What these campaigns undoubtedly do is create and build cloud computing in discourse. They define and teach individuals and organizations what cloud computing is and what good it can accomplish. This is important to fill a void in the absence of any clear understanding, and especially significant as a means of countering journalistic and research accounts that identify significant problems with cloud computing. By associating cloud computing with perfecting individuals, families, and organizations, promoters of the cloud construct an alternative to stories about environmental risks, power outages, pervasive surveillance, and threats to jobs in the IT field.

Blogging the Cloud

Commercial advertisements were once the overwhelmingly dominant way to promote a product. While they remain significant, there are now many more ways to construct a discourse around the cloud and, through this, to sell cloud computing. Among the many signs of this change, where once we talked about advertising agencies, today they are just agencies whose creative talent designs many forms of communication, including, but certainly not limited to, advertising. The expansion of media forms in the twenty-first century has certainly helped to open new promotional opportunities. For example, as one would expect, all of the major and minor cloud-computing providers promote their services on their own websites and blogs. Their sites are generally informative, but it is easy to dismiss them as corporate self-promotion. Nevertheless, they do serve additional functions. When the Microsoft site reported that its research found that two-thirds of small and medium-sized businesses lacked a marketing strategy, a widely circulating private blog picked up the item in its lead to a story on how cloud-computing companies can improve marketing (*Cloud Tweaks* 2013). Here a corporate website provides information to a site that has a greater claim to objectivity, thereby conveying legitimacy for the Microsoft figures. In this respect, company sites provide nourishment for the growth of the promotional food chain.

Cloud discourse is also built by the many online sites, including blogs, newsletters, and reports on research, that promote cloud computing without a clear association with any particular cloud enterprise. This enables them to enjoy a sense of objectivity even as they advance a partisan view. Most of these bear the cloud label: *Cloud Tweaks*, *Talkin' Cloud*, and *Asia Cloud Forum* are among the many. Some are connected to larger companies that do IT research and sell cloud products. Others are just the product of an enterprising individual or small business. A number of these sites are directly linked to a sales effort. For example, to download a white paper on overcoming challenges facing cloud computing, I was asked to provide a street address and phone number. I did so, found the paper useful, and received a phone call the next day inquiring about my interest in buying a cloud service for my company. Another blog followed a similar process but was even more clearly aimed at helping IT people convince their bosses to move to the cloud. Titled "How to Beat a Cloud Skeptic," the paper I downloaded from that site "details four key steps to dispel skeptics' fears so your organization can take advantage of the cloud's many benefits" (Shields 2013). The article "Five Different Ways to Sell Cloud Computing" conveys the sales message on *Cloud Tweaks* but with a humorous touch (Kenealy 2013).

Some of what they do involves general consciousness-raising about cloud-computing companies: what are the top ten or top one hundred cloud companies or what are the five or ten companies to watch in the coming year (Panattieri 2012)?

The blog site *Cloud Tweaks* is a good example of an informational blog whose goal is to promote interest in the cloud and in sales of cloud services. Established in 2009, it is one of the older sites. Its readership is made up of IT professionals, government workers, financial institutions, and corporate executives who subscribe for free by providing identifying information. For this they receive information on jobs, vendors, conferences, courses, and white papers that contain research on the cloud industry. *Cloud Tweaks* is supported by advertising, which is primarily placed by cloud-computing businesses and the companies that service them. An issue posted on January 8, 2013, provides insight into how sites like this bring together informational and promotional characteristics to advance the construction of a cloud-computing discourse. It starts by raising concerns about how cloud companies, especially small and medium-sized firms, market or fail to market their product. Many cloud companies, the article maintains, believe that the cloud is so extraordinary that it will sell itself and so they rely on a single person or a small consulting company to promote the sales effort. This is viewed as a mistake and a set of remedies is suggested. First on the list is securing a serious "channel" program. A channel is lingo for how a seller communicates with potential customers, typically by opening an online presence such as a website or blog. Furthermore, while branding the channel is important, companies need to be cautious about using the term *cloud* in a nonspecific way since most companies, especially small ones, likely know more about the specific service they need than about the concept of the cloud. Next, in a recognition that cloud promotion takes place in many different ways, the site recommends involvement in the cloud-computing community by posting on cloud blogs, contributing guest articles, and participating in online discussions. All of these are forms of company promotion. Finally, it is essential to participate in trade shows and conferences that focus on cloud computing because they, too, are vital promotional opportunities (Kenealy 2013).

Many other online sites are directly involved in providing promotional information on such topics as how to market cloud computing. It is especially important to pay close attention to these because they offer concrete insight into the ongoing process of constructing the cloud in discourse, including protecting the image of the cloud from critical accounts that might damage the industry. For example, *Cloud Computing Journal* offers an article on how to "Avoid Failure When Marketing Cloud Computing." The piece first declares just how essential it is to learn how to market the cloud: "Research organizations are predicting that 'the cloud' will dominate every facet of the software industry; no matter how concerned customers are with security, access, and customization, the Software as a Service (SaaS) market is guaranteed to grow" (Wilson 2012). The appeal to research delivers a measure of legitimacy for what follows and the admission of problems is important because it provides what the literary scholar Roland Barthes (1979) referred to as an inoculation that is important, if not essential, for maintaining the mythic status of an object. In this case, the admission of the security, access, and customization problems with the cloud inoculates the myth of the perfect cloud with the recognition of problems, which in most cases strengthens the argument for its essential importance. The gentle nod of recognition gives greater weight to the primary point that the cloud will dominate the software industry and that its markets will grow. So get onboard. But how?

When it comes to specifics, one can see how this form of communication departs from the pure promotion of a commercial advertisement. Maintaining that the cloud gives customers more power, cloud marketers are advised to stay ahead of the process by assuming that any prospective customer has done the necessary research prior to the personal sales pitch. It is essential for cloud companies to develop the online presence that makes it easiest for potential customers to determine what's right with their cloud services before companies and customers talk. This includes white papers, blog posts, and demo videos. In fact, the piece recommends that cloud providers avoid spending more than a minimal marketing budget on offline advertising such as print ads, direct mailing, or presence at trade shows. In addition to communicating online, cloud companies need to use their websites to launch free software trials for customers because customers want to know how software works (Wilson 2012). Another site, *Business Solutions*, offers tips on how to sell cloud computing to business. It advises that first, if the customer appears to be environmentally conscious, a provider should sell the cloud as a green technology that will cut the corporate electricity bill. Second, for a company worrying about the potential disruptive effects of natural disasters, sell the cloud as a system that practically guarantees continuity of service. Finally, sell those concerned about dependence on a particular platform such as Apple or Microsoft on the ability to use any platform at any time, a step on the way to full virtualization (McCall 2012).

Other cloud sites offer advice on how to market to specific constituencies. One describes how the marketing pitches to chief information officers (CIOs) should differ from those directed at chief financial officers (CFOs). The former are primarily concerned with security, followed by the ability to scale cloud resources, and then with the availability of applications. Along the way, the posting identifies the correct answers to the kinds of questions that CIOs typically ask. By definition, CFOs are concerned about costs, specifically with how much the company will save by moving to the cloud. But they are also worried about regulatory issues and the overall impact of shifting to the cloud on the company's business model. Given potential clashes between the interests of CIOs and CFOs, the piece concludes that finding common ground is critical to making both feel comfortable with the transition (Ko 2012).

Still other sites concentrate on how to sell specific kinds of cloud-computing services. For example, *Gigaom* offers suggestions to both sellers and buyers on how to market IaaS, which, as described in Chapter 2, is a form of cloud service where the cloud provider manages servers that customers use to store and process their data. For sellers, the site recommends eliminating the fits and starts that often come with human contact by "ensuring a seamless and human-free process to try your service." Moreover, because selling IaaS or any cloud service involves a big financial commitment from more than one executive at the client company, "Don't expect that a self-service trial process alone leads to sales." Finally, it recommends that cloud sellers bring in a team of specialists in areas like systems integration and telecommunications, even if that means partnering with other companies. As for buyers, the guide recommends choosing applications that minimize dependencies, something that is difficult to do when a client is purchasing a cloud service that requires using a cloud provider's proprietary software and applications. It also recommends that buyers actively convince others in their organizations that the IaaS solution is best because it is sometimes necessary to take small steps, if these can be advanced as exemplars of success. Lastly, buyers need to demonstrate that the service they want their company to buy is one that is sold and used by many firms. Defending their choice as part of a widely known set of such choices eases concerns within the organization (Orenstein 2010). This advice is particularly interesting because it acknowledges that constructing the cloud as a general business solution requires salesmanship from both sellers and buyers. The notion that "we are all in this together" overcomes structural divisions (buyers/sellers; CIOs/CFOs) and attempts to create an aura of common sense, community, and consensus around the decision to move to the cloud.

Private Think Tanks Promote the Cloud

Online newsletters and blog sites help to build the promotional culture for cloud computing without the commercial appearance of advertising. They are informative, educational, and service-oriented, while at the same time demonstrating key characteristics that are found, albeit more explicitly, in commercials. These sites present the cloud as a technological breakthrough that will have widespread influence on all businesses and throughout society. While noting the occasional problem, such as security, they are quick to point to solutions, such as purchasing strong encryption services from cloud security firms. Otherwise they are overwhelmingly upbeat about the cloud and focus on directing readers to follow their lead by pointing out jobs in the industry, suggesting training opportunities, and identifying key players (from top-ten companies to attention-grabbing start-ups). More than anything, they demonstrate how to sell cloud-computing services with general advice and specific suggestions for different cloud constituencies and segments of the cloud marketplace. These sites are dependent on cloud-computing firms for much of their information, but they also depend on another category of key players in the cloud-computing arena: private research and consulting firms. By comparison to newsletter and blog sites, companies like Deloitte, Forrester Research, Gartner, and McKinsey & Company are a step or two closer to the perception of providing what are perceived to be objective accounts. Although they do not always offer positive reports, private research and consulting firms tend to advance a supportive and generally promotional story that highlights growth and positive influence.

Private research firms are careful to define themselves as independent sources of objective information that businesses and governments should find valuable enough to purchase, even when the price is steep. In 2009 Deloitte focused its research attention on cloud computing with a report whose cover sported various types of clouds, each in different weather, appropriate to a document subtitled "Forecasting Change." From the start, it distinguished the report from promotional material, even as it made an explicit promotional pitch for the cloud: "The goal of this brochure is to enable 'hype-free' discussion on cloud computing and align actors around a common understanding. We hope that, like us, you will be convinced of the compelling power of cloud computing, not just because of its advantages, but also by understanding the risks it entails, and what can be done to address these" (Deloitte 2009, 3). Even as it aims to avoid hyperbole, Deloitte wishes to convince readers of the cloud's compelling power. The report quickly leaves one wondering about the definition of "hype-free" because two pages later it declares without qualification that "Cloud computing will be the next technological disruption to transform enterprise IT delivery and services" (ibid., 5). The report itself is more nuanced, but nevertheless is consistent when it comes to one central theme that unites most reports like this: inevitable growth. Here is a representative assessment: "Many experts state that the cloud market will drastically expand in the coming years. For the 2008–2013 period, Gartner predicts an impressive growth of the Cloud computing market from 9.1 to 26.6 billion USD, which represents a CAGR (compound annual growth rate) of 24% (these numbers exclude revenues derived from Cloud-based advertising)" (ibid., 29). These are strong numbers for an industry that is just getting started, but using the authority of another private research firm, Deloitte is convinced that the cloud will expand significantly. And if we need a reminder, the report summarizes its key points (ibid., 34):

- Economic, technological, and social factors favor cloud computing growth
- Industry trends show significant five-year, worldwide growth
- Customer surveys indicate a high level of interest in cloud computing by IT stakeholders
- With many organizations starting to benefit from the cloud, companies of all sizes should evaluate its potential fit

These points are significant beyond any specific test of their accuracy because, whether or not the report accurately predicts the industry's future, it succeeds unambiguously in advancing the promotional discourse. In addition to providing a singular form of legitimacy for the cloud, the report's influence is multiplied when, as is almost inevitably the case, it is highlighted in newsletters, blogs, and other promotional literature. In this case, blogs, including *Software Strategies Research* (Columbus 2012a) and *The Storage Effect*, a blog produced by the storage manufacturer Seagate (Wojtakiak 2012), and a research report (Dalwadi 2012) are among the numerous examples. The result is a circle of affirmation where reports with legitimacy get referenced, amplified, and reconstituted by other points in what amounts to a global chain of discursive production. In this case, the product is a narrative promoting the inevitable growth of the cloud computing industry.

Forrester Research, which describes itself as a research and advisory company, is another excellent example of a firm that uses its legitimacy to advance the promotional culture around the cloud. The company, which focuses on providing proprietary research to the IT industry, has given considerable attention to cloud computing, including in a 2011 report called "Sizing the Cloud." Forrester uses the report to restate the growth mantra by predicting that the market for the cloud will expand from under $41 billion in 2010 to over $240 billion in 2020. While the report itself requires a budget beyond that of most readers ($2,495 a copy), growth appears to be a key theme (Reid and Kisker 2011). Like the Deloitte report, this one has been picked up by bloggers who single out the growth theme and see it as part of the general view among experts: "Thus, the "Sizing the Cloud" report supports a common view among analysts that the cloud computing market will witness tremendous growth in the foreseeable future. The market will grow six times within a decade, according to Forrester, which is typical only for new and relatively under-developed markets" (Kirilov 2011). Forrester reiterated this view at the end of 2011, when one of its researchers used a blog to make this prediction for 2012: "All cloud markets will continue to grow, and the total cloud market (including private, virtual private, and public cloud markets) will reach about $61 billion by the end of 2012. By far, the largest individual cloud market continues to be the public SaaS market, which will hit $33 billion by the end of 2012" (ibid.). As with other such reports, there is nuance—some cloud markets will grow faster than others, and much will depend on the overall state of the world economy. But on balance, cloud computing will continue to advance as a central force in the global IT economy. It is difficult to determine whether this forecast proved accurate because there is no clear measuring stick and many companies, including industry leaders like Amazon, do not separately identify cloud-computing revenues. The estimate of the total cloud market appears reasonable, but that for the public SaaS market most likely overstates its actual growth. The point is that the specific forecast is less important than its trajectory, whose arrow almost universally supports the promotional discourse.

Once again, the report and its optimistic forecast circulated widely. This was particularly important because Amazon Web Services had suffered a major outage shortly before it appeared and commentators were pleased to see that Forrester's findings were able to relieve some of the understandable anxieties about the cloud marketplace. A blog that serves CIOs headlined its coverage "Forrester: Public Cloud to Surge, Especially SaaS." More important is its summary connected to the AWS failure: "Long after the buzz about Amazon's two-day cloud outage dies down, the public cloud will be a growth trajectory" (O'Neill 2011). The article goes on to repeat Forrester's growth projections, all heading upward, to the year 2020. The Forrester report made it easier to view the failure at Amazon, in spite of significant coverage by journalists, as an isolated event rather than as a portent of disasters to come (Miller 2011). There certainly was no guarantee that potential cloud customers would quickly come back to the cloud given the widespread negative reaction to the Amazon event. Consider this from one IT executive: "'We don't think the cloud is enterprise-ready,' said Jimmy Tam, general manager of Peer Software, which provides data backup for businesses. 'Are you really going to trust your corporate jewels to these cloud providers?'"(ibid.). This was certainly no isolated comment, as others also chimed in: "'Clearly you're not in control of your data, your information,' said Campbell McKellar, founder of Loosecubes, a Web site for finding temporary workspace that was among those that lost service. 'It's a major business interruption. I'm getting business interruption insurance tomorrow, believe me, and maybe we get a different cloud provider as a backup'" (ibid.). It is impossible to say whether Forrester's affirmation of the surging cloud succeeded in calming fears, but it is important to contrast the Forrester predictions with the news of the day because doing so demonstrates the importance to the industry of having a discursive apparatus at work to offset critical concerns raised by journalists and researchers.

Gartner describes itself as "the world's leading information technology research and advisory company" and boasts, "We deliver the technology-related insight necessary for our clients to make the right decisions, every day. From CIOs and senior IT leaders in corporations and government agencies, to business leaders in high-tech and telecom enterprises and professional services firms, to technology investors, we are the valuable partner to clients in 12,400 distinct organizations" (Gartner 2013). Even discounting for the hyperbole that often accompanies such self-descriptions, there is general agreement that the company exerts considerable influence in the IT industry through its research and forecasting. As a result, it can command top dollar for its assessments. A Gartner report, described shortly, forecasts the development of the cloud through 2016, runs to nine pages, and costs $9,995. Like its counterparts at Deloitte and Forrester, Gartner's predictions about cloud computing have contributed substantially to promoting the vision of unrelenting expansion. For example, in July 2012, in an article headlined "Gartner: Cloud putting crimp in traditional software, hardware sales" the company's "cloud forecaster" predicted that the sector would grow by 19 percent in 2012, going from $91 billion in 2011 to $109 billion. By 2016 Gartner expects it to be a $207 billion industry, which, while still representing a small percentage of the total IT sector, nevertheless means that it will be growing considerably faster than the overall sector (Butler 2012a). This rosy forecast came a few weeks after even rosier predictions about consumer adoption of the cloud. While only 7 percent of consumer data was stored in the cloud at the time of the forecast, it concludes that by 2016 the cloud will contain 36 percent of all such data. This will result in increased demand throughout the industry for data centers, for synchronization services, and for flawless uploading and downloading capacity. According to Gartner, "Cloud storage will grow with the emergence of the personal cloud, which in turn will simplify the direct-to-cloud model, allowing users to directly store user-generated content in the cloud" (ibid.). Aside from some minor potential problems such as the threat of commoditization as personal storage expands, the immediate future is clearly positive for the expanding cloud. The Gartner results spread widely among those producing cloud newsletters and websites and made it into the business press, including such influential publications as *Forbes*, which ran a compilation of upbeat market forecasts that included the Gartner study (Columbus 2012b). According to another report, cloud computing has penetrated every facet of the global corporate supply chain. As a result, it concludes, Gartner's forecast that the IaaS cloud will grow by 42 percent by 2016 should not be shocking (SmartData Collective 2013).

The final example of a private research organization that is helping to create a promotional discourse around the cloud is McKinsey & Company, which describes itself as "the trusted advisor to the world's leading businesses, governments, and institutions" (McKinsey & Company 2013). Founded in 1926, the company boasts that it works with two-thirds of *Fortune* magazine's top 1,000 corporations. McKinsey's relationship to cloud computing began with some controversy when in 2009 it defied the early boosters and argued that, especially for large companies, moving to the cloud was not necessarily the best choice. Its report "Clearing the Air on Cloud Computing" concluded that the service was overhyped, particularly as a cost-saver, because cloud services like Amazon Web Services charged more than it would cost companies to keep their data processing in house by using their own data centers and servers. Ideally, McKinsey recommended keeping it all in house but virtualizing the servers or, in essence, carving up servers into multiple virtual machines, enabling software to maximize power from one machine and adding the ability to scale according to the company's changing needs. Even these recommendations were qualified, as McKinsey recognized that small and medium-sized firms would not be able to enjoy the same scale economies for in-house systems as their larger counterparts (Rao 2009). This early research continues to resonate, as the report of one independent study concluded: "Large enterprises with highly optimized IT shops tailored to their business' needs may find cloud computing to be more expensive. But, if a company has workloads that ebb and flow in their use of compute power, then the cloud can yield substantial savings" (Butler 2013a).

The suggestion that large firms should shun the cloud was met with consternation and criticism from cloud-computing supporters. Most were dismayed that such a reputable research firm would rush to judgment and charged that the report "neglects to address a few key trends that are occurring in cloud server services. Innovation is rapidly changing in the cloud.

The space is still very much a work in progress and big cloud computing services, like AWS, Google, Sun Microsystems and Microsoft, are regularly coming out with different products. As these companies throw their hats into the 'cloud computing ring,' AWS will face increased competition in the market and could cause prices to go down to fight for market share" (Butler 2013a). For some analysts, too much attention paid to current prices ("the report seems to hype the cloud costs") and too little to the prospects for innovation doomed the report (ibid.).

The first McKinsey report does not sound promotional at all. But what makes this example particularly interesting is that the company has completely changed its tune. At a 2012 conference, a senior partner with the company delivered an altogether different outlook. In an interview Bertil Chappuis described "an entrepreneurial groundswell for the cloud." His point is that the cloud has not just been good for companies selling cloud services; it has been good for all business and for entrepreneurship as well. Regarding the latter, Chappuis makes it clear that he is not just talking about a Silicon Valley brand of entrepreneurial business formation, but about all forms of business activity, large, small, and individual. What changed from 2009 to 2012? For this Chappuis concentrated on three key developments. In a reversal from the expectation contained in the first report, it's "cheap computing." Specifically, he cites a threefold difference in cost between running your own server system and shipping it to the cloud. In fact, owing to "massively scaled and efficient data centers" the cost of a complete cloud service is lower than the cost of providing the power for in-house servers. Furthermore, cloud services are far more agile for provisioning infrastructure. Whereas it takes anywhere from 60 to 150 days for an enterprise to provide for a server system, access to the cloud is practically instantaneous. In fact, he cites cases of people "buying compute power on their credit cards." On top of this he notes the capacity of the cloud to enable new experiences: "social, local, mobile, big data." These require rapid, agile development to satisfy the requirements across multiple device platforms that have what he calls very "bursty" processing profiles. Putting together cost, agility, and the possibility for new experiences creates "a reinforcing cycle that will enable these cloud environments to propagate in all sorts of environments." As a result, cloud computing actually becomes far more significant than even what its early boosters predicted. In addition to serving or even transforming business, it becomes a critical force in creating entirely new lines of business (Chappuis 2012).

Chappuis supports this view with several examples, including a pharmaceutical company that was motivated to revamp its entire customer-relationship management (CRM) system when it decided to incorporate detailed molecular information into its existing system. Since the company did not have the resources to do the job in house, it contracted with a cloud provider, which provided an app that did the job so well that it convinced the firm to rethink its entire CRM strategy. In another example, an HR manager wanted to apply analytics to his employee database, and the cloud provider that solved the problem convinced the manager to restructure all of its HR systems. Next, a small business with twenty-five employees, which did everything in-house, contracted with a cloud company to host its email. This worked so well that the firm decided to port its online video to the cloud. When that, too, succeeded, the company shifted all of its IT to the cloud, saved 55 percent of its IT costs, and was able to focus on its core business. Finally, Chappuis turns to AWS, which received heavy criticism in the 2009 McKinsey report for its high prices. Now the story is about an IT manager who, facing long provisioning times to stage an app, saved months by turning to AWS, which completed the job in minutes. Problems associated with locked-in contracts and endless subscriber payments disappear from consideration as outsourcing to the cloud becomes, as the cliché goes, a win-win situation (R. Cohen 2013).

To paraphrase a familiar line, we can be assured of three things: death, taxes, and changing weather. So it should come as no surprise that McKinsey's forecast would change from "partly cloudy" in 2009 to absolutely sunny in 2012. But the firm's changing forecast also offers an important lesson in the development of a promotional culture. The evolving agreement in much of the IT world that cloud computing is "the next big thing," guaranteed to grow well into the future and to transform business in the global economy, does not automatically become common sense or what scholars call *hegemony*. Rather, hegemony takes time to grow and inevitably changes in the face of both internal tensions such as the differences in early forecasts between cloud supporters, and external tensions such as the disagreements between cloud boosters and journalists who have challenged the cloud because of environmental, security, and labor concerns. The development of a hegemonic promotional culture is not a mechanical process that arises simply from the balance of societal forces, but an organic one that emerges, changes, and can wither, disappear, or thrive depending on the extent to which key participants continue to actively affirm its importance. McKinsey's change of view may represent simply the recognition that it once misread the cloud or did not appreciate the extent to which it could improve in a short time. But one can also see it as a key turn in the development of the cloud's promotional culture because a major participant in one of its key sectors, the private research and consulting community, overwhelmingly affirmed the dominant view after having raised significant concerns three years earlier.

Promoting the Cloud to the World

In addition to advertisements, websites, and the reports and forecasts of private research and consulting firms, it is important to consider the work of global research organizations that take a further step in building hegemony in support of the cloud. An excellent exemplar is the World Economic Forum (WEF), whose *Global Information Technology Report 2012* (Dutta and Bilbao-Osorio 2012) focused on cloud computing as the essential new ingredient in a networked world. The forum describes itself as "an independent international organization committed to improving the state of the world by engaging business, political, academic and other leaders of society to shape global, regional and industry agendas" (World Economic Forum 2013). It is best known for the annual Davos conference, which brings these leaders together to discuss global issues and build consensus in support of policy initiatives. In the last two years, cloud computing has attracted the forum's attention and the report is its first effort to mobilize international support for a common approach to the cloud and give it the stamp of approval from a major global economic organization. The forum report contains a number of individually authored chapters written by people who work for some of the most important corporations in the information-technology and telecommunications industries; private research organizations (a group of researchers with McKinsey wrote one chapter); international bodies, including the WEF itself, the UN's Unesco, and the International Telecommunications Union; and universities. There are two chapters about the cloud, including "The Wisdom of the Cloud:

Hyperconnectivity, Big-Data, and Real-Time Analytics," written by two executives with the software company SAS, and "Harnessing the Power of Big Data in Real Time through In-Memory Technology and Analytics," produced by the software and cloud-computing firm SAP.

Although the report contains work by people from different professions, there is little doubt that it speaks with an overwhelmingly corporate voice. With no work from the large community of non-governmental organizations in the global IT sector, there is also little doubt about whose voice is silent. Accentuating the corporate stamp is the collaboration between the Forum and INSEAD, a global business school with campuses in France, Singapore, and Abu Dhabi. It is arguably even more interesting that the full report is sponsored by the Chinese firm Huawei, a world leader in electronics and, some would say, a corporate leader in controversy. In 2012 the company surpassed Ericsson as the world's largest telecommunications-equipment maker and leaped over Nokia and RIM to become, after Apple and Samsung, the third largest producer of smartphones in the world. The company manufactures for markets around the world but has benefited from the explosion in smartphone use across China particularly because, unlike Apple and Samsung, Huawei produces inexpensive devices. But make no mistake about it: Huawei's reputation for low-cost devices does not make it a low-end firm. In fact, half of its worldwide labor force is involved in research and development, employed at some twenty research and development institutes around the world. Partly because of its commanding position in global electronics production and partly because the company has rapidly become a dominant force in leading-edge research, Huawei has attracted widespread attention, but not all of it is good.

In 2012 the U.S. House Permanent Select Committee on Intelligence charged that Huawei, along with another Chinese telecommunications firm, served as an intelligence front for the Chinese government and its military "that could undermine core U.S. national-security interests" (Rogers and Ruppersberger 2012, vi). Not everyone in the United States agreed with the House report, citing the lack of strong, direct evidence (Mathias 2012). Nevertheless, the charges spread and other governments, including the Australian and Canadian, raised serious concerns about Huawei and banned the company from bidding on critical government infrastructure projects (Marlow 2013). In this context, the WEF report gains further importance because it enabled Huawei to launder its reputation as a global security risk and mitigate, at least in a small way, the fears that, as one commentator explained, "if China stops playing by Davos rules, then the golden years of the World Economic Forum will be over" (Rachman 2013). Huawei's work with the WEF helped the company build legitimacy as attacks on its actions continued. In 2013 it took another step by becoming a partner with CERN (the European Organization for Nuclear Research), providing cloud storage for the world's major particle-physics center, no minor task since the lab requires twenty-five petabytes of data each year. As an analyst concluded, "CERN has now put the company back on the 'nice list'" (Harpreet 2013).

The content of the report is important because it gives concentrated and repeated attention to three themes. First, it promotes the vision of information technology in all of its forms as the key to economic growth and to the overall success of the global economy. Second, it identifies cloud computing as the leading edge of IT development and the essential ingredient for organizational success, especially in business. Third, the report insists that the primary challenge to the effective use of cloud computing is the adoption of technical standards that would enable the seamless convergence of machines and devices responsible for storage, processing, distribution, and use. Almost as important is the form that the content of reports like this takes. To reach as broad an audience of decision and opinion makers as possible, the report is written in a clear style with practically no jargon. Moreover, it is replete with the kinds of summary text, figures, and tables that both simplify arguments and add the legitimating weight of quantitative data. Finally, it contains numerous lists that rank order nations according to how well they embrace information technology—for instance, readiness to enter the world of hyperconnectivity. These appeal to those who might only have the time to flip through the report, but who would be interested to locate and compare where their own country appears on a list. Although certainly more nuanced than a commercial ad or a short blog post, and with more legitimacy than a commissioned private research report, the document is careful to offer the clarity and simplicity that advances the promotional project. Unlike a journalistic or scholarly account, which can often read like a contested terrain of clashing views, the report is singular in its positive, promotional message about IT and the cloud. Where nuance exists, it is only to highlight the technical hurdles that leave some question marks along the road to full convergence between the cloud and those "pipes" and devices that deliver and display content from the cloud.

From the start, the report resembles those that, in the early days of the Internet, created mythical visions of a digital sublime (Mosco 2004). We do not just live in a connected world, the cover subtitle tells us; ours is "hyperconnected." The preface, written by the chief business officer of the WEF, does little to temper the hyperbolic enthusiasm for a world shaped by information and communication technology (ICT). It describes the document as a detailed analysis of "the main drivers and impacts of this ICT-enabled hyperconnected world and contributes to the work of the World Economic Forum's Hyperconnected World Initiative, which establishes a holistic means of understanding the systemic nature of change in a hyperconnected world" (Dutta and Bilbao-Osorio 2012, v). The chairwoman of Huawei chimes in with her iteration on the theme of digital enthusiasm: "Ubiquitous super-broadband will make almost everything faster and better while delivering an improved user experience" (ibid., ix). The echoes of hyperconnectivity continue through the executive summary, where representatives of both the WEF and INSEAD mix hyperconnectivity and social transformation to create a rich stew of technological euphoria: "We live in an environment where the Internet and its associated services are accessible and immediate, where people and businesses can communicate with each other instantly, and where machines are equally interconnected with each other. The exponential growth of mobile devices, big data, and social media are all drivers of this process of hyperconnectivity. Consequently, we are beginning to see fundamental transformations in society" (ibid., xi). This establishes the model for the document: technology is creating a hyperconnected world that is, with a few minor disturbances, an unalloyed blessing for the world. The only reasonable response of governments to this inevitable development is to figure out how best to adapt. Consequently, the report produces a "world readiness framework" whose primary index measures "the friendliness of a country's market and regulatory framework in supporting high levels of ICT uptake" (ibid., xii). Even before we enter the body of the document, it is clear that we are entering a mythic universe filled with the reification of a technology that drives the world to progress, provided that people figure out how to properly adjust to its requirements. It is mythic because it tells a story of a larger-than-life character, Information Technology, that offers the world the magic of hyperconnectivity. The myth turns on the drama of whether we will adapt ourselves and our societies sufficiently to the needs of technology, by creating, for example, those business-friendly policies that encourage, as the report puts it, "high levels of ICT uptake."

The body of the WEF document details the promise of information technology to deliver ever greater levels of progress to the world's people. Like most myths, however complex the story appears, it is fundamentally a simple narrative: the more IT, the more progress. But the WEF report is more than a promotional blurb for "the next new thing." This is demonstrated in its willingness to admit to challenges that can get in the way of, and perhaps even slow down, the arrival of the inevitable progress that IT delivers. Since it is intended for a knowledgeable readership, the report cannot simply dismiss problems. Rather, it redefines them in a way that deflates their power and their significance.

Consider privacy, a central issue in debates over information technology and the cloud. While not going so far as to see it in quite this way, the report does name privacy among the issues facing a hyperconnected world (ibid., 4). However, from the standpoint of promoting IT, the key is to rethink privacy to minimize, if not completely eviscerate, it as an issue worthy of careful policy attention. Interestingly, this is made clear in a discussion of what some would see as the central place where privacy matters—the collection, storage, processing, and use of health data: "Is privacy a concern? It certainly has to be front and center with respect to virtually any effort connected to healthcare data. However, some experts are gradually adopting a somewhat contrarian view on this topic, believing that our society must move past the fear of data and privacy breaches. Many technological innovations that have revolutionized medicine might not have been possible without sharing data. Any data—electronic or paper-based—are vulnerable. But here, too, hyperconnectivity will enable new tools to fight crime, fraud, and abuse" (ibid., 99). In essence, privacy is a concern, but not really. Specifically, first, get over it. Second, if you want medical progress, then your data must be shared. Third, all data, including paper-based, are vulnerable. Finally, technology, in the form of a hyperconnected IT world, will find solutions to problems presented by privacy breaches. This is a version of what Evgeny Morozov (2013b) calls "solutionism," the view that problems and solutions will be defined and solved within the parameters of the technologies that major IT companies identify. With each reason not to worry about privacy, one is led to wonder why it should be a concern at all. The myth of a digital sublime is strengthened by inoculating it with the identification and subsequent dismissal of what many see as a major limitation on its power to bring universal progress.

Cloud computing makes up a second major theme of the World Economic Forum report, with one chapter on the cloud and another on big data. It is particularly interesting that the cloud-computing chapter returns to the issue of privacy and, even before getting to the specific details that make the cloud important, deflates fears about privacy and security: about concerns over "infringement of privacy . . . we cannot escape the fact that big data offer meaningful social and economic benefits that mitigate these legitimate concerns because of the hugely favorable social and/or economic impact they impart—on private commerce, international economies, and economic development. Certainly data security issues are important, but if big data are to become the currency of the future, we need governance, transparency, and security, as opposed to reactionary plans to lock up the data and throw away the key. As with any currency, suppression is not a sustainable way forward" (Dutta and Bilbao-Osorio 2012, 97). In essence, the report concludes that economic benefits trump privacy worries and, more importantly, it sets up a dichotomy between progressive policies that unleash the power of big data and retrograde approaches that lock it up. There is only one intelligent choice, one way to move forward.

With privacy essentially out of the way, we are free to unleash the power of big data and, more specifically, its power to benefit business in a very big way. Aside from the financial benefits of using the information "hidden in the world's existing data sources" (ibid., 98), such as the estimated $600 billion revenue gain from using personal location data globally and the 60 percent potential gain in retail operating margins, there are the enormous qualitative benefits to companies, particularly those that mine social-media data. Among the benefits are the ability to "protect a brand, engage the most influential voices in a market, understand what trends lead to sales, identify an untapped market, enhance market research, understand the impact of industry changes, gather competitive intelligence, improve warranty analysis, create a better customer experience, and manage a crisis" (ibid., 99). Acknowledging what it views as the "irony" that social-media data are generated not by businesses but by individual users who are linked through Facebook, Twitter, and other social-media sites, the chapter simply assumes that all of the data generated should be fully available to businesses seeking to turn user actions into revenue streams. Such is, as the chapter title suggests without irony, "the wisdom of the cloud." As another chapter notes, "social media present new opportunities for savvy organizations to capture 'the wisdom of the cloud' and leverage the flood of unstructured data that is being created" (ibid., xvi).

By approaching user-generated data as freely available to businesses to use in whatever ways generate profit, the report demonstrates the difference between promotional literature and research. As exemplified in the WEF report, promotion affirms a position that its creators wish to advance in order to accomplish the goal of convincing others to follow their lead. On the other hand, research raises questions about positions that generate thought and debate rather than simply assent. For example, in 2013 the private tech-analysis firm Ovum reported on the results of a survey of 11,000 people in eleven countries on corporate use of personal data. Among its many interesting findings were that 68 percent of respondents would use "do not track" software if it were readily available to them on a website. More troubling was the finding that only 14 percent of respondents believed that Internet companies were honest about their use of personal data (Gross 2013). Ovum's research demonstrated a profound lack of trust in online commerce that finds no place in promotional literature. Based on its results, the Ovum report concluded, "More and more consumers are deciding to effectively become invisible in data terms on the Internet. It will shake the Internet economy as more and more users decide they don't want to be tracked" (ibid.). Facing the reality of that decision, the report raised serious questions for its business clients: "Unfortunately, in the gold rush that is big data, taking the supply of little data—personal data—for granted seems to be an accident waiting to happen" (ibid.). But that is what promotional literature like the WEF report aims to do: take for granted pliable users who will ignore data-protection opportunities. Genuine research does not, even if it means facing hard questions and making difficult choices, such as developing a business strategy that addresses the reality that, as a technical analyst for Ovum concluded, "You are getting this squeeze between a hardening consumer attitude and tighter regulation" (ibid.).

The WEF report is promotional in part because it completely ignores results like this. Instead, not unlike the commercial advertisements described earlier, it chooses to focus on the cloud as a source of intelligence that turns inefficient businesses into smart organizational machines. The key is the ability of cloud computing to perfect the process of convergence, which, over the history of communication technology, has advanced the connections between the production, dissemination, and use of information. For the WEF, this is the heart of the matter: "Cloud computing services provide a catalyst for ICT convergence. Telecommunications carriers will gradually move IT systems and Internet data centers into the cloud, and telecommunications and IT industries will develop uniform standards to facilitate rapid cloud development" (Dutta and Bilbao-Osorio 2012, xiv). The cloud is important not only because of its superior storage and processing power, sufficient to absorb the Internet and all of today's IT, but also because it provides the missing link enabling telecommunications providers to serve the entire world faster, more cheaply, and more efficiently than ever. As a result of joining the "pipe" and the "device" in what is close to a literal cloud of convergence, "the cloud has reshaped the IT industry" (ibid., 38). But this, as the report recognizes, is too simple. It may be promotional, but this is not a slick commercial during which someone announces, "To the Cloud," and, with the snap of the fingers, transports us to a world of seamless integration and sublime convergence. Instead it is the report of a well-respected international organization, which needs to avoid the appearance of the myth-making that is taken for granted in thirty-second commercials.

So in addition to promoting the wonders of IT in general and the cloud in particular, the document acknowledges that "there are obstacles to this integration, including insufficient openness in the ICT industry; a lack of unified technical standards; and a lack of connection among cloud computing, telecommunications networks (the pipe), and smart devices. Overcoming these obstacles and unifying ICT's technical standards is a top priority if we are to improve interoperability within the industry" (ibid., ix). For the WEF, the major problem facing the future of IT and cloud computing is not the environmental consequences of building enormous data centers around the world and powering them with several levels of backup, including banks of spinning flywheels and thousands of lead-acid batteries. It is not the potential to violate privacy built into a system that generates revenue precisely by scooping up and analyzing personal information. It is certainly not the security problems of storing data in nations that will not protect it, but, instead, will use it to meet their own needs. Given Huawei's own security problems, one should not find it surprising that no mention is made of the problems posed by storing data beyond a nation's borders. Nor is it the massive changes in the global division of labor resulting from transferring the IT departments of the world's organizations to the cloud. Rather, the primary issue of significance to the cloud-computing industry is determining the best way to create a global system of uniform standards that will guarantee the smooth performance of a cloud-based global grid. Given the heavy telecommunications-industry involvement in the report's creation, including sponsorship by the world's leading electronics-equipment company, it is not a great surprise that the document would concentrate on technical standards. Indeed the chapters that focus most heavily on technical convergence are the ones written by Huawei and representatives from the International Telecommunications Union. Moreover, it is an issue that the telecommunications industry has worried about and worked on for generations and one that private research organizations insist needs careful attention in order to properly maintain cloud-computing networks (Bernnat et al. 2012). But there is more to this than promoting a major issue for the industry.

The report represents the *technicism* that is common in most promotional documents. It is constructed to represent the general public interest, but is written from a particular industry interest. To avoid tensions between the public interest and the needs of business, promotional reports avoid social and political issues and focus instead on technical problems like standards and convergence that are both real and unlikely to threaten the goal of equating a specific industry interest with the general public interest. For the report's writers, there is no questioning the general value and legitimacy of information technology and the cloud. Any thought of restricting their development, for example, to protect the environment, secure privacy, or save jobs, is foolish and irrational because it means giving up the benefits. It is, however, legitimate to raise technical issues that stand in the way of their full development. *Technicism*, a focus not just on how technology determines things but on how it becomes the singular source of solutions to problems, is a major means of uniting the specific interest of the industry and the general interest of the world's IT and cloud users.

Lobbying for the Cloud

Two additional forms of promotionalism are important to consider: the expansion of lobbying by firms involved in cloud computing and the proliferation of corporate trade shows dedicated to the cloud. There are certainly overlaps among the various forms of building a vision of the sublime cloud. While it might not take place as directly at Davos, host of the World Economic Forum, as it does in Washington, D.C., lobbying is intrinsic to political activity in both places. Nevertheless, there is enough difference to warrant distinguishing among the contributions made by the advertising spots that promote the cloud's ability to create the perfect family, the sponsored blogs that chronicle the cloud's seemingly unstoppable growth, the report that documents a hyperconnected world in the cloud, and the hand-to-hand networks that lobbying and conferencing build.

Perhaps because the first waves of IT entrepreneurs believed that the technology would sell itself to decision makers in Washington and other world capitals, there was little organized lobbying until recent years. This is particularly surprising because the telecommunications and electronics industries are legendary for their lobbying prowess. In the United States, AT&T and General Electric were at the top of a long list of firms that were prominent in the corridors of power. Scholars attribute much of AT&T's ability to maintain its monopoly control over the telephone industry to its army of lobbyists, who made the case that Ma Bell embodied the needs of local subscribers, a massive workforce, and the millions of shareholders, all of whom held America together in one seamless network (Tunstall 1986). To tamper with the network in any way, whether with companies that might want to compete by building a better or cheaper service, or just those who want to sell a pink telephone, would be harmful if not downright un-American. AT&T's lobbying clout built a particularly cozy relationship with the Pentagon, which could be counted on to defend the telecommunications monopoly as a matter of national security. According to the company line, multiple providers would endanger secure networks that were essential for national defense. It was not until AT&T met its lobbying match that it lost its monopoly control over the telecommunications marketplace. That could only happen when the banks, insurance companies, retailers, and others who paid a premium to sustain a telecommunications monopoly decided to form user associations whose combined lobbying power exceeded that of AT&T (Schiller 1981). Even then, AT&T almost sidestepped the move to competition when its lobbyists convinced a near majority in Congress to support legislation cementing Bell's monopoly. But that move fell a few votes short and when the Department of Defense recognized that lobbyists representing major users would win the day, it withdrew support for the monopoly, opening the door to market competition.

In spite of this and many other models of lobbying power, the burgeoning IT industry of the 1990s chose to maintain the bare minimum of a lobbying presence in Washington. As one account described, "Until the mid-1990's, politics was a foreign subject to executives at most technology companies—just as software, hardware and the Internet were foreign concepts to most members of Congress" (Rivlin 2004). A business user explained, "There was benign neglect on both sides, Washington and Silicon Valley. The valley generally took the attitude, 'As long as they ain't in my face, just ignore them'" (ibid.). What contact existed mainly took the form of politicians making the pilgrimage to Silicon Valley for a generous sprinkling of the gold dust that turned politicians into visionaries. This view began to subside once the new century arrived and the dot-com bust rocked the industry. First, since they no longer had the Midas touch, Silicon Valley lobbyists had to line up along with those from other industries and make sure to bring their checkbooks. Politicians, many of whom lost a lot of money in the crash, were no longer there just for a photo op. As one lobbyist for the IT industry said in a 2004 article, "Back in the late 1990's, Silicon Valley assumed that all they had to do is show up and politicians would fall at their feet, and for a while they were right. Now it takes a checkbook to get that meeting" (ibid.). Second, the policy issues that seemed low on the priority list when IT executives were rolling in venture capital, like tax rules on stock options and visa programs for foreign workers, now grew in significance.

Although lobbying grew in the wake of the downturn and especially when social media and cloud computing started new waves of IT expansion, it did not really pick up steam until social media and the cloud began to raise significant concerns, including the need to promote government's use of cloud services. While other issues might attract more press attention, cloud companies' success in getting the U.S. government, both civilian and military, to fully commit to shifting services to the cloud has been one of the great victories for the industry. In addition, IT and cloud companies have used lobbying to actively resist efforts to tighten privacy protections in the United States and Europe, to demand higher caps on immigration visas for skilled foreign tech workers or remove them altogether, to stop efforts to tighten controls over online advertising, and to prevent reform of tax laws that have enabled companies to perfect the dark art of tax avoidance (Nelson and Duhigg 2013; Houlder 2013).

Google led the way with a major boost in its lobbying outlay in 2010, just as concerns were growing about what some charged were the company's anti-competitive practices (Rao 2010). As the Federal Trade Commission (FTC) continued to look closely at potential antitrust violations, Google, fearing a repeat of earlier rulings that severely damaged Microsoft, intensified its lobbying activities. As one report summarized, "instead of ignoring Washington—as rival Microsoft did before its costly monopolization trial in the 1990s—Google spent about $25 million in lobbying, made an effort to cozy up to the Obama administration and hired influential Republicans and former regulators. The company even consulted with the Heritage Foundation and met with senators like John Kerry to make its case. In other words, these traditional outsiders worked the system from the inside" (Romm 2013a). In 2012 alone Google spent $16 million on lobbying, more than twice that of any other tech company, and, with twelve different lobbying firms working on its behalf, it succeeded in forestalling any major restrictions on its market control (T. Lee 2013).

Learning from Google's success and concerned about its post-IPO bottom line, Facebook significantly increased its lobbying outlays from $1.34 million in 2011 to $4 million in 2012 (Dembosky 2013b). The last thing the company needed was stiffer privacy legislation that would cut into its plans to boost revenues by providing companies with information about its one billion users. So when the U.S. Federal Trade Commission began an investigation into nine data brokers that do business with Facebook, the company boosted its Washington lobbying significantly. Facebook stated, "Our presence and growth in Washington reflect our commitment to explaining how our service works, the actions we take to protect the billion plus people who use our service, the importance of preserving an open internet, and the value of innovation to our economy" (ibid.). In 2013 Facebook set up its own lobbying coalition, FWD.us, to engage in a broad-based lobbying effort primarily promoting its members' support for expanding the number of visas for foreign workers (Wallsten, Yang, and Timberg 2013). However, its activities created turmoil and an advertising boycott on Facebook itself when the coalition lobbied on behalf of oil companies and for Republican Party causes in the South (Edwards 2013). Other companies also boosted their lobbying budgets,

ft's effort to rein in Google, they
n themselves against each other.
h, as it faced off against Apple in
from practically no Washington
on lobbying the American capital
th quarter alone (Quinn 2013).
capitals, though. Because cloud-
that offer cheap land, low utility
them spend time lobbying local
slatures for the best possible deal.
ild a data center on seventy-five
n required considerable corpo-
local government to provide tax
n half the U.S. national average.
ompany's use of polluting diesel
ory taken up in Chapter 4. Lob-
gton is seen over and over again
e world. In North Carolina, for
nefits to Apple when the company

Current Check-Outs summary for La, Hoa
Tue Oct 11 08:45:32 PDT 2016

BARCODE: 31215001403002
TITLE: To the cloud : big data in a turb
DUE DATE: Nov 01 2016
STATUS:

proposed to build data centers in the state, partly to take advantage of low labor costs and low-priced power. To attract the company, the state legislature approved $46 million in tax breaks, and local governments cut Apple's real-estate tax bill by 50 percent and its personal-property taxes by 85 percent (Greenpeace International 2011, 19).[4] Additionally, North Carolina rewarded Google's efforts with tax breaks, infrastructure upgrades, and other benefits worth $212 million over thirty years and Facebook received a similar payoff (Greenpeace International 2011). When cloud-computing companies in Boise, Idaho, found themselves with a hefty tax bill levied by a state authority that determined cloud computing to be the taxable sale of software, they enlisted the local Chamber of Commerce to help roll back the tax (Glanz 2012a; Moeller 2013).

Lobbying helps organizations representing companies promote the common industry interest. But this is sometimes a mixed blessing. Buoyed by the success of their lobbying in the United States and with a bigger stake in the global economy, tech firms, including cloud providers, began lobbying the European Union (EU) for favorable treatment, including more business-friendly privacy policies. Brussels (the EU's de facto capital) is not as sold on cloud computing as is Washington, D.C., in part due to threats the cloud poses to privacy and security, and its proposed policies, especially on data protection, take a stronger position than those advanced by the U.S. government. Brussels was also not happy about hearing from the lobbyists of major U.S. tech firms and made its views clear. Specifically, the head of an industry coalition that is working to develop EU-wide data-protection rules criticized U.S. tech giants, especially Google and Facebook, for hiring lobbyists to pressure the EU to weaken its privacy laws. Setting aside diplomatic niceties, Jacob Kohnstamm, chairman of the Dutch Data Protection Authority, declared that European officials were "fed up" with U.S. businesses putting their corporate interests ahead of what Europeans see as their fundamental rights to data security. Calling out the U.S. government as well as its big tech firms, he maintained that Congress would not be as tolerant if the tables were turned: "If such a lobby from the European side were organized towards Congress, we would be kicked out of there." Americans, he insisted, simply do not understand that for the United States privacy is a consumer protection, whereas in Europe it is considered a fundamental human right. A German politician summarized the extent of the lobbying pressure: "Throughout the last year there has been a massive campaign from the side of AmCham [the American Chamber of Commerce], which organised events throughout Europe and met with many MEPs [members of the European Parliament] in Brussels and Strasbourg. But now, since January when my report was published, lobbyists, especially from Silicon Valley, have stepped up their campaign to water down the EU privacy regulation" (Dembosky and Fontanella-Khan 2013). While the Obama administration, the American Chamber of Commerce, and lobbyists for the IT industry may succeed in forcing Europe to synchronize its data-protection laws by paring them back to where those of the United States stand, this is one case where lobbying can easily backfire.

For some observers, major IT and cloud providers face an even more significant challenge than opposition from the EU. Lobbying, they maintain, turns firms known for their inventions, innovations, and entrepreneurship into ordinary companies that would rather focus on influencing Washington to protect what they have than on developing "the next new thing." One business publication harkened back to a 1999 speech by Nobel Prize–winning economist Milton Friedman, who referred to lobbying as the IT industry's "suicide impulse" (Crovitz 2013). When Google lobbied the Federal Trade Commission—successfully, it turns out—to forestall an antitrust investigation, the commission's chairman questioned the lobbying strategy: "Stop! Invest your money in expansion and innovation. Google's lobbying expenses had no effect on the care, diligence or analysis of the agency's incredibly hard-working staff or the decisions reached by any of the FTC's five commissioners" (ibid.). But even if its lobbying was successful, there is still an argument to be made that lobbying distracts companies from their core mission. "Instead of the 'suicide impulse' of lobbying for more regulation," one analyst concluded, "Silicon Valley should seek deregulation and a long-overdue freedom to return to its entrepreneurial roots" (ibid.). These observations are understandable. Did Facebook really need thirty-eight lobbyists in 2013, an increase of fifteen over 2011? Do Apple, Google, and Microsoft really need to pad their high-paid ranks with former FTC staffers? Is this not "spinning the revolving door that fuels the growth of lobbying" (ibid.)? And what about Amazon, whose owner appeared to trump his lobbying competitors by purchasing the primary newspaper in the American capital, thereby giving him, and presumably his company, privileged access to the corridors of power (Cassidy 2013)?

Well founded as they are, these criticisms also reveal a simplistic view of government as a completely negative influence on business, especially in new industries, such as those that took root in Silicon Valley starting in the 1950s. It is simplistic because, while government can slow the growth of innovation through excessive regulation, it is also the case that businesses have historically depended on government for infrastructure support, for maintaining a stable intellectual-property environment, and for a market in the early days of experimentation. Government was all of these things for Silicon Valley and it is reasonable to maintain that Silicon Valley would not have succeeded without government support (Mazzucato 2013). This is not just because government funded early research on information technology through its own research labs such as at the Defense Advanced Research Projects Agency (DARPA); it also provided a market when no private firms stepped up in the first rounds of semiconductor production. Lobbying can be essential to making sure government provides a stable environment for growing businesses. Moreover, criticisms presume that lobbying is only about achieving a specific goal. Google lobbies to stave off antitrust regulation, Facebook to avoid privacy controls, and Microsoft to weaken environmental rules and win low-cost power for its cloud data centers. But, important as these are, lobbying means more than accomplishing short-term goals. Lobbying also helps companies promote the general interest of the industry, including selling its products to government, which often helps to make a market and to win government support for a favorable business climate abroad. Looked at in this way, lobbying is every bit as promotional as commercial advertisements, blog postings, and high-level business reports.

Cloud Expo: Promoting Cloud Computing through Trade Shows

Lobbying is also interesting because, in an era that touts the wonders of social media and moving everything to the cloud, it remains a decidedly interpersonal, real-time activity. So are trade shows and conferences that aim to advance both knowledge and support for IT and the cloud. In the IT sector there are endless rounds of these events, but over the years arguably the most important have been the COMDEX (Computer Dealer Exhibition) trade shows, which took place from 1979 to 2003, and the Consumer Electronics Show (CES), which brings together companies aiming to have their new products named "the next new thing." CES began meeting in 1967 and continues as an annual event in Las Vegas. COMDEX was the major IT event until 1999, when it tried to restrict media coverage to writers accredited with a handful of the leading trade publications. Competition contributed to a drop-off in attendance from a peak of 200,000 attendees and, when major companies decided to make big product announcements at CES or other venues, COMDEX discontinued the event. CES picked up the slack, topping 150,000 attendees in 2012 and again in 2013 (Takahashi 2013).

Trade shows are important because they circulate technical and marketing information about products and because they build networks of promoters who share the wonders of information technology. It is only a slight exaggeration to say that trade shows are similar to religious events that bring together believers in a magical setting full of icons and symbols that affirm their mutual faith. On a more practical note, they provide opportunities for widespread coverage in mainstream and social media that amounts to free advertising of new products.

Nevertheless, attendance at these shows is leveling off, a sign that the days of the grand trade show that aimed to be all things to all participants are nearing an end. The sheer number of participants as well as the diversity of interests (or faiths) they represent appears to be overwhelming the goal of offering anything resembling a clear focus on common themes. The mass trade show is suffering some of the same effects as the religious pilgrimages, such as the Camino de Santiago de Compostela in Spain, which became so popular that it is more and more difficult to maintain the conditions of quiet contemplation and austerity so attractive to its supporters over the years. "Pilgrims" decked out in the latest hiking gear from REI and carrying iPhones updated with the latest pilgrimages apps (each route has its own) do not exactly convey the spirit of sacrifice and poverty before God that the thousand-year-old event was meant to instill. While Las Vegas is not Santiago de Compostela, the variety of pilgrims making their way to CES is so overwhelming that many of the big companies, such as Apple and Microsoft, no longer show up or appear only through their partners' products, choosing to focus on their own or specialized events with much less clutter than the big trade show. Such is increasingly the case for cloud computing, which holds specialized events throughout the year. In June 2013 I attended the leading cloud-computing and big-data conference and exhibition, Cloud Expo, in New York City. Over four days I heard speakers from a cross-section of cloud companies; participated in cloud bootcamp, a set of sessions spanning the technologies that comprise cloud computing and data analytics; and spent hours on the exhibition floor observing and speaking to as many of the 500 or so vendors as I could.

The show's website announcement should dispel any doubt about its promotional nature: "Recent IDC [International Data Corporation] research shows that worldwide spending on cloud services will grow almost threefold, reaching $44.2 billion by 2013. And a recent Gartner report predicts that the volume of enterprise data overall will increase by a phenomenal 650% over the next five years. These two unstoppable enterprise IT trends, Cloud Computing and Big Data, will converge in New York City at the 12th Cloud Expo—being held June 10–13, 2013, at the Javits Center in New York, NY." Moreover, the website proclaimed, "In the most transformative technology shift since the personal computer and the Internet, it's apparent that migrating business to the cloud has reached a tipping point in 2012, where it is no longer a trend but rather an absolute business requirement." And if we needed an exclamation point: "Join us as a media partner—together we can rock the IT world!" (*Cloud Expo* 2013). All pilgrimages exact a price; even *las peregrinas* who walk the Camino have to pay for equipment, accommodations, and the much-encouraged donations. But the pilgrimage to the cloud in the Big Apple costs considerably more. To simply attend all of the conference sessions over four days runs $2,500. So, unlike the Camino, the cloud pilgrimage, whether to New York or to any of a number of cloud-trade-show venues, is limited to those who can afford the high entry fee.

Trade shows build community in several different ways. The registration fee itself makes certain that only people who are strongly motivated to be part of the community participate. The content ranges across every dimension of promotionalism. Registrants who need basic training in the wonders of the cloud can join a cloud-computing bootcamp and take a cloud-essentials course. All participants have access to exhibitors representing every type of cloud-computing and big-data company. The exhibition hall is a massive marketing and sales space. As in any promotional event, whether people are selling spirituality or computer services, some are singled out as especially gifted in the field, and these take up roles as keynote speakers who sell the cloud and big data from their own positions within the industry. Whether they are covering the trade-offs between the cloud and on-premises computing, the potential of big data to identify customers or voters, or the transformation of the IT profession from operations to service delivery, there is a pattern to the keynotes and the breakout sessions. They tend to begin with a broad overview that praises the cloud as a general and profitable business tool. This might involve cost comparisons between different types of cloud arrangements: public, private, and hybrid. Next, they identify a problem that businesses face, such as maintaining data security or entering the Asian market. Finally, they conclude with a pitch on how the products and services of the speaker's company, whether Rackspace's hybrid cloud or Pacnet's experience in the Asian market, will solve the problem. Whatever the subject, the outcome is the same: follow our lead, buy our product, and watch your business take off.

Despite the best efforts of the self-proclaimed cloud evangelist who chaired Cloud Expo and introduced the keynote and general sessions, occasional discordant notes reverberated throughout the event. At a lunch panel discussion, big-data experts were asked to state what comes to mind when they hear the term *big data*. Following the unwritten script, the experts chirped the expected—"opportunity, challenge." One, however, refused to follow their lead and instead proclaimed it "a bullsh*t marketing term." As the saying goes, you could hear a pin drop.[5] But soon thereafter, the evangelist MC returned to the upbeat message that might convince the audience to buy a big-data analytics service from Hadoop or Teradata. This event was no exception to the widespread use of props and inducements to spur attendees to buy the cloud. As an academic unused to the special effects that fill these events, I was a bit surprised to hear loud rock music, including heavy metal, blaring in the run-up to a general session. Also unexpected was the presence of models in short shorts, thigh-high boots, and sparing no makeup opportunity, walking the conference floor and chatting up delegates. The spokesmodel presence was right out of an old-fashioned auto show except for the high-tech tool each used to scan attendee conference badges for information useful to the company that hired her. In addition, there were the cheesy freebies such as buttons (I "heart" the cloud; Do IT in the cloud), yo-yos, wind-up toys, and T-shirts (mine supports the hybrid cloud). To trade on the icons of tech work, the exhibition hall featured bean-bag seats for plopping, as well as foosball and air-hockey games for unwinding. Exhibitors offered more serious enticements to attract shoppers, such as lottery drawings for tech equipment. One enterprising speaker, in what was actually an interesting session on cloud security, kept the audience in the room by raffling two state-of-the-art, high-capacity Intel solid-state drives at the end of the session. In addition to equipping their spokesmodels with scanners, the conference made use of another modern conference add-on by live-streaming the entire event to a worldwide audience of paying viewers. High-tech gear aside, one of the most remarkable, and remarkably ironic, points in the conference arose when a massive line snaked its way through the exhibition hall. It was by far the longest queue of the four-day event, with a thousand or so people waiting patiently for a very low-tech reward: free copies of a hardcover book on how cloud computing will change everything (Erl, Puttini, and Mahmood 2013).

Cloud Expo helped advance my understanding of cloud-computing technology, big-data methodology, and the leading companies that produce both. But it also underscored the role of large conventions in the promotion of cloud computing and big data. The conference and others like it are promotional because they insist on the absolute necessity of adopting cloud computing. They are also promotional for what they do not address, primarily the pressures that the cloud imposes on the built environment and on the electrical grid, the tendency to concentrate power in a few large companies, and the challenge to employment arising from big changes in the international division of labor. Data security and privacy attract a bit of attention, but largely as a threat to cloud adoption.

The forms of cloud promotion that this chapter has considered—commercial advertising, blog posts and social media, promotional research reports, lobbying, and trade conferences—do not exhaust the major examples. They cover a great deal of ground, but there are other topic areas, including government promotion. In the United States, the 2010 federal government chief information officer's report hailing the cloud and ordering agencies to adopt cloud computing was one of the first in a series of government promotional steps. In addition, there was a 2011 National Institute of Standards and Technology (NIST) report that promised major cost savings for government agencies moving their information technology functions to the cloud (NIST 2011). Then in 2012 the National Science Foundation joined the chorus supporting the NIST report and committed the government to carry out research on all aspects of cloud computing (National Science Foundation 2012).

All of the promotion and the hyperbole are important to mobilize support, which, as the history of communication technology demonstrates, can be fickle, as people continuously flock to the next new thing. So it is essential for those who envision the cloud as an engine to drive informational capitalism to continually promote its revolutionary capabilities.[6] Promotion is also essential to protect the cloud from criticisms about its challenges, problems, and even dangers. The next two chapters address these and, in doing so, raise questions about the wisdom of moving to the cloud.

CHAPTER 4
DARK CLOUDS

The inherent nature of the mobile Internet, a key feature of the emergent Cloud architecture, requires far more energy than do wired networks.... Trends now promise faster, not slower, growth in ICT energy use. (Mills 2013, from the report "The Cloud Begins with Coal")

SECRETS ARE LIES
SHARING IS CARING
PRIVACY IS THEFT (Eggers 2013, 303)

Cloud computing is nothing more than the next step in outsourcing your IT operations. (McKendrick 2013c)

There is no quicker way to descend from the cloud than to look in on an old-fashioned, down-to-earth dispute about money and power. Such was the case when the veteran *New York Times* reporter James Glanz, known for his work as Baghdad bureau chief and for an investigative history of the World Trade Center (Glanz and Lipton 2004), arrived in the town of Quincy in central Washington to do a story on cloud-computing data centers. There he found a dispute between a computer giant and a small power company. Now, this was no ordinary big computer company—it was Microsoft, the business that, in the minds of many, saved the state of Washington from the fate of other declining industrial regions by setting up its headquarters there rather than in Silicon Valley. In 2006 Microsoft decided to expand by buying seventy-five acres of an old bean farm and building a data center to support its cloud services. The company was drawn by the abundance of hydroelectric power produced by generators operated from the nearby Columbia River. It was also attracted by utility rates priced, thanks to its effective lobbying, at less than half the national average, which brought a reliable flow of power made possible by dams along the river, including two operated by the local power company. Finally, Microsoft sought and received generous tax breaks from the state because it paid property taxes to the town, helping to pave roads and build a new library for Quincy's 6,900 residents. The head of the power company summarized a general feeling when the company came to town: "You're talking about one of the largest corporations. You're talking Microsoft and Bill Gates. Wow!" (Glanz 2012a).

It did not take long for the wow to turn into pow when a Quincy citizens' group took legal action against Microsoft for pollution spewing from forty diesel generators that, as is common at data centers, the company deployed for its primary backup system. The software giant's facility is located near an elementary school, and parents and neighbors feared the toxic effects, especially for young students. The term *backup generator* does not sound particularly harmful, but those used in data centers are not the kind homeowners keep in the garage. They are over ten feet tall and weigh thousands of pounds each, enough to generate 2 million watts per generator. Just as significant, they get used a lot more often than the term backup would indicate, particularly during frequent periods of building construction. The state had initially permitted Microsoft to use them for 6,000 hours over the course of a year for emergency backup power or for "maintenance purposes" (ibid.). It appears, however, that the company actually used the generators so frequently during a period of data-center expansion that it asked to be unplugged from the electrical grid to run entirely on diesel. In 2010, Microsoft ran its Quincy diesel generators for 3,615 hours, sending into the air particulate matter that studies of other Microsoft data centers found contained enough carcinogens to pose a threat to people living and working in the area. No assessments were made in Quincy, but residents knew when the diesel generators powered up. According to a forklift driver who works at a local fruit warehouse, "When they first start up, a big, huge cloud of black smoke comes up. It just kind of makes you nauseous" (ibid.). As more companies and more data centers moved into town, even more diesel was used, all of which generated environmental hearings, lawsuits, and a lot of delicate negotiations, leaving an environmental engineer with the state's Department of Ecology to conclude in some exasperation, "I find it hard to believe that this is the best way to store data. Something's flawed in that thought process" (ibid.).

Alongside the fight over diesel, another dispute arose between Microsoft and the utility over power usage. As is generally the case, the utility requires estimates of power usage from its large customers in order to efficiently manage the grid. This issue is so important that power companies are permitted to fine firms that significantly miss estimates. In this case Microsoft overestimated and was levied a fine of slightly more than $200,000. Much to the surprise and chagrin of locals, the computer giant not only refused to pay the fine, but proceeded to burn millions of watts of power in what it admitted was an "unnecessarily wasteful" manner until the utility agreed to slash or completely erase the fine. In Microsoft's view, if it was going to be fined for overuse, then it would simply burn off enough power to raise its power consumption above the level that had triggered the fine. One might think Microsoft would pay the fine and enjoy some positive publicity for using less power than it estimated. Indeed, Yahoo! faced just such a fine and paid it. However, Microsoft decided against doing so, and its power use jumped from 28.5 to 34 million watts in three days. Under pressure, the utility board voted to cut the fine to $60,000, and Microsoft ended its fuel-burning protest.

It is little wonder that a utility commissioner and local farmer commented, "For a company of that size and that nature, and with all the 'green' things they advertised to me, that was an insult" (ibid.). Microsoft, for its part, claimed that this was an isolated incident. But it was actually just one more in a long list of issues creating tension and outright conflict between the company and the farming community. A mere three days after the ribbon-cutting ceremony welcoming the computer giant and presenting the local general manager with a bag of beans from the last harvest on the land and a sign announcing, "Preparing the Site for Another Farmer: Microsoft," tensions rose over the ability of the town to meet the company's electrical-power needs. The data center's general manager complained that the utility was slow to bring on board a substation that would provide 48 million watts of power to the Microsoft facility, or enough to power about 30,000 homes. Arguing that slow construction "dramatically affects our agility as a business," the Microsoft official informed the utility that "our confidence is becoming quite shaky" and wondered if, in the absence of speedier construction, the company might be eligible for $700,000 in reimbursements. This struck one utility official as demonstrating "a level of arrogance" and confounded others, including a retired schoolteacher who had felt that "Microsoft would bring a little class to the town" (ibid.).

Despite its problems with Microsoft, the town has not turned its back on data centers, approving construction for Yahoo! and Dell, also attracted by the promise of cheap power and tax breaks. By the end of 2012, little Quincy had two supermarkets, two hardware stores, and six data centers, with five more under construction, but no movie theater or Main Street. Some town residents and businesses worry that, with many companies now chasing lower utility costs, the power company might have to raise rates for local customers. They are also concerned that power-hungry data centers might create an actual power shortage, a remarkable irony given the town's proximity to the Columbia River and its hydroelectric dams. A local fruit grower in the area concluded that the overall impact has been much less positive than most people imagined: "I don't think it's benefiting Quincy." Although he recognizes the importance of data centers to the American economy, "I think," he said, "we're taking one for the team, to tell you the truth" (ibid.).

While details may differ, there is nothing particularly unusual about Quincy's experience with the cloud. Many people are now "taking one for the team" to build and operate cloud computing systems. Indeed, incidents of legal action for alleged violations of environmental regulations, utility agreements, promised employment for local residents, and other related issues come up time and time again after the cloud arrives. This led Glanz to conclude, "When these Internet factories come to town, they can feel a bit more like old-time manufacturing than modern magic" (ibid.). Nor do they feel like the clouds described in promotional accounts. As long as environmental officials in Washington State and local citizens in places like Quincy continue to think of data centers as clouds rather than as factories, they will continue to have problems making sound decisions. It is striking, but not surprising, to observe how confused people appear to be about the cloud. I have talked to people with graduate degrees who still think it has something to do with actual clouds, with communication satellites, or with the weather (e.g., the system can go down in the rain). Surveys confirm the public's confusion about the cloud (Linthicum 2013a). At best, the general public sees it as "one big storage space," which at least comprehends one piece of the cloud puzzle (Abdul 2013).[1] Getting a handle on the language matters a great deal, especially in an era that lauds advertising and promotion, suitably dressed up in terms like strategic communication. Giant power projects in the desert are called *solar farms* (Soto 2011), and diesel-spewing information-processing factories are known as *clouds*. Factories, whether in the desert or in a small town, are not inherently bad, but people need to know what they really are before they approve construction, determine whether or what kind of incentives to provide, and establish an appropriate regulatory regime.

This chapter takes a step toward providing a critical understanding by examining some of the major problems associated with cloud computing, concentrating on environmental and power issues, privacy, security, and employment.

E-pollution

Advertising aside, we have known for some time that computers are not a green technology. Chemicals used in their components are among the most carcinogenic. Silicon Valley long led the list of extreme toxic-waste sites in the United States, and today China and many poor nations contain mountains of computer parts making up a dangerous chemical stew. According to Maxwell and Miller (2012a, 3), by 2007 between 20 and 50 million tons of e-waste were generated annually, most of it from cell phones, televisions, and computers that people sent to the dump. E-waste is mostly produced in the developed West and disposed of in Latin America, Africa, Eastern Europe, India, Southeast Asia, and China. In recent years, India and China have joined the leaders in waste production. Over the ten-year period from 1997 to 2007, the United States alone discarded 500 million computers containing over 6 billion pounds of plastics, over 1.5

billion pounds of lead, 3 million pounds of cadmium, almost 2 million pounds of chromium, and 632,000 pounds of mercury, as well as many other dangerous and carcinogenic chemicals, like beryllium and gallium arsenide (Maxwell and Miller 2012a).

E-waste has been described as a "growing toxic nightmare" and with good reason. As Leyla Acaroglu describes it,

> In far-flung, mostly impoverished places like Agbogbloshie, Ghana; Delhi, India; and Guiyu, China, children pile e-waste into giant mountains and burn it so they can extract the metals—copper wires, gold and silver threads—inside, which they sell to recycling merchants for only a few dollars. In India, young boys smash computer batteries with mallets to recover cadmium, toxic flecks of which cover their hands and feet as they work. Women spend their days bent over baths of hot lead, "cooking" circuit boards so they can remove slivers of gold inside.... Most scientists agree that exposure poses serious health risks, especially to pregnant women and children. (2013)

From their earliest days, one major argument made about computers has been that they provide an environmentally sound alternative to the productive engines of the industrial era. Scholars, including most who are otherwise critical about information technology, have generally ignored their impact. Moreover, as Maxwell and Miller (2012a, 13) note in one of the few sustained accounts of the environmental problems associated with media technology, well-regarded academics who are quick to point out the excellent use environmentalists make of new media have nothing to say about the profound irony of this activity. At best, research advances the view well stated in a 1998 article by a trio of scholars who, in the first wave of the Internet's growth, sought to understand the relationship between environmentalism and the information society: "On the one hand, there is the potential for reducing the stress on the environment: the emergence of information technologies and services can lead to a dematerialisation of production and immaterialisation of consumption" (Jokinen, Malaska, and Kaivo-oja 1998). This puts succinctly the promise of IT to promote a more sustainable world. Computers linked to communication systems can create smarter systems of production that require less material input and create less material waste. Just as important, the process of getting goods to consumers is made less material, in part because an information society requires fewer material products and also because the process of getting things to consumers is made smarter and more efficient.

One can certainly understand why this view would receive support. I wrote this book putting practically no ink to paper because I used my laptop and drew from the vast stores of online information for research. To its credit, and unlike the many positive forecasts about green IT, the 1998 article also raises the risk that "positive environmental effects might be overcome by the 'rebound effect' caused by excessive economic growth" (ibid.). That success on the environmental front can encourage people to consume more is not dissimilar from other counterintuitive effects, such as the link between advanced braking systems and the number of accidents. Trusting the brakes can lead to more reckless driving, just as progress on environmental controls can encourage people to buy more, especially more "green" products.

The counterintuitive effect embodies good dialectical thinking, but it nevertheless retains the view that information technology is inherently green. The consequences of using IT may indeed lead to greater consumption and resource depletion; however, the thinking goes, this is due not to the technology but rather to what we do with it. The expansion of cloud computing demonstrates the limitations of this view, particularly when one considers the genuine materiality of production that takes place in the large data centers around the world. On the outside, they appear to be enormous rectangular warehouses, perhaps distinguished by their lack of unique identification and minimal exposure to outside light. Inside, they are far from the storage facilities that typically define a warehouse. Instead they are filled with active devices and systems, including rack upon rack of servers processing data and multiple power and cooling sources. According to a lawyer for Microsoft, "The heart of the cloud are these data centers, and the data centers are really at the heart of Microsoft's business" (Glanz 2012a).

We now have tens of thousands of data centers spanning the world, permitting people to instantly download their Google mail, search on Baidu, buy music and movies from iTunes, and purchase products of every kind from Amazon. But all of these benefits come at the cost of increased power use and more stress on the environment. Cloud data centers are filled with thousands of servers, each comprising common and rare materials whose disposal raises serious issues of water and soil contamination. There are few more arresting images than those in Edward Burtynsky's documentary *Manufactured Landscapes* of elderly village women in China picking through mountains of hazardous computer waste for something to sell. This scene, repeated again and again throughout the many places where detritus from the cloud finds a not-so-final resting place, belies the image of an immaterial information age. Admittedly, this problem does not make for the dystopian drama of nuclear-waste disposal, a reality that has itself slowed the development of nuclear power by providing political ballast for its foes. Moreover, the mushroom cloud associated with nuclear weapons is a far more arresting deterrent than the puffy clouds of our information age. But in some respects, the challenge of the cloud's e-waste is more insidious because its hazards are not so immediately threatening and because the bulk of the damage is done in poor countries, where most such waste is dumped, or in the poorer regions of richer nations, such as in rural China.

The need to keep the heart of the data center beating requires a constant stream of power. As a result, the facilities need reliable sources of electricity for their 24/7 operations and, for those times when even the best electrical systems shut down, backup systems, including the diesel-powered generators described in the Microsoft story. Furthermore, in most cases, additional backup is provided by a massive supply of lead-acid batteries and banks of flywheels whose spinning offers additional reserve power. Even with all of this expensive, polluting backup, there is still no guarantee of 24/7 performance, as Microsoft itself learned when it experienced a worldwide crash of several major cloud services because it failed to renew a security certificate in 2013 (Ribeiro 2013).

The need for reliable, low-cost electricity for both power and cooling is a complicated coupling that influences locational decisions and helps to shape the politics of data centers. The power demands alone are astounding. As an engineer who has designed hundreds of the centers described, "It's staggering for most people, even people in the industry, to understand the numbers, the sheer size of these systems. A single data center can take more power than a medium-size town" (Glanz 2012b). Estimates vary, but experts agree that data centers' power consumption accounts for roughly 2 percent of all the electricity consumed in the world, and their carbon emissions are set to quadruple by 2020 (*Data Center Journal* 2013).

Over the long run, these rates of electrical consumption are less than sustainable, and companies are actively trying to find solutions. But this is not easy because data centers are profit-making enterprises that keep customers by maintaining 24/7 access. Moreover, their systems need more than just a constant supply of power to operate. They also need a means of maintaining a sufficiently cool environment to prevent their servers from overheating. It should therefore come as little surprise that the coal industry expects a revenue bonanza from cloud computing. In a detailed report, the association representing Big Coal in the United States contradicts all the forecasts that cloud computing will eventually diminish energy requirements for companies that use the cloud and for the cloud industry itself (Mills 2013).

Companies can do some things to moderate power consumption, including locating their facilities in places like Scandinavia and Canada that provide better natural cooling. But, as the section on security issues shows, storing data outside one's borders raises other concerns. Companies can also better attune their power systems to times when servers are actively engaged in processing. But this is difficult to accomplish because cloud providers like to keep the power flowing so that, in the event of a sudden spike in processing demand, their servers do not crash. Cloud companies know that customers do not like to see any delay or down time in their email use, in digital product downloads, or in access to social-media sites, and they worry that customers will turn to another provider or lose interest and cut back on their discretionary activities in cyberspace. Nevertheless, some firms are taking action.

HP has developed new servers that require less power, an initiative that has helped its bottom line even as it earns less than it used to on all of its other lines of business (Sherr and Clark 2013). Companies are also developing innovative power systems to substantially reduce, if not eliminate, the need to cool servers electrically.[2] Yahoo! made the decision to build a data center outside Buffalo, New York, that uses hydroelectric power, which substantially lowered its carbon footprint (Greenpeace International 2010, 3). Although Google killed its thermal power program, the company has used wind power for a data center in Iowa and set up an electricity subsidiary to sell power back to the grid (Barton 2012). Especially since it suffered a barrage of negative publicity for locating one of the largest data centers in North Carolina and choosing to deal with a company,

Duke Power, with a notorious environmental and labor record, Apple has taken some steps to develop sources of renewable energy (Clancy 2012). Finally, Salesforce has developed new metrics, including carbon produced per transaction, to better monitor its energy use (Makower 2012).

Even if companies manage to increase renewable energy sources for cloud data centers, significant environmental problems will remain. That is because most people access cloud systems wirelessly, and, as a 2013 report concluded, wireless access consumes enormous amounts of energy and does so less efficiently than the data centers that have come in for most criticism (Center for Energy-Efficient Telecommunications 2013). Moreover, it is important to observe that most of the green shoots in an otherwise bleak landscape sprout within the United States. There are exceptions. Greenpeace named the giant Indian technology outsourcing company Wipro the greenest electronics company in the world (Swinhoe 2013). However, the material construction of cloud computing requires global supply chains whose many links outside the United States give rise to daily stories of environmental ruin. So even as Apple was trying to burnish its reputation for producing solar power in North Carolina's coal country, one of its suppliers in China was discovered to have killed a river outside Shanghai with e-waste resulting from the production of Apple products. According to an account in the *Financial Times*, the Apple contractor has been turning the river a milky white just about every week over the two years it has run the industrial park facility, prompting this comment from one waste-treatment plant worker: "Before that, there were fish and shellfish in the river that we used to eat. But now there are no fish at all. And when the water turns white, we can't even use it to water the vegetables any more" (Mishkin, Waldmeir, and Hille 2013). The local company is facing sanctions from the Shanghai government, but it is unlikely that the river can be brought back to life. Stories like this provide an important reminder that the cloud is grounded in a global system of production that is material, industrial, and, unless there are major changes, unsustainable.

One result of the "always-on" commitment is that server operation is woefully inefficient. When the *New York Times* commissioned McKinsey and Company to examine the energy use of data centers providing cloud services to a variety of customers, it found that they were using only between 6 and 12 percent of the electricity powering their servers to perform actual processing operations (Glanz 2012b). Companies keep the electricity flowing for fear that service will not be available when it is needed. Customers leasing facilities do not want to hear about down time and are not reluctant to find another cloud provider if 24/7 service is not provided. So engineers working for cloud companies labor in fear of losing their jobs if they are caught with their servers down. Better to power unused servers than to face an angry customer. According to one executive at a utility firm, "It's a nervousness in the I.T. community that something isn't going to be available when they need it" (ibid.). There is practically no incentive to save energy and every incentive to keep the system going. As a senior industry executive told the *Times*, "This is an industry dirty secret, and no one wants to be the first to say mea culpa. If we were a manufacturing industry, we'd be out of business straightaway" (ibid.). The term *dirty* is appropriate in more than one sense.

Another not-so-little secret is the reliance on very un-cloud-like backup systems to guarantee against an electrical power failure. These include diesel generators like those described in the case of Microsoft's data center in central Washington. Data centers throughout Silicon Valley have been cited on the state of California's Toxic Air Contaminant Inventory for diesel air pollution. Since many jurisdictions lack such a tracking mechanism, they cannot monitor the effects of diesel use and so must suffer the effects of toxins and carcinogens or try their luck with legal action, as did the citizens of Quincy. Diesel generators are not enough for an industry determined to provide instant service, on demand, any time. These also tend to be backed up by thousands of lead-acid batteries of the type used in trucks and cars and by enormous flywheels whose spinning generates more backup power. A staffer at an institute that studies electrical power usage is not impressed: "It's a waste. It's too many insurance policies" (ibid.). Of course, data-center managers under intense pressure to deliver all the time would disagree. Microsoft is not the only company to be penalized for violating environmental regulations. In October 2010, Amazon was issued a fine of slightly over $500,000 by the state of Virginia for building, installing, and continuously running diesel generators without obtaining the necessary permits to do so. After appeals, the fines were cut to about half that amount, but four inspections and a total of twenty-four violations ranked "high" do not make for a record to boast about, especially for a company claiming leadership in cloud computing (Barton 2012).

The cloud industry, which profits by storing and processing other people's secrets, is among the most secretive itself. Companies do not reveal the location of their own data centers, which tend to be housed in nondescript warehouse-like buildings with no signs or markings. Making matters more difficult, the United States and other nations with large numbers of data centers have no single agency responsible for overseeing them. The United States knows how many government data centers it has—2,094 in 2010—but does not know how much energy they consume. This does not just create a regulatory issue; it also creates the conditions for disaster. As one technology and power industry consultant concluded, "It's just not sustainable. They're going to hit a brick wall" (ibid.).

Public awareness is growing as pressure mounts from environmental groups, especially Greenpeace. In 2010, the activist organization issued a report on cloud computing that challenged the major providers to do a much better job of taking into account environmental damage. Specifically, it took Facebook to task for building a data center in central Oregon serviced by a utility that primarily uses coal-fired power stations, the largest source of greenhouse gas emissions in the United States (Greenpeace International 2010). Greenpeace used the report to launch a campaign dubbed Unfriend Coal, complete with a Facebook page that attracted 700,000 supporters and set a Guinness World Record for most comments on the social-media site in a twenty-four-hour period. In 2011 the organization issued another study on cloud computing that provided specific details and graded cloud companies on their performance. This report gave Facebook an F in "Infrastructure Siting" for the social-media company's continued reliance on coal-fired plants (Greenpeace International 2011). A year later, Facebook reached an agreement with Greenpeace by pledging, among other things, to change its data plant siting policies. Aside from the commitment to reduce dependency on coal-fired plants, Facebook was short on specifics. But Greenpeace took this as a step in the right direction.

The Greenpeace reports did not just call out Facebook for failure to "like" the environment. No company fared especially well. In the 2011 report Twitter came out the worst, with F marks in all three categories of transparency, a measure that included openness about its environmental policies, infrastructure citing, and mitigation strategy. In keeping with the secrecy with which new media companies operate, Amazon received an F for transparency but squeaked out D marks in the other categories. Apple, which fared slightly better (two Cs and an F), had the worst record for coal intensity, faring a bit worse than Facebook. However, the most striking finding, and the most disappointing for anyone expecting different behavior from companies that like to polish their own halos, is that, with rare exceptions, cloud-computing companies, including all the big names in hardware, software, social media, and big data, behave no differently from their industrial predecessors.

Greenpeace has not only taken the lead in shining a light on the sad environmental record of IT companies. It has also been a leader in activism. In April 2012, people with the organization climbed to the top of Amazon's new corporate headquarters in Seattle, directly across the street from Microsoft's corporate center, and rappelled from the roof to hang a banner in the shape of a cloud that read, "Amazon, Microsoft: How Clean Is Your Cloud?" Following the event, Greenpeace's IT analyst explained the protest to *Wired* magazine: "If we want to get to a renewable energy economy, we can't get there without leadership from these companies. For too long, too many of the energy decisions have been dictated by a small set of companies who are very happy with the status quo" (ibid.). The companies insist that they are making positive strides, but they also maintain that large data centers are intrinsically better for the environment than having every individual or organizational user house its own data (ibid.). Environmentalists insist that Amazon will have to do much more than build photo-op-ready greenhouses in downtown Seattle.

It is difficult enough to contemplate a sustainable cloud from the supply side, but it is even more challenging when one considers the seemingly unstoppable demand for cloud services from organizations and individuals. Supply and demand are interconnected, as is evident throughout the promotional culture of cloud computing. For those who market the cloud, customers should not only want cloud services, but also demand them as a right. A 2013 advertisement for Sprint makes this abundantly clear as a young male voice recites a spiritual ode to technology while a sublime montage zips by:

> The miraculous is everywhere.
> In our homes, in our minds.
> We can share every second

in data dressed as pixels.
A billion roaming photojournalists …
Uploading the human experience.
And it is spectacular.
So why would you cap that?
My iPhone 5 can see every point of view …
Every panorama. The entire gallery of humanity.
I need to upload all of me.
I need, no, I have the right to be unlimited.
Only Sprint offers Truly Unlimited data
for iPhone 5. (Sprint 2013)

"I need to upload all of me." Why not? Since most people believe that digital bits are different from atoms, this is a consequence-free choice. However they might have been burnt, or at least jaded a bit, by the dot-com bust of the early 2000s, many remain with former director of MIT's Media Lab Nicholas Negroponte (1995) and former editor of *Wired* magazine Kevin Kelly (2010), as well as countless other myth makers, who insisted that the digital world not only differed from the world of material atoms; it represented another order of reality. Being digital, as Negroponte insisted, meant living in a world of limitless possibilities unbounded by the physical, material, and environmental limits that constrain the world of atoms. As powerful as this vision has been for drawing a world into the ether of cyberspace and now the cloud, it is fundamentally flawed. The resource and environmental problems of the digital world demonstrate that the digital and the material are inextricably bound.[3] Negroponte and those who followed in his path were wrong. The world of atoms is not ending; it weighs upon us ever more powerfully, with every additional petabyte, in the digital world's seemingly relentless growth. Cloud companies like Google argue that the centralization and rationalization of power use that a shift to the cloud enables will diminish overall business power consumption. But a model based on research funded by Google that appears to demonstrate this has met with skepticism (Bourne 2013). Moreover, reports funded by Greenpeace International (2010, 2011, and 2012) and by the U.S. coal industry (Mills 2013), typically adversaries, conclude that overall business energy consumption will instead grow substantially.

Building an environmentally sound or sustainable digital world requires fundamental changes in the behavior of IT companies, including those leading the flight to the cloud. Just because they are producing, processing, distributing, and displaying a digital product does not mean that companies can avoid the environmental consequences of their activities. But it also requires a fundamental change in the people and the organizations that download, upload, transmit, receive, and display the digital world. It is no more reasonable, and no less environmentally impactful, to demand a world of limitless data than it is to demand a world of limitless goods. Neither comes without a cost, and neither is sustainable without major changes in consciousness and material practices. As Maxwell and Miller eloquently conclude, "There are technological fixes for the Internet's environmental problem—moving data centers off the coal-fired power grid and onto hydro-electric, solar, geothermal and other sources; designing energy efficient devices; and using smart grids to regulate and reduce domestic and workplace energy consumption. But these fixes will not succeed without a corresponding transformation of our consumer culture into a culture of sustainability, one that ensures that social, political, and economic development does not exceed or irreversibly damage the Earth's abilities to supply and renew the natural resources upon which we depend" (2012b). This will be difficult, and there is little time to lose. As Maxwell and Miller also note, there are now 10 billion devices to power, and these soak up 15 percent of all global residential energy. If the current rate of adoption continues—that is, if there is no change in the belief that these devices impose no, or little, burden on the environment—then they will require 30 percent of the world electrical grid by 2022 and 45 percent by 2030. Meanwhile, the power demands of cloud data centers are expanding at an even faster rate, growing by 56 percent between 2005 and 2010, at a time when worldwide industrial energy growth was flat (ibid.).

Privacy and Security

Privacy and security concerns are coming together to form another question mark over the IT industry, including cloud computing and big data. In order to properly assess these concerns, it is useful to begin by considering different ways to think about privacy and security. At the risk of some simplification, consider three alternatives that range from weak to strong privacy protections. Starting at the weak end, one can view privacy and security as tradable commodities. We believe in the right to be left alone and to feel secure but are willing to give up some of the protections afforded in order to achieve other goals. This increasingly includes the decision to trade some of our privacy and security to live in the cloud by posting on Facebook or Twitter and downloading videos from Apple's iCloud. For the ability to do these things, we risk losing some of our identity to hackers or giving up information about ourselves, including the content of our postings or the profile established by our purchases, to the companies that provide the service, as well as to outside parties that purchase information about us from Facebook, Twitter, and Apple. Sometimes the deal with a cloud provider is not clear. I know a person who, after letting her Facebook friends know about a serious illness, began receiving ads for "bucket lists." Of course, she wasn't looking for a bucket list when she gave up some of her privacy in order to let friends know about her health issue. Nor was the person who started receiving ads for multiple sclerosis support services after doing an online search of sites devoted to the condition (Singer 2013). The outcome is not always this offensive, but it can also be worse, as when innocent online searches for pressure cookers and backpacks led to a home visit from six members of a terrorism task force, who, we soon learned, regularly check on people whose use of the Internet provokes suspicion (Bump 2013). Whether the deal is clear or not, in this first view, privacy and security are among the several things we desire, and we make choices about them in the context of other things we want.

In the middle of the continuum, privacy and security are no longer tradable commodities; rather, they are untradable values that define a citizen's right to be left alone and secure from violations. From this perspective, there is no trade-off in money, services, or goods because privacy and security are not commodities. Rather they are rights to freedom from identity loss and from physical or mental violation. Seen from this point of view, law and custom should protect the right to be left alone, which cannot be taken away without violating a right of citizenship and therefore cannot be traded for money, goods, or services. When Google, Amazon, or Microsoft tracks us, we lose some of our privacy. What we appear to get in return is actually unrelated to privacy. It is a service provided by the company for which we might or might not pay. But since, from this point of view, privacy is not a commodity, we cannot use it as a currency. When we agree to a website's "privacy policy," we are actually only accepting that we know about its privacy violation policy. We rely on government to protect this citizenship right, and when it allows corporations to diminish our privacy, or when government itself takes away our privacy and security, it is failing to uphold a fundamental right.

Both of these approaches provide useful ways of thinking about privacy and security. But they are weak in conveying a sense of what privacy and security do for us or why we should care deeply about them. For that we turn to a third perspective that tries to address these points as it provides the foundation for the strongest private protection. According this view, privacy and security are significant means of providing the space, the breathing room, or the buffer between our selves and the world that is necessary for self-development. They offer an essential space between the individual and the world, including those elements of the world that might benefit from taking, purchasing, or otherwise carrying out surveillance that violates this space and makes it more difficult to safely develop a self and an identity. In this reading, privacy violations are attacks on our capacity for self-development.

Dissatisfied with what they perceive as weak versions of privacy and security that fail to address why these values are important, a number of observers and scholars have adopted the self-development perspective. As writer Jathan Sadowski explains, "Since life and contexts are always changing, privacy cannot be reductively conceived as one specific type of thing. It is better understood as an important buffer that gives us space to develop an identity that is somewhat separate from the surveillance, judgment, and values of our society and culture" (2013). Scholars have deepened this view. For law professor Julie E. Cohen, it means "creating spaces for play and the work of self-making" (2013, 1911). For Woodrow Hartzog and Evan Selinger, privacy protection goes well beyond keeping businesses from gathering information about us for profit; privacy—or, in their terms, obscurity—is essential for democratic societies because it guards "autonomy, self-fulfillment, socialization, and relative freedom from the abuse of power" (2013). Finally, for Michael Lynch, privacy is essential for the growth of human autonomy; putting it in strong terms, he insists, "However we resolve these issues, we would do well to keep the connections between self, personhood and privacy in mind as we chew over the recent revelations about governmental access to Big Data. The underlying issue is not simply a matter of balancing convenience and liberty. To the extent we risk the loss of privacy we risk, in a very real sense, the loss of our very status as subjective, autonomous persons" (2013).

When Facebook develops tools, like the social search engine Graph Search, that combines pieces of our identity with third-party data and then markets this information to advertisers, it takes over the space of self-development, limits our breathing room to carry out the task of forming an identity, and lessens our ability to develop the autonomy necessary to live as citizens in a democratic society. It turns citizens into data points, commodifies their identifies, reduces democracy to another act of consumption, and leaves less room for genuine autonomy. Attacks on privacy and security are not just matters of trade or abstract rights; they diminish our psychological and social well-being, a point often submerged in debates about the impact of privacy legislation on commerce and politics.

Privacy is a perennial issue in communication, especially since the arrival of media technologies in the mid-nineteenth century. With the telegraph and then the telephone, people learned to trust strangers with their secrets. One way to build trust was to promise that messages would remain private and secure, even if that required close surveillance of those who worked the telegraph key and delivered messages, as well as those who took call requests at a switchboard. In the 1960s, as television was transitioning into cable and experiments in "interactive" video previewed a future of on-demand entertainment, people learned quickly, to the embarrassment of some, that the systems making it all possible also kept a record of the choices made. Later, the worry grew when video stores kept track of rentals, first of cassettes and then of DVDs. Questions arose regarding the public's right to know about a politician's viewing habits, questions that could not feasibly be raised in the "rabbit-ear" broadcasting days. The Internet upped the ante by globalizing once largely local privacy and security issues.

Cloud computing is the next step—neither a simple extension nor a radical rupture in the challenges it poses for privacy and security. By definition the cloud raises serious concerns in these areas because it entails moving all data from relatively well-known settings where the home computer hard drive is under personal control or the computer at work stores data behind an employer's firewall at an on-site data center. These certainly do not guarantee privacy and security, but the move to the cloud diminishes them further. It is one thing for a scholar to keep data on a laptop or portable hard drive or, to save space and money, on a university server. It is quite another to relocate data to the servers and data centers of businesses with whom nothing more is shared than an impersonal, customer-company relationship. There are many layers to the privacy and security problem with cloud computing, including growing opportunities to hack and steal data, incentives for companies to make commercial use of cloud data in various forms of surveillance capitalism, and opportunities for governments to use cloud data to track people within and beyond their borders and to apply their own laws to data originating outside their boundaries, giving rise to a surveillance state.

A headline on the *Washington Post* Ideas@Innovation blog wondered, "Is This the Year Everybody Gets Hacked?" After near-daily accounts of one hacker after another successfully attacking the sites of some of the biggest players in the cloud, it was hard to consider this hyperbole (Basulto 2013). After all, it was only February 21, 2013, and already Facebook, Twitter, and the once invulnerable Apple had been hacked. Four days later, as if in response to the question, hackers struck Microsoft. It is difficult to say what precisely the attackers were after, but experts agreed that they were probably looking for customer data or proprietary company information for which black market customers might pay top dollar to better tailor phishing attacks (M. Schwarz 2013). In April, the Twitter account of the Associated Press news service was hacked and a tweet posted announcing a White House bombing that had seriously injured President Barack Obama. In the ensuing brief panic, stock markets dove, and both Twitter and the Associated Press were left to issue major apologies and promises of solutions. This hack followed closely on the heels of similar attacks on the Twitter accounts of Burger King and Jeep (Romm 2013b).

Arguably the award for the biggest hacking story of the new year went to a February 19 report that China's People's Revolutionary Army was responsible for systematic hacking attacks directed against American corporations and government agencies. Attacks included the theft of terabytes of data from Coca-Cola, once involved in a feud with the government of China. Significant as this strike against the world's leader in soft drinks was, security analysts believe that attackers care more about companies responsible for critical infrastructure projects, including electrical power grids, gas lines, and waterworks (Sanger, Barboza, and Perlroth 2013). A survey of U.S. companies with businesses in China concluded that about a fourth claimed to have been hacked (Reuters 2013b). Details remained murky, and it was reasonable to wonder about the connection between the proliferation of hacking reports and the U.S. government's drive to pass controversial cyber-security legislation that itself raised privacy questions because it would increase information-sharing between intelligence agencies and private companies (Finkle 2013). Furthermore, as two hacking experts note, "It's good business today to blame China. I know from experience that many corporations, government and DOD organizations are more eager to buy cyber threat data that claims to focus on the PRC than any other nation state" (Raimondo 2013).

The United States was not just on the receiving end of cyber-attacks. Particularly notable was one it launched with Israel to send the malicious Stuxnet malware to disrupt Iran's nuclear program. China also claimed that the United States was responsible for massive cyber-attacks on its computers and data centers, especially those containing sensitive military data. According to a spokesman for the defense ministry, China's two main military websites are under constant attack from the United States: "Last year, the Chinese Defence Ministry website and Chinamil.com were attacked 144,000 times a month on average. Attacks originating in the U.S. accounted for 62.9 percent" (Hille and Thomas 2013). Moreover, China's Huawei, a world leader in the provision of telecommunications equipment, which itself has been charged with stealing sensitive data in the United States, Australia, and Canada, maintains that its computers are attacked about 10,000 times a week (ibid.). For the *People's Daily*, "In fact, it is America which is a real hackers' empire worthy of this name" (ibid.). Indeed, given the connection revealed by Edward Snowden between Verizon and the National Security Agency (NSA), even Western experts wonder whether the special attention to Huawei is justified since we now know that at least one of America's telecommunications giants has been directly involved in massive cyber-surveillance (Pilling 2013). Furthermore, Snowden's contention that hacking attacks on Hong Kong and China have emanated from the United States for years did not help the American claim that China is the primary source of cyber-mischief (Lam 2013).

All of these attacks and counterattacks called the security of the cloud enough into question to lead some well-respected experts to argue against adopting cloud computing (Darrow 2013; Stapleton 2013). According to the Privacy Rights Clearinghouse, in the first two months of 2013, twenty-eight breaches attributed to hackers were made public, resulting in the loss of 117,000 data records (Gonsalves 2013). If hackers can steal data from some of the largest computer and social-media firms, the largest soft-drink company in the world, and vital infrastructure companies, then whose cloud data is safe? Indeed, among the many attacks reported in the winter of 2013, one that stood out made use of cloud computing facilities to launch a concerted attack against major U.S. banks. Here the major suspect was Iran, perhaps in retaliation for Stuxnet. However, the most interesting part of the tale was not the culprit but the means. Hackers mobilized the combined resources of several cloud data centers to create what one account called their own "private cloud," from which they launched denial-of-service attacks that disrupted service for customers of Bank of America, Citigroup, Wells Fargo, U.S. Bancorp, PNC, Capital One, and HSBC, among others (Perlroth and Hardy 2013).

These hacking attacks are just those publicly reported. Many others are known only to those affected because organizations do not want to call attention to their vulnerabilities or to those they believe are responsible. In fact, there is considerable debate in business and government about whether attacks should be revealed at all. As one expert argued, "This is just the tip of a vast iceberg, and the overwhelming majority of companies today are terrified of talking too publicly about the issue, for fear of suffering stigma or sparking panic. That means it is tough for any outsider to get precise information about the overall scale of attacks" (Tett 2013). The culprits also vary considerably from individuals intent on demonstrating their prowess, to genuine thieves out to steal identities, company secrets, and money, to others who are looking to disable corporate systems and critical infrastructure (*New York Times* 2013b). Far from diminishing security threats, the move to the cloud increases them. That helps to explain why attacks on U.K. businesses went from two a day in 2010 to five hundred a day in 2012 (Robinson 2013). As one analyst explained, "All the vulnerabilities and security issues that on-premise, non-virtualized and non-cloud deployments have still remain in the cloud. All that cloud and virtualization does is enhance the potential risks by introducing virtualization software and potentially mass data breach issues, if an entire cloud provider's infrastructure is breached" (Gonsalves 2013).

Compounding the problem of hacker attacks is that, for all the charges and countercharges, there is genuine uncertainty about where they come from and why. When it appeared that China was going after computers operated by the company that monitors more than half the oil and gas pipelines in the United States, the company set out to determine why they were doing it. Were they interested in bringing down a major piece of American infrastructure in the event of a military confrontation, or were they just trolling for secrets to pass on to China's utilities? Six months after the attack, American officials claimed that they still did not know. The same was the case with attacks against five multinational energy companies in 2011. They appeared to come from China, but no one knows for sure and certainly not why. Moreover, U.S. security experts are uncertain about which is the bigger threat, China or Iran. The latter, they suspect, continues to work on retaliation for Stuxnet but lacks the technical sophistication of China. But no one knows whether either is a primary threat given the number of operations emanating from all over the world, including from within the United States (Perlroth, Sanger, and Schmidt 2013). Indeed, given the mountain of revelations about the NSA, it is reasonable to conclude that the major threat to the privacy of communication and information in the United States, and perhaps the world, is the electronic surveillance operations of the NSA, other U.S. intelligence agencies, the Pentagon, and their partners in the United Kingdom, Canada, Australia, and New Zealand (Bamford 2013).

More than external attacks violate privacy and security. The very act of maintaining these protections can bring down computers, a demonstration of the often repeated principle that complex systems fail because they are complex (Perrow 1999). In order to block unauthorized access to their cloud services, some companies deploy an https protocol, which requires regular renewal. In February 2013 Microsoft failed to renew the certificate to run its cloud service Azure, leading to a worldwide shutdown of its main cloud services. The embarrassing failure kept Azure users from accessing files stored in Microsoft's data centers. Even after four hours, customers were still only able to see the statement "We apologize for any inconvenience this causes our customers" on the company website (Ribeiro 2013). In this case, systems set up to protect the privacy and security of cloud services led to a global crash. The Microsoft case demonstrates that even when armed to the teeth with security protection, cloud companies are not guaranteed to continue providing services. Indeed, the very act of protection, of adding that extra layer of complexity that needs to be managed, can lead to a catastrophe. This snafu was not an isolated case. Cloud companies regularly lose data, and accidental loss, mainly through deletion, was considered the second most significant security problem facing cloud companies in one survey (Gonsalves 2013).

In another survey of 3,200 companies, 43 percent admitted to losing files stored in cloud computers and had to use backups to retrieve them. Still, almost every company reported at least one failure in the recovery process. Although a leading provider of security services conducted this survey, the problem is serious enough to alarm even independent security experts (ibid.; *Investor's Business Daily* 2013). Moreover, the growing trend to "bring your own device" to the workplace has created major security problems. Companies might spend millions to keep out hackers only to find that their own executives are causing major security breaches because they use unprotected smart phones, tablets, and laptops in the workplace (McCarthy 2013). The proliferation of cloud-computing providers is also a source of security concerns because small, inexperienced companies are also less likely to provide strong privacy protections, as users of the start-up Digital Ocean learned when they found other users' data, including passwords, showing up in their accounts (McMillan 2013). But whether the cloud company is large or small, experienced or not, it is increasingly difficult for firms to discard data that clients want deleted. Explained one analyst, "Companies are losing control of where their unstructured data are. And if they don't even know where it is, they will not be able to delete it." As a result, data that one believes has been deleted actually lives on to threaten a client's privacy (Palmer 2013a).

Failures like these lead security companies to keep layering systems that pay for added protection with greater complexity. In the wake of the big start to the "Year Everybody Gets Hacked," the Cloud Security Alliance (CSA), a nonprofit organization comprising industry security experts, released, through its Top Threats Working Group, a position paper titled "The Notorious Nine," a collection of threats to cloud privacy and security, each with a set of protocols to minimize the threat risk (*Market Watch* 2013). Following on this, the CSA published a report on how to address the threats of big-data analysis to cloud security and privacy (Goldberg 2013). Organizations like the CSA represent one small piece of the very large and growing business of IT security, which was worth about $65 billion in 2013 and is growing at the rate of 9 percent annually, faster than the IT business as a whole (Waters 2013a). Despite this enormous investment in protection, experts, including those with no ax to grind with the cloud security business, are not optimistic that current forms of security are keeping up with the increasing sophistication of the attacks. Indeed, it appears that the environmental impact of the cloud is just one of the industry's "dirty secrets." Another, as one analyst notes, is the failure of traditional measures to successfully address current problems: "The dirty secret that the security professionals can no longer keep to themselves is that their old defenses—which were aimed at protecting PCs and other devices that comprise the endpoints of computer networks—no longer work" (ibid.). The old defenses mainly consisted of antivirus software, which continues to work well against the bulk of attacks but is no longer effective against today's more sophisticated hacking.

It is particularly interesting that while attacks on cloud data centers are the most problematic, security companies believe that the big data processed in the cloud may provide the best solution. Big data presents opportunities for pattern recognition, which can distinguish between normal and anomalous behavior in a network. What the security people call "big intelligence" is actually big surveillance because to succeed requires massive monitoring of network activity. When attackers make it through standard defenses, surveillance spots the patterns they make in the cloud. Some see this as little more than useful rhetoric, a means of giving hope to computer security customers in language they might understand. But as one commentator observed, "Besides the improved rhetoric, there's another benefit to these new approaches: some of them might even work" (ibid.).

Raytheon, the fifth-largest defense contractor in the United States, developed one especially promising system. The company mines social-media sites and tracks people's movements to predict behavior. With a name chosen from the land of bad science fiction or good science satire, Riot, or Rapid Information Overlay Technology, provides a snapshot of an individual's online life, including likes and dislikes, opinions on issues, friends, and places visited. Using one of its employees as an example,

Raytheon developers put together a profile and used it to demonstrate how Riot could predict where he would be (a specific gym), on a particular day (Monday), at a particular time (6 a.m.) (Gallagher 2013). The Riot software was developed with the support of industry and government experts, and by 2013 it was featured in a patent Raytheon pursued for a system designed to gather information from social media, including social networks, blogs, and other sources, to determine whether a person should be judged a security risk. Public advocates like the Electronic Privacy Information Center raised concerns about the arrival of Big Brother into the seemingly innocuous world of social media: "Social networking sites are often not transparent about what information is shared and how it is shared. Users may be posting information that they believe will be viewed only by their friends, but instead, it is being viewed by government officials or pulled in by data collection services like the Riot search" (ibid.). Actually, the cloud may be even darker than this. First, more than just governments are interested in tracking people and predicting their behavior. Businesses are also eager to follow people's moves in the cloud, especially if a system like Riot enables them to forecast what products or services they are likely to purchase. Furthermore, an arguably more significant problem with Riot and systems like it is that they often make mistakes with significant consequences. Riot and other such applications appear so flawless that they receive the benefit of the doubt in disputes about accuracy. Others doubt whether such systems can work successfully to track down criminals and terrorists who operate in a less than rational fashion, such as the brothers who engineered the Boston Marathon bombings in 2013 (G. Silverman 2013).

The dark cloud of attacks on privacy and security is only part of the story. The biggest challenges come not from outside attackers but from within the cloud itself as companies increasingly recognize that an excellent, if not the best, revenue stream flows from the data provided by their own users. In fact, whereas 2013 may be remembered as the year we all got hacked, perhaps it should also be known as the year we all got tracked. As Maija Palmer maintained, "The new digital economy's biggest resource is data. From Google's recording of internet search habits to Amazon's storing of credit card numbers, companies are busy pumping and extracting data, all to grease the wheels of commerce" (2013b). No enterprise is more aware of this than Facebook, which bases its business model on making the most profitable use of information about its users derived from their posts on its site. Rolling out this model has created problems for the company because each step in the process encroaches on Facebook's own privacy policy, which it initially used to attract and keep users. This began when the social networking site introduced advertising on user pages. To attract more advertisers and justify charging them more, it allowed companies to direct ads to users based on what they post to their page. Since my page describes me as a Canadian, I receive ads from Canadian companies, but since I also post links from the *New York Times*, the newspaper that delivers all the news that's fit to print also sends me ads. The next step was to vastly expand the information Facebook gathers on users by making deals with large data vendors that collect and manage information on users' offline purchases. This enables the social-media giant to match offline purchasing data with information that users post to provide a more complete guide to advertisers who want to better target users with ads. Member profiles, advertiser records, and offline databases provided by third parties are anonymously matched through user email addresses and phone numbers to improve targeting. Each step in the privacy erosion dance meets with a negative reaction from privacy advocates. In this case the executive director of the Center for Digital Democracy immediately alerted the Federal Trade Commission, the Government Accountability Office, and key lawmakers who work on privacy policy because "clearly the integration of these powerful databases and purchasing records to be used for targeting is a serious privacy concern and needs to be investigated. We need new privacy controls and marketing policies to protect sensitive information" (Bachman 2013).

Even though it must abide by a twenty-year consent decree with the Federal Trade Commission to give users clear and prominent notice and obtain their consent before sharing information beyond its privacy settings, Facebook pushed its commercialization project a major step forward with the introduction of Graph Search, its challenge to Google and, some would add, its challenge to privacy. The service, which began a rollout in 2013, takes every post, including pictures, likes and dislikes, age and birth date, schools attended, work history, sexual orientation, political views, religious preference, and comments on members' own and other sites. It combines this information with public data available to users of a conventional search engine, puts them in a database, and makes use of a search algorithm that both Facebook friends and the general public can access. Graph Search determines its results by matching phrases and objects on a site rather than just key words. By combining the information on a user's site and the relationship of the user to friends and to objects, Facebook is able to return results that take into account how users feel about people and things. The "like" function is especially important in this respect because it enables Graph Search to produce results such as friends who like the films *Life of Pi* and *Zero Dark Thirty* and single women in Manhattan who were born in France.

There is more to it than these relatively innocuous search possibilities suggest. Graph Search takes putting together social combinations to a new height or depth, depending on your point of view. Which employers are most likely to hire racists (i.e., people who identify their employer and "like" racist or racist-friendly organizations) or people who like sadomasochism (in an early search the "prize" went to Home Depot). How about people who like the banned religious group Falun Gong—the government of China might be interested to know which of its citizens have relatives in the United States who like the outlawed organization. All this and more is available on the powerful new search engine, and none of it is subject to fact-checking (Giridharadas 2013b). Making this all the more remarkable is that most of the work is done by Facebook members who, of course, labor without compensation so that companies, governments, and, yes, friends can do a better job of advertising to them, tracking their behavior, and keeping in touch. It is little wonder that one organization that tried out Graph Search in its early days declared "the end of privacy by obscurity." Or we can view it as the end of privacy through a business model that turns every bit of information posted by members into a marketable commodity and delivers those same members to advertisers effectively and efficiently.

With all of these elements in place, there remained one key element. How would the company determine the effectiveness of advertising on its own and other sites? The first step was to partner with the data-mining company Datalogix, which tracks the connection between ads that users see on Facebook and their in-store purchases. This provided an important indicator of just how successful the social-media company could be in turning ads into actual sales. But this was not enough. Facebook wanted to determine how ads on its site stacked up against those located on others, and that would require another investment. In this case, it was Atlas Solutions, which Facebook bought from Microsoft. Through this purchase, the social-media firm expanded its ability to measure the efficiency of ads because Atlas compares advertising and purchasing across a range of companies that display an ad, as well as across different platforms, including computers, smart phones, and tablets (Dembosky 2013a). Atlas provides Facebook with an assessment of the relative strength of the site and of the range of devices that carry Facebook ads. Nevertheless, questions arose about the accuracy of this research, particularly when hacking schemes like the March 2013 "botnet" attack hijacked 120,000 personal computers and falsely added 9 billion ad views a month to over two hundred sites (Bradshaw and Steel 2013). With or without mischief like this, audience analysis is becoming more and more difficult, leading one media industry analyst to decry "the measurement mess" (Winslow 2013).

There is no guarantee that any or all of Facebook's strategy will work. In fact, it can become painfully counterproductive, as when it led Facebook to place ads for major brands next to deeply offensive content, which prompted companies to cancel campaigns on the social-media site (Budden 2013). Through the first half of 2013, the company's share price remained mired considerably below that of its initial public offering, a signal that Wall Street at least was not optimistic. Nevertheless, some research suggests that Facebook advertising pays off for most sponsors, a point that contributed to the turnaround in its share price in the last half of 2013 (Manjoo 2013). Whatever the outcome, Facebook is a prime example of a major cloud company whose business model fundamentally derives from using information provided by members about themselves and others to sell advertising. In essence, in return for using the social-media site, participants give up their privacy. They lose it not because of deviant acts by domestic or foreign hackers but because Facebook, like Google, Twitter, and most other companies that use the cloud, take it from them in the normal course of doing business.

It is not just corporations whose normal practice makes privacy in any form increasingly difficult to secure. Citizens lose privacy through the ordinary practices of governments whose security concerns often outweigh the protection of privacy rights. On this subject, fingers typically point toward China, Iran, and the Arab states of the Middle East, which practice surveillance widely and legally constrict privacy. China's surveillance practices are particularly worrisome because of the country's strong commitment to become a world leader in cloud computing, as evidenced by its plan to construct the world's largest data centers, build entire cities around cloud facilities, and spread the cloud across the country, all part of a program to more than double its cloud data center capacity by 2016 with a government investment of $370 billion. Moreover, China has welcomed big names in the cloud to help achieve this goal. By 2013 IBM already had three large cloud facilities up and running in the country (J. Lee 2013a).

Although most of its data center capacity will be used for domestic civilian and military data, there is little doubt that China will want to profit from its investment by offering data storage, processing, and other cloud services to foreign companies operating within and even outside its borders. The country has already demonstrated that its low-cost production model has been overwhelmingly successful in luring foreign companies to use it as the foundation of global supply chains. With massively increased cloud capacity, China will most likely be in a position to offer a low-cost alternative for Western companies looking to beat the competition for new cloud customers. Given that it is common practice for the Chinese government to monitor the online activities of its own citizens and to engage in spying and hacking practices on computers in the United States and elsewhere, it should come as no surprise that files stored in cloud data centers in its territory would be routinely inspected, copied, and used.

Dark clouds over China will likely grow in the coming years as it challenges the United States for world leadership in cloud computing. For now, however, the United States is well ahead of the pack, and it is important to focus on problems that this presents for its own citizens and for people beyond its borders. Electronic privacy is a problem in the United States not just because hackers from abroad are stealing secrets but, more importantly, because the country has some of the weakest privacy protections in the developed world, certainly weaker than those of the European Union (EU) or Canada. There are several reasons for this, but the primary one that American policy makers will point to is the need to balance the right to privacy with the nation's need for security, particularly in the wake of the 9/11 attacks and the ensuing struggles against terrorism. We will get to the security side of this issue shortly, but it is also important to point out that weak privacy protections have made for a strong IT industry, particularly as social-media firms have built world-dominant companies like Google, Facebook, Amazon, Apple, Microsoft, and Twitter that profit from selling information about users to advertisers. It would be much more difficult for these firms, especially Facebook and Google, to profit if they were not free to market this information. Most of the $1.1 billion in profit that Facebook earned in 2012 came to the company because advertisers were interested in targeted marketing to its users.[4] By strengthening companies reliant on selling user data, weak privacy protections better enable them to compete in global markets. Such has been the case for leading search and social-media companies in the cloud, particularly as they target markets in the developed world, such as in Europe and Canada. However, in these places companies run into resistance from those who prefer a stronger privacy regime, especially one that does not subject them to the USA PATRIOT Act and other cyber-security laws. Even though Americans are increasingly restive about data privacy (Gross 2013), U.S. business has fought back fiercely against EU attempts to strengthen privacy laws with lobbying led by the American Chamber of Commerce and IT companies, headed by Google and Facebook, that would benefit the most from loosening data security in the EU.

Until 2013, the EU was adamant in its resistance to the lobbying barrage and high-level pressure (*RTT News* 2013). However, in a weakened economic position and desperate to boost economic activity, the EU began to back off from its resistance in 2013. In fact, one can date this change almost precisely to March 6, 2013, one of the more remarkable in the history of the EU's dealings with the United States, because it began with a decision that demonstrably affirmed the EU's determination to enforce the law and ended with what can only be described as capitulation to American power. The first announcement out of Brussels was for a $732 million fine against Microsoft because the company failed to live up to an agreement to offer Windows customers easy access to alternatives to Internet Explorer, the company's own web browser. Microsoft claimed that a "technical error" kept the company from offering user choice on some of its products and, in addition to paying the fine, agreed to make a correction. Since it took over a year for the company's failure to come to light, and then only after its rivals, including Google, brought it to the EU's attention, the commission was chastised for lax enforcement. Nevertheless, the size of the fine gave some indication that Brussels was prepared to get tough when necessary (Kanter 2013). That conclusion was questioned, however, especially by privacy advocates, when later that day the EU reported that it would loosen its data security requirements, thereby easing the ability of American companies that make heavy use of the cloud to expand into European markets (Fontanella-Kahn and McCarthy 2013). For privacy proponents this was a major step backward because establishing a unified privacy policy for the twenty-seven-nation body that included heavy fines for failing to secure explicit consent from users before processing and using their data, as well as incorporating a "right to be forgotten" for online users who want to be erased from the web, would significantly strengthen privacy protection in the EU and worldwide. Eager for opportunities to expand economic growth, leading EU nations, including the United Kingdom and Germany, appeared to toss in the towel on strong privacy protections in order to advance a free trade agreement with the United States. But further turmoil broke out when Edward Snowden's revelations about massive global surveillance by the NSA, including across the EU, led to renewed calls to strengthen data privacy in the EU cloud (Bryant 2013).

One reason why the European Commission has sought its own data privacy regime is that U.S. legislation could violate the privacy of EU citizens. The USA PATRIOT Act and the Foreign Intelligence Surveillance Amendment Act (FISA) give the U.S. government enormous leeway to collect information on people without requiring a warrant based on probable cause. The pursuit of global markets by American companies using cloud computing, including, for example, Google's cloud mail service Gmail, draws foreign citizens into their orbit. Consider a concrete example from Canada. Gmail earns revenue by selling advertising to companies that target ads to users based in part on the content of their emails. That in itself troubles privacy supporters. In order to expand into new markets, Google has been offering deals to organizations as well as to individuals. Scrap your current internal email system, goes the company's pitch, eliminate the labor costs incurred by your IT department to manage an internal system, join us in the cloud, and slash your IT budget. That pitch has been made to countless organizations, including Toronto's York University, which was fully prepared to accept Gmail in the cloud, along with its advertisements, in return for help meeting the fiscal crisis that, like most other public institutions, the university faces. The fly in the ointment was a presentation by the Canadian Association of University

Teachers (CAUT), which explained the privacy consequences of going with the Google system. Under the university's existing email system, U.S. law enforcement authorities, intelligence services, and corporations do not have direct access to communication, unless it passes entirely through a server located in the United States. Furthermore, the cooperation of Canadian authorities is important, if not essential, in making the judgment call about pursuing intercepts. With Gmail, all email—including messages, attachments, links, and any transaction data—is subject to the provisions of the PATRIOT Act and FISA. Neither a warrant, nor probable cause, nor even suspicion of criminality is required to permit intercepts. Government authorities would simply have the right to scoop up most of what scholars consider the exercise of academic freedom. Moreover, corporations like Google are required to comply with government requests for email and associated communication and are prohibited from informing the target that such a request has been made (Turk 2013). For Canadian universities like York, this means weighing major cost savings against the threats to the security and privacy of its students, faculty, and staff.[5]

These conclusions received the complete support of Microsoft's chief privacy officer, who, in a submission to the European Parliament, determined that all U.S. cloud-computing companies, including Microsoft, were subject to the surveillance and investigatory powers outlined by CAUT. Specifically, he asserted, "it is lawful in the U.S. to conduct purely political surveillance on foreigners' data accessible in U.S. clouds" (MacLeod 2013). He notes that FISA in particular provides broad surveillance powers directed at "foreign-based political organization(s) . . . or foreign territory that relates to . . . conduct of the foreign affairs of the United States." The cloud is singled out in 2008 amendments that, in addition to permitting "warrantless wiretapping," give the go-ahead to investigate communication contained in "remote computing"—that is, the cloud (ibid.). In an interview with a Canadian newspaper, the Microsoft official concluded that the U.S. government "for the first time [has] created a power of mass-surveillance specifically targeted at the data of non-U.S. persons located outside the U.S., which applies to cloud computing" (ibid.). He called the U.S. legislation a "grave risk" to European data security and told the Canadian newspaper "everything I've said about the situation of Europeans applies also to Canadians" (ibid.). For example, Canadian organizations mobilizing against energy projects that threaten the environment or marching against more pipelines to the United States should expect their communication stored in U.S. company cloud systems to be subject to investigation without any recourse, even if they did know, which they most likely would not, that such investigations were taking place. The head of one of the largest advocacy groups in Canada concluded, "It does indicate for many who take advocacy positions that they really need to be very cautious about what they're doing for the want of saving a few dollars," and counsels against outsourcing computer services to U.S. cloud-computing companies (ibid.). Although Canadian federal and provincial governments have put in place privacy protection measures, most experts agree, according to a journalist with the leading newspaper in Canada's capital, that "the FISA Amendment Act overrides any privacy and data protection offered by third-party vendors, international agreements on data transfers and Canadian domestic legal protections" (ibid.).

There is little hope of removing FISA in the near future because the U.S. Supreme Court, in a 5–4 decision supported by both its conservative majority and the Obama administration, ruled against plaintiffs who challenged its constitutionality. In what has been described as the catch-22 of FISA and other laws intended to combat terrorism, the Court majority argued that opponents of the law could not demonstrate that it would harm them. However, since this and other laws of its type keep all warrantless surveillance secret, to the point of preventing service providers from notifying customers, it is impossible to demonstrate the law's specific harm (Liptak 2013). As one law professor determined, "The coalition could not challenge our secret surveillance laws because they are secret. There is no one who can complain of his or her rights having been violated, because anyone whose rights have been violated doesn't know it. That's the catch when it comes to assessing the legality of the government's secret activities" (Calo 2013). It is therefore likely that significant concerns about privacy and security will continue to face providers and users of cloud computing well into the future.

Working (or Not) in the Cloud

Each year *Fortune* magazine produces a list of the top one hundred companies in the United States to work for. It covers the range of objective criteria, such as pay and benefits, as well as such subjective considerations as sense of community and camaraderie. By the looks of its 2013 list, the sixteenth annual for the company, cloud computing does not have a labor problem. Of the top ten, three are leading cloud companies, including numbers one and two. Google takes the top prize for the fourth time, as its 34,311 employees in its headquarters location enjoy three wellness centers, a seven-acre sports complex, and the benefits of knowing that the company continues to list dozens of vacant positions. In second place is SAS, the data analytics company, with its own artists in residence and an organic farm for its cafeterias. It is no wonder that turnover is less than 5 percent annually. The data storage company NetApp holds down sixth place. Like the first two, it provides both an on-site fitness center and domestic-partner benefits for same-sex partners. The rest of the list includes other major cloud companies, including Salesforce (19), Rackspace (34), Cisco (42), and Microsoft (75), as well as some firms that, while not primarily cloud-computing companies, are involved in some aspects of the cloud, such as Autodesk (54) and Intel (68) (Moskowitz and Levering 2013).

While it may surprise some that the list does not contain Apple, Amazon, Facebook, or Twitter, the cloud is well enough represented that one might question the inclusion of work in a discussion of dark clouds. This is certainly understandable because when we think of leading IT firms, including those in the forefront of the cloud, we tend to think of the top slice of workers, what Giridharadas calls "the tech aristocracy"; for him, "this emerging aristocracy is, of course, the technocracy—the thousands of men and women who are striving, through the gadgets and services they sell, to change the texture of being human: to change fundamental things about all of our relationships with time, with our brains, with each other" (2013a). These privileged few get to enjoy workplaces filled with luxuries beyond the imagination of most of the world's workers. Google's New York offices contain, in the words of one touring reporter, "a labyrinth of play areas; cafés, coffee bars and open kitchens; sunny outdoor terraces with chaises; gourmet cafeterias that serve free breakfast, lunch and dinner; Broadway-theme conference rooms with velvet drapes; and conversation areas designed to look like vintage subway cars" (Stewart 2013). Hundreds of software engineers get to design their own desks and workspaces, including the precise ergonomics of furniture and whether to include company-provided exercise equipment. Workers are free to come and go as they please, as long as they satisfy the requirements of their work group. However, most remain at the office for an average of nine hours a day because of all the perks. Here is an account of a Google employee's description: "In the course of our brief conversation, she mentioned subsidized massages (with massage rooms on nearly every floor); free once-a-week eyebrow shaping; free yoga and Pilates classes; a course she took called 'Unwind: The Art and Science of Stress Management'; a course in advanced negotiation taught by a Wharton professor; a health consultation and follow-up with a personal health counselor; an author series and an appearance by the novelist Toni Morrison; and a live interview of Justin Bieber by Jimmy Fallon in the Google office." The free food alone is enough for some to return to the office on their day off. Practically every element in the workplace is research-tested and appears to work, in the words of one Google executive, "to create the happiest, most productive workplace in the world" (ibid.). Google turns workplaces into communities, encouraging freedom and serendipitous interactions that contribute to the innovations that make the company a world leader. Most other companies that employ the tech aristocracy fall short of Google's standard but only in degree. Big cloud companies like SAS and Rackspace report similar degrees of comfort and freedom.

Nevertheless, the tech aristocracy is just a thin sliver, the privileged few at the apex of companies that not only employ thousands of workers at their corporate centers but also manage global supply chains. It is critical to resist the temptation to mistake the sliver for the whole because doing so means missing serious problems looming for the cloud computing industry at two very different levels of labor. The supply chain, or the chain of accumulation, responsible for the success or failure of cloud computing extends well beyond the corporate headquarters. In order to understand the industry, especially its labor issues, it is essential to scan the broader supply chain that includes, at one end, the workers who manufacture the material that makes cloud computing possible, where workplace conditions are comparable to the "dark satanic mills" of the early industrial age, and at the other, the work of the IT professionals who are most directly affected by the transformation in labor that cloud computing is bringing about. The first group of workers toils primarily in the industrial centers of China where contractors for big computer manufacturers produce the hardware that fills data centers, offices, and homes. This sector has experienced remarkable growth as production has shifted from the West to China, but it is now undergoing an upheaval with significant implications for every company in the cloud. As a result, it is important to consider the dialectical relationship between chains of accumulation and chains of resistance.

The second major development is the reorganization of information technology labor. A main reason why companies move to the cloud is to save on IT labor by outsourcing work to the cloud. While the head of Amazon Web Services sees this as a two-decade-long project, he is confident enough to conclude that the cloud "is replacing the corporate data center" (Miller and Hardy 2013). The centralization and resulting industrialization of professional craft IT work are one of the primary means of saving costs in the cloud. But it is important to understand that "IT" now includes a much wider range of specialties than it once did. It now encompasses not only those who work in IT departments but also those tech-savvy people whose expertise also lies in a substantive profession like education, journalism, or law. In other words, there is an increasingly significant category of workers whose work in a professional field requires considerable expertise in the use of information technology. As a result, the threat the cloud poses to information technology professionals by virtue of its capacity to absorb the IT functions of individual businesses extends to a growing number of workers.

The employment issue has been debated throughout the history of computing. In fact, it arose as early as the 1940s when the celebrated cybernetics pioneer Norbert Wiener (1948, 1950) speculated that computers would lead to massive workplace automation. The issues he raised continue to provide the foundation for a more general debate about the role of technology in structural unemployment (Krugman 2013; Sachs 2013). Once again, the problem of the quantity and quality of jobs is not new to computers and communication, but the cloud adds significant elements to the debate. The complexity of managing the global supply chains that the cloud requires demands a degree of labor stability that may not be possible. Moreover, cloud computing promotes the elimination of skilled jobs through centralization and automation.

It sometimes appears that the global supply chain is anything but unstable. Has not most every material thing been produced in China for as long as anyone, at least anyone under forty, can remember? It may seem that way, but this is not the case, especially in the IT industry, where fundamental changes in the global division of labor are the norm. Beginning in the 1950s, for example, computer electronics production began in the rooms and garages of amateurs who, like the amateur "Radio Boys" of the 1920s, started an industry through interpersonal networks of tech friends playing with modified off-the-shelf components. It also began in the laboratories of a small group of universities where the building blocks of computer communication were invented and then sent into production with industry partners. IT production moved first to the factories of big computer firms like IBM and DEC whose skilled workforce in the U.S. Northeast, including upstate New York and the Boston area, firmly established the computer industry. But providing a strong foundation does not guarantee labor stability. During this time, production began to shift to the U.S. West Coast as Silicon Valley emerged as a center of digital technology production. This was partly because the expansion of a division of labor in IT production made it possible to hire low-skilled workers for an important part of the process that could be completed in a factory or even at home. There were considerable workplace hazards associated with this work because it involved dangerous chemicals, which were often cooked up in the apartments and homes of immigrant workers. One consequence was the rise of a significant toxic-waste issue in Silicon Valley, which the Environmental Protection Agency singled out as the site of the most toxic of the many "Superfund" sites in the country (Pellow and Park 2002).

While remnants of hazardous production remain in California, it was not long before the industry went in search of offshore production sites where authoritarian governments could enforce a regime of low wages, labor discipline, and weak environmental protection. The first stop was Southeast Asia—Malaysia, Singapore, and then Vietnam—where the IT production process began. But that too was short-lived as the transition to a state-directed capitalist economy in China overwhelmed other production sites with cheap labor subject to the near-complete control of companies like Taiwan-based electronics firm Foxconn or China's own Huawei, a world leader in the provision of telecommunications equipment. Based in the new industrial heartland of eastern and southern China—which replaced the old one, now a rust belt in northeast China, established with the help of the former Soviet Union—these firms anchored the unprecedented mass production of electronic technologies for export to the world.

The success of Foxconn is undeniable. Its 1.4 million workers labor in over a dozen factories in China, and the company also operates manufacturing plants in Brazil, India, Japan, Malaysia, Mexico, and, especially since it experienced bad publicity for its China operations, three low-wage European countries (the Czech Republic, Hungary, and Slovakia). It is no exaggeration to conclude that Foxconn plays a vital role in the global division of information labor, and although 40 percent of its revenues come from contracts with Apple, the company manufactures products for nearly every major IT company (Yang 2013). Clearly, however, Foxconn's China factories employ the most workers and attract the most attention, both good and bad. The largest of these facilities is located in the city of Shenzhen across from Hong Kong in the south of Guongdong province, where over 250,000 people toil in electronics plants that make products for almost every major IT firm in the world, including leading cloud-computing companies such as Amazon, Apple, Google, Microsoft, Cisco, and HP, as well as Japan's leading tech firms. Most of these workers are immigrants to the region who come from China's hinterland in search of a living. The Foxconn facility in Shenzhen is part of a walled complex that includes dormitories for most of the workers and company stores that provide them with meals and other essentials. One key to the firm's success in making this facility, as well as others that attract rural workers, highly productive is the workforce's utter dependence on the company for their livelihoods, if not for their lives. Low wages and long hours building PCs, iPhones, iPads, servers, and many of the other ingredients that comprise the cloud have made Foxconn a world leader.

We encountered Huawei earlier in the book in connection with both the World Economic Forum report on cloud computing and concerns raised by Western governments over alleged spying by company staff in the United States, Canada, and Australia. The company, now one of the largest producers of telecommunications equipment in the world, is also based in Shenzhen. Huawei employs fewer people than Foxconn, about 150,000, almost half of whom work in research and development in China and at sites around the world. Manufacturing has tended to be concentrated in the Shenzhen area.

Much of the world that, with the considerable help of the Chinese government, Foxconn and Huawei have built is beginning to change as this stage in the dynamic electronics industry supply chain faces growing turbulence that is likely to impact the cloud-computing industry. The quiescence of a poor, rural, immigrant workforce, cut off from their homes in some cases by thousands of miles, is coming to an end. Working conditions that generated big profits for Foxconn and built big cloud-computing companies have taken their toll on workers who endure long workdays of twelve hours or more with at best one day off per week—and not even that during peak demand periods. In 2010 Foxconn made headlines around the world when fourteen workers reportedly committed suicide because of stress produced by long hours and low pay. Photos of how the company dealt with the issue made even more headlines. Instead of moderating working conditions, the Foxconn plant in Shenzhen installed nets around the roof of the building to make it more difficult for workers to take their own lives. While reported suicides did decline, worker protests spread. Foxconn generally ignored them or called on the police and the military to maintain order.

In January 2012, the *New York Times* reported on systematic violations of basic worker rights, including the hiring of underage workers and routinely requiring greater than sixty-hour workweeks over long stretches without a day off. It also cited Foxconn's failure to comply with minimum standards of workplace safety that led, in one case alone, to injuries to 137 workers at plants manufacturing Apple products and to explosions at other Apple plants that killed several workers (Duhigg and Barboza 2012). Apple itself reported that in 2012 children worked at eleven of its manufacturing facilities (Bradshaw 2013). A May 2012 report by a workers' rights group that examined company documents and interviewed 170 workers concluded, "Exhausting workloads, humiliating discipline, and cramped dormitories are still 'the norm' for workers at Foxconn factories in China" (Musil 2012). Workers who refused to follow strict discipline were made to read "confession letters" aloud and to clean toilets. Foxconn did nod to worker demands by supplying stools so that they would no longer have to stand for entire shifts. However, the company insisted that workers sit on only one-third of the stool in order "to remain nimble" (ibid.). Living conditions remained cramped; typically twenty to thirty people shared a three-bedroom apartment stacked with bunk beds. Use of high-energy appliances, such as hair dryers, kettles, and, ironically, laptop computers, was prohibited, and workers who used them risked their confiscation until they were no longer working for the company.

Nevertheless, it became increasingly obvious that the supply chain was fraying. When Apple tightened pressure to meet iPhone production schedules, Foxconn resorted to more extreme measures, such as drafting high school students to work as unpaid interns for the company. For example, the government of a nearby province sent students by the thousands to labor for a month or so at the Shenzhen plant. Students were given the choice of obeying or dropping out of school. Some complained, but not wanting to ruin whatever hope they had for a career, most complied (Perlin 2011, 191–196). This practice continued well into 2013, when the company, faced with strong evidence, admitted to employing students and forcing them to work overtime and through the night (Mishkin 2013). Nevertheless, this does not appear to be a long-term solution, as publicity blows back against the Western firms that contract with companies engaging in these practices. Indeed, in 2013 HP and Apple responded to revelations about student labor by announcing limits on student and temp work in China (Bradsher and Barboza 2013). Apple also tried to diversify production by contracting with one of Foxconn's competitors, but that company too was charged with numerous labor code violations, including employing underage workers (Osborne 2013).

Foxconn responded to global protests with two substantial changes. First, it moved factories away from increasingly militant urban centers like Shenzhen and into less populated regions, especially to western China, where it expected that workers would be more malleable and information about working conditions would be less likely to reach beyond China's borders. Second, in a complete reversal of corporate policy, Foxconn supported the formation of trade unions at its factories. Although it was unclear how the unions would be organized, most people believed that the company would control them (Jacob 2013). Nevertheless, wages are beginning to rise, and even if the prospect of unions does not increase worker power, it is likely to raise wage rates. Meanwhile, the company was hit by strike actions against several of its facilities in China (Tang 2013). All of these moves suggest that Foxconn is in trouble. It benefited for a few years from drawing immigrant labor into China's booming cities and walling them into industrial fortresses to support manufacturing, especially electronics production, for export. But it did not take long for these former peasants to doubt the wisdom of the system and to start turning the chain of accumulation that their work sustains into a chain of resistance. At the very least, they succeeded in forcing Foxconn to move production to new centers and to provide for some form of worker representation.[6] Nevertheless, given the country's one-child policy, it is becoming increasingly difficult for the electronics manufacturer to replace workers who decide that the global assembly line is not for them or whose rebellion leads to their dismissal. This raises questions about the long-term viability of China's export-led growth policy and the political consequences of shifting to a model that concentrates on China's consumers.

Just as it is easy to expect that the massive control China has maintained over the world's industrial economy, especially in electronics, is here to stay, it is also tempting to overstate contemporary signs that it is eroding. Given the coercive power of the state in China, it is always possible for a crackdown to restore some degree of order, however imperfect. Nevertheless, the instability at the base of the computer supply chain should be a source of serious concern for the cloud-computing industry. Neither the stable flow of material products essential to the cloud industry nor the low prices made possible by oppressively low wages and horrendous working conditions can be guaranteed for much longer.

There is also instability at the top of the cloud-computing supply chain. As one analyst after another has concluded, the primary value of cloud computing—what really compensates for all of the risks involved in yielding control over data and information services to another company—is the savings in IT labor. Some companies can eliminate their IT departments altogether, and others are able to cut them substantially. For IT consultant Dan Kusnetzky, "Cloud computing is nothing more than the next step in outsourcing your IT operations" (McKendrick 2013c). Put another way, cloud computing advances the industrialization of skilled knowledge labor by centralizing and concentrating it in cloud companies. According to this view, the enterprise can run more efficiently and leave most of the IT work to others. As another IT labor market expert concluded, "Automation has massive implications, especially for the jobs market. It will not only affect manufacturing but also knowledge workers in the service sector" (Solman 2013).

It is especially telling that one of the major boosters of cloud computing, the Gartner Group, is also among those most insistently predicting the demise of IT labor through the cloud. For Gartner, such a development is positive because it means a significant reduction in labor costs for the companies that employ its services. Speaking at a conference of IT professionals, two Gartner analysts forecast that by 2020 demand for IT staff to support cloud data centers will collapse. For them, "the long run value proposition of IT is not to support the human workforce—it is to replace it" (Dignan 2011b). The process will take many forms, but the basic pattern will start with outsourcing computing to the cloud, which will become an IT utility. Business processes will then be outsourced to software, which will affect all economies, but it will hit developing economies the hardest because nations like India now dominate the outsourcing of high-tech jobs. As software takes over the jobs of high-tech service workers, countries like India, which have employed millions through outsourcing from the West, will suffer. Furthermore, cloud companies will virtualize their data centers, leading to a decline in the number of people required to maintain that infrastructure. Workers whose jobs are connected to building and designing data centers will also suffer as the need for physical infrastructure declines. Consequently, "many IT workers will face hollowed out job prospects just like factory workers did as the U.S. manufacturing base disappeared" (ibid.). The outcome appears inevitable, according to the Gartner analysts and a tech expert who describes their views. As IT utilities emerge and spread, workers will disappear along with other physical assets. Gartner could not be clearer: "CIOs believe that their data centers, servers, desktop and business applications are grossly inefficient and must be rationalized over the next ten years. We believe that the people associated with these inefficient assets will also be rationalized in significant numbers along the way. We foresee a substantial reduction in the U.S. IT workforce, especially among those supporting the data center and applications, in end-user organizations" (ibid.). This forecast is already playing out among some of the major users of cloud services, such as Europe's largest bank, HSBC, which in March 2013 announced a significant reduction of its IT workforce due to the growing ability to outsource to the cloud. In the first round of cuts, it trimmed software staffing from 27,000 to 21,000 and planned further cuts across all of its IT departments (Jenkins 2013). As if to add insult to injury, companies are now using cloud computing to develop and train robotic systems to replace human labor (Harris 2013a). Even some cloud companies are shedding jobs. For example, Cisco, which built a business based on providing hardware, software, and services to on-site data centers, announced layoffs of 4,000 workers in 2013 because it has not been able to overcome the declining business of serving on-site IT with cloud services (Wortham 2013).

This is a significant development for the IT workforce. Undoubtedly, new jobs will emerge requiring expertise to manage IT utilities, to mediate relationships between centralized cloud providers and individual businesses, and to make use of big-data analytics. They are also likely to grow in certain specialized areas such as security because, as more data and business functions are moved to the cloud, opportunities for hacking and surveillance will also increase. The growth of cyber-security laws and regulations to minimize security problems will also require considerable expertise to address the complex problems of complying with new legal and regulatory regimes. Nevertheless, these additional jobs are not likely to keep up with the mass downsizing of individual IT departments in corporations and government agencies. Concerns over security might also slow the process as organizations choose to adopt the private over the public cloud in order to better control their own data. But this is more about whether the transition will take place over five rather than ten years, not whether it will happen at all. Not only do most observers believe that it will, but many see the shrinking of the IT workforce as only one piece of an even larger process of transforming most knowledge labor through IT and cloud computing.

One way to understand this larger process begins with recognizing that not all IT work takes place in IT departments. Such work occupies an increasing share of all knowledge labor, which includes most jobs involved with the production, processing, and distribution of information (Mosco and McKercher 2008). This encompasses work in schools, libraries, and media industries like newspapers, as well as in the audiovisual and social-media industries. It also includes jobs in health care, law, banking, insurance, transportation, social services, and security. The power of cloud computing and the increasing reliance on big data, algorithms, and analytics for decision making make it possible to subsume into technology much of what the professions in the information and cultural industries labor at today. As one observer put it, "In the next 40 years analytics systems will replace much of what the knowledge worker does today" (Dignan 2011a). This conclusion draws from another Gartner presentation, which maintained that cloud computing and analytics will lead to massive job elimination and increasing polarization in the workforce (ibid.). We are beginning to see this happening today as colleges and universities rely more on online education to deliver curricula, including the spread of massive open online courses (MOOCs) (Lewin 2013; *Chronicle of Higher Education* 2013). Moreover, while MOOCs get the attention, we tend to neglect elementary and secondary schools where it is expected that the cloud will take up 35 percent of annual budgets by 2017 (Nagel 2013). Librarians are giving way to automated systems that deliver e-documents from the cloud (Goldner 2010).[7] The journalism profession is in rapid decline as print advertising has evaporated and freelance and unpaid or low-paid intern workers replace full-time reporters. Moreover, centralized editing from the cloud is replacing editorial staff associated with specific publications (Pew Research Center 2013). There is an inevitable decline in the quality of work for these and other professions whose labor can be centralized and concentrated in the cloud. But it appears that institutions are willing to accept some erosion in quality for massive savings in labor costs.

Cloud computing essentially deepens and extends opportunities to eliminate jobs and restructure the workforce. Whereas technology once only displaced workers in industrial settings, it began to be deployed to eliminate knowledge workers in the 1970s, at a time when accelerating energy costs and the emergence of industrial centers in non-Western societies challenged companies to cut costs and restructure by drawing on a global workforce. Combined with the growing analytical capabilities of computer systems that give new life to the "scientific management" of the workplace, the cloud is creating opportunities to eliminate several levels of decision makers in organizations (Lohr 2013b). Already there is widespread fear in IT and human resources departments that job loss is inevitable and, where jobs are saved, control will be lost because companies will rely on automated decision-making systems based on big-data analytics (Linthicum 2013b)—hence the conclusions of the Gartner experts about the erosion in jobs, including at most levels of management, and the polarization in the workforce between those in low-skilled/low-pay service work and those in the upper reaches of organizations. In more descriptive language, Harvard economist and former Treasury secretary Lawrence Summers warned, "As economists like to explain, the system will equilibrate at full employment. But maybe the way it will equilibrate at full employment is there'll be specialists at cleaning the shallow end and the deep end of rich people's swimming pools. And that's a problematic way for society to function" (Freeland 2013). Citing the unprecedented break between productivity and wages that has afflicted Western economies in recent years, MIT economist Erik Brynjolfsson concluded, "Most of the debate in Washington is really playing small ball and is missing the tectonic changes in the way the economy works, which are driven by technology. This is the big story of our time, and it is going to accelerate over the next 10 years" (ibid.).

What might change or slow this trend? I have already alluded to two possibilities. Supply chain disruptions may make it more difficult to deploy cloud systems around the world, and organized resistance from workers may alter the potential to profit from the cloud. The labor force in China, the base of global electronics supply chains, has grown restive in recent years, prompting higher wages and a redeployment of electronics manufacturing sites. It is unlikely these measures will do anything more than delay the inevitable choice between substantially raising the living standards, including the wages, working conditions, and political freedom, of China's workforce or face escalating mass civil unrest. One can deploy suicide prevention curtains for just so long. The acknowledgment of unrest in China's once placid factories has reached the mainstream Western press, where a recent account in *Time* magazine offered this startling set of observations:

> "Resentment is reaching a boiling point in China's factory towns. People from the outside see our lives as very bountiful, but the real life in the factory is very different," says factory worker Peng Ming in the southern industrial enclave of Shenzhen. Facing long hours, rising costs, indifferent managers and often late pay, workers are beginning to sound like an angry proletariat. "The way the rich get money is through exploiting the workers," says Guan Guohau, another Shenzhen factory employee. "Communism is what we are looking forward to." Unless the government takes greater action to

improve their welfare, they say, laborers will become more and more willing to take action themselves. "Workers will organize more," Peng predicts. "All the workers should be united." (Schuman 2013)

It is not only the base of the global supply chains created by major cloud companies that can create disruptions. Chains of resistance can also form in the advanced nations of the West where the labor process is certainly better than in Chinese electronic assembly plants but very far from what applies in the headquarters of these companies. Resistance can arise from how management uses the cloud to monitor and control the minutest actions of its workforce, including those in white-collar occupations. According to one analyst, "As Big Data becomes a fixture of office life, companies are turning to tracking devices to gather real-time information on how teams of employees work and interact. Sensors, worn on lanyards or placed on office furniture, record how often staffers get up from their desks, consult other teams and hold meetings" (R. Silverman 2013). Today's technology enables employers to control workers in ways that Frederic Winslow Taylor, the father of "scientific management," could only dream about. Whereas once an employer could only systematically monitor workers when they punched their time cards at the beginning and end of the workday, today they can measure practically every activity of workers employed in call centers and logistics operations. As a specialist in workplace surveillance comments, "If you have a plentiful supply of labor and don't need to worry about quality, the temptation is to nail your workers for every minute of the day" (Gapper 2013a; see also Neff 2012).

While sensors raise significant privacy issues, a more ominous portent comes from Amazon, which is fundamentally challenging the rights that workers in the West secured over years of struggle and organizing. One hot spot for labor tensions is Germany, where the company has established eight distribution centers employing 8,000 workers. Germany is important for the company as the source of 14 percent of its revenues (Wingfield and Eddy 2013). The country has not received a great deal of attention in struggles over global supply chains, but it has a long history of battles with Walmart, which abandoned Germany in 2006 rather than bend its worldwide labor standards to meet the expectations of German workers and especially their union Ver.di, which represents over 2 million employees in the service sector. German workers and their unions have considerably greater power than their counterparts in the United States and the United Kingdom. Mobilizing workers across the nation, Ver.di's actions succeeded in ending Walmart's presence in the country. The battle has now erupted over Amazon, which, in the view of German workers, is attempting to impose "American-style management" by relying on ruthless labor practices such as hiring thousands of low-wage and mainly foreign temporary workers and the security police necessary to maintain control. This has enabled the company to cut prices and drive out competition, including one German firm. According to a union leader, Amazon applies rigid controls to its workforce: "Everything is measured, everything is calculated, everything is geared toward efficiency. People want to be treated with respect" (Ewing 2013). The company denies these claims, arguing that it hires foreign temps because there are not enough local workers. But the online giant faced embarrassment when it had to fire a security firm hired to police one of its plants because some of the firm's employees, decked out in outfits associated with neo-Nazi groups, roughed up people trying to film activity outside the plant. The company maintains that it could not possibly vet the backgrounds of all those it hires and insists that, while it refuses to negotiate with the union, it does pay workers well.

What will happen in this key node of Amazon's global supply chain is uncertain. Workers mount regular protests using mass mobilization, guerilla theater, and online global petition drives (37,000 signatures received by March 2013). But Amazon has refused to back down. In May 2013, workers at the giant Amazon distribution center in Leipzig walked off the job, marking the first reported strike at an Amazon facility (Wilson and Jopson 2013). As the story continues to unfold, there are important implications to consider for labor in the cloud and for the cloud over labor.

While a great deal of its labor process can be automated and lodged in the cloud, Amazon still requires a large workforce in the developed world to efficiently locate and distribute its products. So in spite of the company's high-tech image, Amazon workers at a typical warehouse walk between seven and fifteen miles every day carrying handheld devices that direct and monitor their every move to locate ordered goods in its warehouses and package them individually. To maximize productivity, the company regularly advises workers on more efficient ways to carry out their activities, making full use of the data in everything from individual personnel decisions to global logistics planning. One business publication, not known for harsh attacks on workplace practices, cites people in one U.K. Amazon plant who complain about the company's practices. A local official, who fought to bring the company to his town with a high unemployment rate, concludes, "They're not seen as a good employer. It's not helpful to our economy; it's not helpful to the individuals" (S. O'Connor 2013). Another uses stronger language: "The feedback we're getting is it's like being in a slave camp." Even an Amazon manager admits, "You're sort of like a robot, but in human form." In the words of one technology reporter, "Digital capitalism produces few winners. Apple, Amazon, Facebook and Google might post huge profits, but many of their staff see little financial benefit" (Naughton 2013).

Amazon labor is restive not only in the material workplace. The company operates a global system of piecework in the cloud that critics have called a "digital sweatshop" (Cushing 2013). The Amazon Mechanical Turk (AMT) employs a large body of "crowdsourced" workers, whom Amazon calls "providers" (also known as "Turkers"). They carry out minute tasks online for "requesters," who pay Turkers piece rates for writing product descriptions, identifying individuals in images, or producing spam (a 2010 study by New York University researchers determined that spam constitutes as much as 40 percent of the jobs) (Ipeirotis 2013). Amazon originally set the system up to carry out work that could be done online but required some human involvement. The typical job was sorting merchandise into categories based on color or style for the company's massive online warehouse. It was so successful that Amazon decided to become a job broker for corporations needing people to do things like look up foreign zip codes or transcribe podcasts.

For managing the service, Amazon receives 10 percent of the value of a completed job, or human-intelligence task (HIT). Although Turkers include professionals, the vast majority are semiskilled workers who provide their credentials to requesters and, once cleared, choose among posted tasks. Workers in the United States are paid in cash, but many foreign workers are primarily given the option to accept gift certificates. Exact figures are hard to pin down, but it is estimated that the industry employs over 200,000 workers and, by 2011, was earning about $375 million annually (Cushing 2013). There is also growing evidence that workers are less than happy with the system. It did not take long for them to realize that, as one complained, "they make it sound like you can just do a few tasks in your free time in between other things, but if you worked like that, I believe you would make about a dollar a day" (ibid.). Because companies have an enormous workforce to draw from, they can pay the lowest possible rates—$1 or $2 an hour is not unusual—and demand swift and accurate completion of jobs. Workers who mess up a job are dropped or banned from reapplying. In January 2013 Amazon stopped accepting new applications from international Turkers because of what the company deemed unacceptable levels of fraud and poor worker performance ("The Reasons Why Amazon Mechanical Turk No Longer Accepts International Turkers" 2013). Since international workers are more likely to accept the low pay and constant demands, requesters have begun to set up their own Turk operations.

Upset about the system, Turkers use their online world to vet requesters and contact other Turkers. The result is Turkopticon, a piece of software that adds functionality to sites that post HITs by adding ratings, reviews of employers, and advice to exploited Turkers.[8] According to one scientist who has worked on AMT 28,000 times, "There's no sick leave, paid holidays, anything like that on Turk. There is no arbitration, no appeal if you feel that you have been unfairly treated, apart from a stinging review on Turkopticon" (Hodson 2013). Furthermore, worker complaints, fraud, and a host of negative consequences resulting from AMT's sweatshop in the cloud have encouraged other firms to set up somewhat more hospitable operations. For example, the firm MobileWorks pays the minimum wage in effect in the country where the work is being done, assigns each worker a manager to deal with problems, and provides opportunities for worker mobility (ibid.). It is uncertain whether the emergence of more worker-friendly companies will restore some credibility to online piecework. Much will depend on whether big companies like Amazon reform the labor process in the cloud. It appears to be in their interest to do so because it has become clear that the race to the bottom for wages and working conditions creates problems for the company as well as for workers.

Worker organizations, especially trade unions, are not often discussed alongside cloud computing. Only a handful of cloud providers, mainly the older computer and telecommunications firms such as IBM and Verizon, have to deal with organized labor. But as we have seen in the case of Apple's experience with Foxconn in China and Amazon in Germany, cloud companies, as they become inextricably bound to global supply chains, face the resistance of organized labor. These are examples of a process at work in the broadly defined knowledge and cultural industries that brings together workers across once discrete sectors. As a result, unions that once represented only telecommunications workers now include creative and technical talent in the audiovisual, writing, service, and technology sectors. The Communication Workers of America and its counterpart in Canada, which in 2013 merged its communications and power workers' union with the union representing auto workers, are good examples of worker organizations that have followed the path of technological convergence in their organizing efforts. The 2012 merger of the Screen Actors Guild and the American Federation of Television and Radio Artists brings together the major Hollywood unions for the first time to face off more effectively against the increasingly integrated Hollywood media industry. Moreover, individual unions are not only expanding across the converging communication and information industries, but they are forming large transnational organizations like Ver.di and UNI Global Union. These transnational unions are better equipped to deal with powerful multinational companies because they have enormous memberships and are well funded. Furthermore, the scope of their membership enables them to better represent the convergences in both the labor process and the working conditions among information, cultural, and service workers and to build bridges across the divide separating workers at different spatial and occupational points in the global division of labor.

Ver.di was founded in 2001 and by 2013 had reached 2.3 million members, primarily in Germany but in other parts of the world as well. It represents workers in thirteen sectors, all of which are increasingly affected by the rollout of cloud computing, including financial services, health and social services, education, science and research, media and culture, telecommunications, information technology and data-processing, postal, transport, and commerce services. Its members work in government and business at almost every level of occupational skill and function. The union can not only mobilize a large and diverse workforce but also draw on the specialized talents of its members, who can help the union to tighten and secure its internal communications or carry out guerilla theater protests that attract widespread media attention. UNI Global Union was created in 2000 when three international worker federations in the information, media, and service sectors came together to form a genuinely global federation of knowledge workers. Today, it gives voice to 20 million workers in 150 countries through nine hundred affiliated unions in a broad range of fields, including information technology and services, media, entertainment and the arts, gaming and sport, finance, commerce, and security, as well as to the growing numbers of workers who toil for temporary employment agencies. Among its major activities is negotiating global agreements with transnational companies to address important issues such as child labor, discrimination, and the right to organize local unions. By early 2013, it had completed forty-eight such agreements with a wide range of companies, including a number in the communication and information technology sector. It was also in the process of negotiating fresh agreements with major transnational firms, including IBM and Disney.

Ver.di and UNI are not alone among converging unions and international labor federations that are having an impact on global supply chains, including those central to the growth of cloud computing. But it is uncertain whether this development is the harbinger of a significant upsurge in global labor activism or a defensive posture that can at best slow down the inevitable decline and demise of organized labor. That depends, in part, on how one defines organized labor, because another important trend is the growth of labor organizations that are not formal trade unions. These worker associations resemble unions but, either out of choice or necessity, remain outside the legal and political structures that govern the operation of trade unions. They operate all over the world, and research has documented their importance in China, India, Europe, and the United States (Mosco, McKercher, and Huws 2010). They are especially active in the information, communication, and cultural sectors where worker associations have represented employees in occupations ranging from call-center agent to software-engineering specialist. Worker associations have won major victories for contract employees at Microsoft and for telecommunications workers in India. Although they do not typically negotiate contracts, worker associations have provided employees with legal representation, group medical insurance, training, model contract language, counseling, and support for collective resistance, without suffering from some of the bureaucratic entanglements that plague traditional trade unions. These associations are particularly active among contract and temporary workers; for example, the Freelancers Union has signed up 200,000 members in a wide range of jobs, including law, app and software development, graphic arts, accounting, writing, editing, and consulting. Worker associations differ from trade unions not just in what they lack—a system of formal bargaining with employers—but in their emphasis on mutual assistance outside, as well as within, the workplace. They follow the social movement tradition of earlier trade unions, which provided workers with social support, including family assistance, housing, insurance, and a source of collective power and community. As the head of the Freelancers Union noted, "The social unionism of the 1920s had it right. They said: 'We serve workers 360 degrees. It's not just about their work. It's about their whole life.' We view things the same way" (Greenhouse 2013).

The dark clouds identified in this chapter, involving the environment, privacy, and labor, present major challenges to the future of cloud computing. The next chapter addresses a cloudy forecast of another sort that takes us into the world of big data and the culture of clouds.

Chapter 5
Big Data and Cloud Culture

This is a world where massive amounts of data and applied mathematics replace every other tool that might be brought to bear. Out with every theory of human behavior, from linguistics to sociology. Forget taxonomy, ontology, and psychology. Who knows why people do what they do? The point is they do it, and we can track and measure it with unprecedented fidelity. With enough data, the numbers speak for themselves. (Anderson 2008)

A long time ago (and, of course, in many parts of society today), people had another name for massive information dumps that occurred spontaneously without any query having been made. They called it God. It was God, or the gods, who spoke out of the burning bush to tell you what you didn't even know you needed to ask. Before Oracle, Inc., in other words, there were oracles. (Alan Liu in Franklin 2012, 445)

The growth of cloud computing continues a process of building a global informational capitalism by concentrating production, processing, storage, distribution, and electronic services in a handful of companies, and, in some cases, governments, that manage labor and consumption through the systems that the cloud enables. This is undoubtedly a contested process as dark clouds gather around the environment, privacy, security, and labor. So it is uncertain that the cloud's combination of massive computer power under near-uniformly private control will be able to produce and sustain a continuously growing capitalist world order. Given the problems, it is doubtful that we will achieve Bill Gates's vision of "friction-free capitalism" (Gates 1995). Nevertheless, the powerful forces promoting the global cloud make it reasonable to expect considerable expansion, however contested, in the near future. This innovation alone makes cloud computing an important development to follow. But the cloud means considerably more because it is also promoting a very specific *culture of knowing* that valorizes certain types of knowledge and ways of knowing that have significant implications across social life. In this respect, friction-free capitalism meets what a *Wired* magazine editor calls the "global superintelligence known as the cloud" (Wolf 2010). This chapter examines this culture of knowing and critically assesses it by taking up episodes in the long history of cloud culture, where a 2,000-year-old play, a medieval manuscript, and a contemporary novel speak to the knowledge culture that is under construction. The political economy of the cloud (how it advances informational capitalism) and the culture of the cloud (what it means for knowledge and for the representation of our world) cohere and clash. Exploring both the harmony and the conflict creates space for a critical understanding of the cloud.

Cloud computing accelerates a powerful and influential way of knowing that is called on to address significant issues facing global capitalism. In its near-magical brilliance at certain tasks, the cloud has seduced many of its proponents to see it as the primary, if not the only, means of solving problems, pushing to the sidelines ways of knowing and seeing the world that have guided humanity over the centuries. In its extreme form, and there are many examples from which to draw, the way of knowing advanced by the cloud will reach a singularity, understood as the one and only legitimate means to know. All the rest is to be marginalized, sequestered in the nether world, reserved for the likes of astrology and conjuring. This is a mistake for two substantial reasons. First, life is so massively complex that no form of knowledge, however dazzling, can claim to be the universal way of knowing. Second, because cloud computing has developed under almost complete private control, its particular way of knowing is constrained by the narrow goal of commercial expansion. To put it bluntly, the cloud addresses most of the world as consumers and subjects, not as active citizens, and this tendency has significant consequences. It is more important than ever to resist singularities, expand what it means to know, and make the cloud more than merely the instrument to build and manage markets for products, services, workers, and consumers. To address these points, we need to understand the particularity of the cloud's way of knowing. What are its strengths and limitations? What are the alternatives and how are these constrained by the culture of the cloud?

A Cloud of Big Data

It is useful to start by examining the relationship between the cloud and what is called "big data." The latter refers to the movement to analyze the increasingly vast amounts of information stored in multiple locations, but mainly online and primarily in the cloud. We cannot reduce one to the other because the cloud encompasses more than big data. The analysis of big data, sometimes referred to as analytics, is one (admittedly important) service provided by cloud companies. Furthermore, big-data analysis can take place outside of a cloud setting, as companies and government agencies often make use of data held on their own computers. However, since the store of material used in big-data analysis is growing in size and complexity, it is increasingly a feature of cloud computing, benefitting from the promotional pitch that cloud companies make to customers. For example, Amazon Web Services (AWS) has grown since its success in supplying the Obama campaign with big-data analysis that most experts agree provided significant help in the successful 2012 campaign, and this success gave AWS a major boost in a battle with IBM to win a $600 million contract with the CIA. It also helped AWS expand its consumer service to challenge that of Dropbox and Google (Barr 2013). The expansion of cloud computing alone advances the interest in big data because, as one analyst said, the cloud "has made it viable to perform sophisticated analytics over huge volumes of data that were never even thinkable before" (Wainewright 2013). The cloud is not alone in giving impetus to big data. The proliferation of smart devices has brought about the massive growth in cloud-based information, including the locational data stored on phones, the devices installed in homes and workplaces that monitor everything from power consumption to the activities of families and workers, and the constant streams of social-media tweets, postings, and messages. In fact, one can safely conclude that big data results from the intimate connection that companies and governments recognize between cloud computing and smart devices.

Cloud providers have also led the way in promoting big-data analysis, viewing it as a means of expanding revenue. Some companies simply enable big data by introducing analytics programs to the applications they provide their cloud-computing customers. Other companies go further by directly analyzing the data they store on workers and customers to find added value. One firm produced a national database on employees who have been caught stealing, information that retailers use to prevent future hiring (Clifford and Silver-Greenberg 2013). Another firm used consumer data to develop a predictive algorithm to let clients know what files its users are most likely to download to local storage. Still others are "productivizing" data by harnessing publicly available archives such as Twitter postings to build new products (Wainewright 2013). This has been the centerpiece concept behind IBM's Smarter Analytics project, a combination of software, systems, and strategies that enable clients to combine their own business or enterprise data with their consumers' unstructured data to better identify and anticipate consumer behavior. IBM refers to the latter as "the data of desire" because it registers popular expressions of sentiment and feeling, such as likes/dislikes, about products and services. This gives its cloud customers the ability to correlate sales records with social-media postings, thereby linking behavioral data with information about customer feelings to provide a deeper view of customer sentiment—not just which customers are buying, but why. IBM credits this system with enabling a communication carrier to predict which customers were likely to defect within ninety days and reduced churn by 35 percent in the first year (IBM 2013). The potential in big data gives traditional companies like IBM opportunities for reinvention. A leader in research on embedding intelligence and communication capabilities in objects, or what is called the "Internet of things," General Electric has also bet heavily on transforming itself into a company that specializes in finding big-data solutions in the cloud (Butler 2013b). So has Monsanto, one of the world's leading chemical and agribusiness companies and the dominant producer of genetically modified seed. In 2013 the company spent $930 million to purchase a Silicon Valley start-up that uses big data to carry out weather and climate analysis (McDuling 2013).

These developments demonstrate the dynamic relationship between big data and cloud computing. Cloud companies that might have been satisfied to limit their business to providing data storage and applications now have a strong incentive to make use of data to sell additional services to customers and to develop new products of their own. But this does not just offer economic advantages. It also raises questions about the rights and responsibilities of cloud companies. Some companies and individuals might wonder why data they expected was only going to be stored in the cloud is instead being used by cloud companies to seek financial gain. Such activity might benefit a customer who stands to share in the added value, but it will also expose customer data to uses that were not anticipated. Moreover, as the cloud continues its inexorable global expansion, the storage facility is increasingly likely to be located in the jurisdiction of another country whose government will apply its own rules, regulations, and policies. In 2013 Microsoft took significant steps toward such a relationship with China, a development that prompted warnings about dire consequences from experts on Sino-American relations (Ragland et al. 2013). The economic synergies touted for the cloud and big data can easily produce significant political complications.

It is therefore now essential to consider big data in a comprehensive assessment of cloud computing and especially to assess its way of knowing. The cloud received a boost when the National Institute of Standards and Technology provided a generally accepted definition, but the same has not been the case for big data. Among the many circulating, the Wikipedia entry is a reasonably good one: "In information technology, big data is a collection of data sets so large and complex that it becomes difficult to process using on-hand database management tools or traditional data processing applications."[1] The authors of a 2013 book on the subject refer to it as "the ability of society to harness information in novel ways to produce useful insights or goods and services of significant value" (Mayer-Schönberger and Cukier 2013, 2).

Like the cloud, big data has often generated a rapturous response from its supporters, with one of the most sober accounts noting that "it has become *de rigeur* to ascribe all sorts of supernatural powers to Big Data"

(Asay 2013). A Microsoft researcher worries about the uncritical acceptance of big-data analysis out of a widespread "big data fundamentalism" (Hardy 2013i). One source of the fundamentalism is the belief that once the easy work of gathering data is completed, the data will speak for itself, yielding profitable gold nuggets of business information. But this is far from the case. Analysis is the hard part and it is growing more challenging as the amount of collectible data expands. It is no wonder that some experts worry that businesses are giving up on big data, leading one to conclude that a "dirty little secret" of the industry is that "nobody *wants* to use the data" (Elowitz 2013). Before examining what might appropriately be called the big-data sublime, it is best to briefly examine what the fuss is about.

Although in application big-data analysis can be a very challenging exercise, its fundamentals are much less complicated than one might expect. Analysts take sets of quantitative data and run correlations to find relationships that yield insights, perhaps anticipated, perhaps not, and they use these findings to make predictions. Let's consider the four important elements in this description. First, the data under analysis are invariably *quantitative* in that operations are applied to numerical values of objects, events, outcomes, ideas, opinions, etc. This does not mean that big data avoids qualitative information, but rather that analysts represent subjective states with quantities—for example, by assigning numerical values to likes and dislikes or to feelings of satisfaction or dissatisfaction.

Second, big data develops generalizations based on *correlations* among variables. According to two big-data specialists, this means internalizing "a growing respect for correlations rather than a continuing quest for elusive causality" (Mayer-Schönberger and Cukier 2013, 19). Such analysis might lead to the conclusion that a voter's age is closely related to support for the president. Specifically, as age increases, support decreases. Correlational analysis can measure the direction of a relationship, positive or negative, and the strength of that relationship. But it cannot say anything, by itself, about causality or even about whether a relationship is genuine or spurious. One cannot, from the data itself, determine whether two variables that are positively related are also causally related—their relationship may be caused by another, yet unrecognized, variable or, worse, their relationship may be a figment of the data and the variables actually have nothing to do with one another. Even correlations achieved at a high level of significance—for example, that out of one hundred samples, the relationship would show up ninety-five times—give no warrant to assert causality and to rule out the possibility of a spurious relationship. Correlations help one to determine which among a group of variables go together, or covary, and to rule out with some confidence those that do not. But people often mistake this for providing evidence of causality or of certainty that they are tied together, independent of other variables that may very well be essential. For example, just because the sale of umbrellas is highly correlated with car accidents does not mean that one causes the other. Rather, it is the presence of a third variable, rain, that influences both. In this case the relationship between umbrella sales and accidents is spurious.

Big-data analysis also tends to be *atheoretical*. In fact, major proponents boast that it frees people from coming up with hypotheses or theories to be tested and allows the data to speak for itself (Anderson 2008). Not every proponent of big data holds as strongly to this view, but most accept that, given our ability to measure and monitor behavior, from the "likes" posted on Facebook to how fast we drive, the goal of science should be to apply mathematical procedures, such as correlations, and let generalizations emerge from the data. The point, as Mayer-Schönberger and Cukier emphasize, is that "no longer do we necessarily require a valid substantive hypothesis about a phenomenon to begin to understand our world" (2013, 55). Theory's guiding hand was necessary in the past because there was not enough data to rely on it alone to provide answers. A world awash in data can now find, in the analogy often used by big-data supporters, a needle in a haystack (Singh 2013). Replacing theories and hypothesis are general areas of interest and specific questions that the researcher believes big data and the cloud might answer. Anything more rigorous would prematurely rule out entire areas where solutions might be found.

The primary goal of big data is to be *predictive*. Find patterns deep in the data and expect that, barring significant structural changes, they will tell us what the future will be like. Determining *why* is less important than predicting *what will be*. As a 2013 overview concludes, "We're entering a world of constant data-driven predictions where we may not be able to explain the reasons behind our decisions" (Mayer-Schönberger and Cukier 2013, 17). Consider the example of Google's search for the needle of insight into the spread of flu, a goal that has eluded experts at the Centers for Disease Control (CDC) who have spent years trying to track the disease. Google's haystack is more like a towering skyscraper, with three billion searches a day saved in Google's clouds. Drawing from this vast store of data, Google compared 50 million of the most common search terms to the CDC's information on the spread of flu from 2003 to 2008 (Ginsberg et al. 2009). The company's researchers looked for correlations between the frequency of certain search terms and the spread of the virus over space and time. They found that "because the relative frequency of certain queries is highly correlated with the percentage of physician visits in which a patient presents with influenza-like symptoms, we can accurately estimate the current level of weekly influenza activity in each region of the United States, with a reporting lag of about one day" (ibid.). Since the best reporting lag up to this point was about two weeks, Google's results, which led to the online tool Google Flu Trends, promised to provide flu fighters and the general public with the best information on how to predict the spread of flu. Moreover, it could do this unobtrusively and inexpensively. Big data found the needle in the form of key search terms and Google cautiously believed its method might serve to refine global and local preparations for the virus.

Big data is now used widely throughout the sciences. Genomics, which uses it to decipher the human genome, and astronomy, which applies it to map the heavens, gave rise to the term big data. According to one assessment of the benefits for genetics research, "Improvements in the speed and functionality of data collection, storage and analysis tools have lowered the cost of sequencing from almost £2bn to around £2,000 today, and cut the time it takes from over a decade to a week. While more incremental gains would have taken place at any rate, such major strides have only been made achievable by the cloud computing services offered by—among others—Microsoft, Amazon and Teradata" (Burn-Murdoch 2012). The Sloan Digital Sky Survey has used big data to analyze more information for astronomy than all the astronomical research amassed before the project began in the year 2000 (Mayer-Schönberger and Cukier 2013, 7). Physicists use big data to model quantum behavior and climatologists use it to produce models of changing weather.

Big data is increasingly used to analyze, model, and forecast human behavior (Boyd and Crawford 2012). Many of these uses are familiar, although not often associated with big data. They include Google, Bing, and other search engines, which apply algorithms to databases to deliver search results. Facebook's Graph Search takes this to a new level by providing search results tailored to the record of subjective choices such as friend requests and "likes." Seeing the value of big data in ordinary online use has added to individual user capabilities and, in the process, lengthened the industry lead of those companies, especially Google, that have invested in their development. For example, Microsoft pioneered the use of large databases to spell-check its word-processing program's documents, but did not pursue the technology further, at least not as far as Google, which used the same technology to develop its search, autocomplete, Gmail, and Google Docs services. In fact, lessons learned from this use of big data helped convince Google to develop a completely cloud-based laptop computer, the Chromebook. These big-data applications are typically cited in descriptions of success stories, but others that receive less attention bear close scrutiny.

The U.S. military is a leader in big-data analytics, with the largest projects run by the National Security Agency (NSA), the country's leading global electronics spy agency and the subject of considerable controversy in the summer of 2013, after a former NSA contractor lifted the lid on the agency's massive domestic and international surveillance operations. Through its global surveillance networks, the NSA has been collecting data for sixty years, first intercepting phone calls and now capturing emails and other online communication, which it stores and assesses through a variety of analytical systems, including keywords that might provide clues about security threats. IBM delivered the NSA its first computer, the top secret Stretch-Harvest, to process surveillance in 1962 (Lohr 2013a). This extended a long tradition of government surveillance of communication technologies, which began in earnest with the telegraph. Back in 1861, just a few years after the technology was deployed, President Lincoln ordered federal marshals to enter every telegraph office in the United States and seize copies of all messages, with an eye to rooting out Confederate sympathizers.

Just as there is nothing especially new about the NSA's activities, there is nothing particularly novel about the warnings over its abuse of power. After all, in the 1970s, shortly after the Watergate scandal, a Senate committee warned about the danger that agencies charged with foreign spying, including the NSA, posed to the American people (Greenwald

2013). The effectiveness of NSA activities has not always been clear, in part because the agency collected far more information than it was able to analyze. For this, big data provides what is hoped to be a solution by strengthening the capacity to process data, apply analytical tools, and make predictions. To deepen its analytical capacity, the NSA has built a close relationship with Silicon Valley, to the extent that one analyst concluded that "they are now in the same business" (*New York Times* 2013a). Others maintain that connections between the NSA, Microsoft, Google, Apple, Facebook, and major telecommunications firms make up a data-intelligence complex, a contemporary version of the military-industrial complex that President Eisenhower criticized when he left office in 1960 (Luce 2013). The Pentagon and U.S. intelligence agencies are an increasingly essential training ground for start-up companies. An NSA employee who left to start a successful tech company praised the agency for putting him "on the bleeding edge, not just the cutting edge of what's possible" (Sengupta 2013). Nevertheless, the relationship between private companies and the intelligence agencies is far from harmonious. The scandal that arose from revelations about NSA spying and the involvement of the major computer and social-media companies led to business fears about a decline of public trust in the online world. As a result, in December 2013 Apple, Yahoo!, Facebook, Twitter, AOL, and LinkedIn joined Google and Microsoft in an open letter to the president and Congress calling for reform and regulation of online surveillance by government agencies (Wyatt and Miller 2013).

The 2013 NSA scandal is unlikely to slow the construction of an NSA cloud data center in Utah for the storage, processing, analysis, and forecasting needs of the agency, estimated to cost $2 billion (Bamford 2012). As journalists who have tried to investigate what is benignly called the Utah Data Center have learned, the site is shrouded in the secrecy that one has come to expect from the NSA (Hill 2013). After all, it is hardly surprising that an agency whose budget is kept secret from public scrutiny (estimates range in the tens of billions of dollars) would not open the doors of its latest big project. According to one of the world's leading experts on the NSA, "Flowing through its servers and routers and stored in near-bottomless databases will be all forms of communication, including the complete contents of private emails, cell phone calls, and Google searches, as well as all sorts of personal data trails—parking receipts, travel itineraries, bookstore purchases, and other digital 'pocket litter.' It is, in some measure, the realization of the 'total information awareness' program created during the first term of the George W. Bush administration—an effort that Congress killed in 2003 after it caused an outcry over the potential for invading Americans' privacy" (Bamford 2012).

The Utah Data Center is a monumental construction project built around four 25,000-square-foot buildings that house cloud servers to process and analyze data, with floor space raised to permit access for cables delivering data files. Fully 900,000 square feet of space will be set aside for technical support and management. The budget includes $10 million for extraordinary measures to secure the facility, which includes a fence reportedly capable of stopping a 15,000-pound vehicle traveling at fifty miles per hour. The entire operation is considered self-sustaining, with its own substation able to deliver sixty-five megawatts of electricity.

Three key developments prompted the construction of the Utah site. The first is the massive growth of information worldwide that requires enormous investment in facilities and processing power. Analyzing public data alone would be daunting, as one estimate has the entire stock of data on the Internet quadrupling between 2010 and 2015, to over 950 exabytes. The total amount of information created from the dawn of writing to 2003 amounted to about 5 exabytes (Bamford 2013). But the NSA needs to go beyond what is publicly available to capture and examine information contained on the deep web, or deepnet, which includes classified reports from governments and businesses that are protected by encryption systems that big data enables the NSA to crack. As one of the foremost experts on the NSA concluded, "With its new Utah Data Center, the NSA will at last have the technical capability to store, and rummage through, all those stolen secrets" (ibid.; see also Deibert 2013).

Second is the expansion in the agency's domestic spy operations (Clement 2013). Initially charged with intercepting electronic traffic to and from the United States, NSA surveillance no longer stops at the U.S. border. In the wake of the 9/11 attacks, according to Bamford and former NSA employees, it installed what amount to taps on major domestic telecommunications switches and satellite earth stations. It also set up between ten and twenty facilities in the United States to analyze electronic traffic within the country and extended the NSA's reach with surveillance loops into major Canadian cities (Bamford 2013; Clement 2013). While the agency is formally prohibited from domestic spying, there are different perspectives on its legality and constitutionality, particularly in light of post-9/11 legislation that expands the government's power to intercept electronic communication within the United States and abroad. With the help of a Boeing software subsidiary, the NSA can now remotely control software from its Maryland headquarters to search U.S. databases, including, it now appears, 2.8 trillion billing records of telephone calls stored in an AT&T facility covering individuals and organizations it targets for recording, transmission, and analysis. The Utah Data Center expands the opportunity to analyze and make use of these massive new stores of data.

Third, as daunting as it is to keep up with the growth in traffic, the NSA has benefited from the expansion in processing power and big-data analysis that enables the agency to actually use what it gathers to analyze intelligence and forecast events. The agency now has the capacity to enter a name into its database and automatically route and record all electronic communication to and from that person. When the NSA considers it necessary, the agency can carry out a detailed analysis of communication content and use it to complete a risk assessment. Along with content surveillance, the agency uses metadata to map the social networks of individuals to determine the implications of strong and weak network connections as well as ties that can be implied by networks of associations among different people. Given the quantitative and qualitative expansion in its capabilities, a former NSA employee, Walter Binney, believes that the agency has shifted from focused collection and analysis of data on foreign threats to gathering as much data on foreigners and Americans as the technology allows (Bamford 2012).[2] Moreover, the predictive capability of big-data systems makes it even more likely that the NSA and agencies like it will collect far more data than they need. That is because improvements in cracking data-encryption codes keep open the likelihood that, if the agency cannot decipher and analyze data now, it will likely be able to do so in the future.

The NSA is at the leading edge of a concerted program that also involves the CIA, the Defense Advanced Research Projects Agency (DARPA), and other military and intelligence organizations that put big data to work, for example, in the controversial use of battlefield attack drones. Considering the sheer amount of data that must be processed to carry out a successful drone attack, it is not surprising that there are significant challenges to successful applications. In fact, some insiders question the expansion of drone programs because they require processing capabilities that exceed today's budgetary and technological limits (Beidel 2012). Pushing ahead, in 2012 the federal government announced spending of more than $200 million on big-data military and civilian research and development. According to the press release accompanying its announcement of the "Big Data Initiative," the Department of Defense (DOD) will "place a big bet on Big Data" with $60 million in new annual spending. The goal is to "accelerate innovation in Big Data" that will "improve situational awareness to help warfighters and analysts and provide increased support to operations. The Department is seeking a 100-fold increase in the ability of analysts to extract information from texts in any language, and a similar increase in the number of objects, activities, and events that an analyst can observe" (U.S. Office of Science and Technology Policy 2012). This funding is expected to significantly expand the military's drone attack program (Beidel 2012).

Along with the DOD initiative, DARPA announced an investment of $25 million a year in its XDATA program to overcome current limitations in big-data analysis. Specifically, it is focusing on developing software and other computational tools, such as improved algorithms and visual representations, to examine the semistructured and unstructured data in text documents and message traffic. The announcement did not include the NSA or the CIA, whose programs are not publicized in press announcements and whose spending is kept separate from DOD authorizations. It is hard to say whether the bad publicity that the NSA has attracted in the wake of revelations about the extent of its surveillance activities, especially against Americans, will dampen the government's commitment to expanding the military use of the cloud and big data. This is unlikely. While the names of programs change (today it is Prism, tomorrow something else), the NSA has been in the surveillance business for more than half a century and its work is vital to U.S. spy operations. Nevertheless, some rethinking is likely because revelations of electronic surveillance on the offices of allies, particularly in the European Union and in Latin America, have created enough anger to damage relations to the point of threatening sensitive trade negotiations (Castle 2013). Indeed, some analysts are wondering aloud whether revelations about NSA activities will significantly undermine support for cloud computing worldwide (Linthicum 2013d). One think tank estimates losses to the U.S. cloud industry at between \$21.5 and \$35 billion over the next three years as a result of fears generated by NSA surveillance (Taylor 2013a). Cisco claimed that it had already lost business in emerging markets because of concerns about U.S. spying (Meyer 2013).

The government commitment to cloud computing is not limited to military/intelligence applications. In addition to advancing research in medicine and health care, it is looking to reduce healthcare costs, and the analysis and predictive promise of big data are means of meeting this goal. To that end the government is funding a joint project bringing together the National Science Foundation and the National Institutes of Health to research "managing, analyzing, visualizing, and extracting useful information from large and diverse data sets" (U.S. Office of Science and Technology Policy 2012). While improving the analysis and display of data is not controversial, the ultimate goal of predicting outcomes based on patient information has stirred concerns that government will use the results to modify behavior in ways considered excessively intrusive. For example, should the government tailor its medical-insurance coverage to the health choices of Americans, with cuts to benefits for those who make what the data suggests are bad choices? Another health-related field, genomics, is also a popular subject in big-data discussions. Here the government is teaming with Amazon Web Services (AWS), which helped bring victory to President Obama in the 2012 election, to store 200 terabytes (16 million file cabinets or 30,000 standard DVDs) of data from genomics research. The data is publicly available, but users have to pay AWS for computing costs. It is interesting to observe another example of the government's dependence on private cloud companies, in this case one of the most important in the world, to store, process, and distribute valuable data sets. Finally, energy and geology research receive funding to advance the capacity of these fields to analyze, visualize, and predict the behavior of resource and geological systems.

Big data is increasingly used in the traditional social sciences and in the humanities. Social-science research is now often conducted by private corporations that see significant opportunities in areas such as real-time fraud detection, health risk assessments for medical patients, continuous process monitoring of consumer sentiment or vital mechanical systems, and network relationships on social-media sites (Davenport, Barth, and Bean 2012). Large data sets are providing new opportunities for research with practical consequences. For example, a United Nations agency supports big-data research on how organizations respond to humanitarian crises. The data include social-media content with the goal of creating recommendations on what works best (Burn-Murdoch 2012). Similarly, in Sierra Leone, the mapping company Esri provides software and a cloud portal that reveals where health clinics are needed (A. Schwarz 2013). Data scientists working with the London-based organization DataKind provide advice to charities about how to deal with problems in the nonprofit sector. Furthermore, researchers associated with Toronto's Hospital for Sick Children have used big data to develop algorithms that anticipate infections in premature babies. Notwithstanding these benefits, because similar types of algorithms can be used by insurance companies to refuse coverage or by social-media companies to manipulate "trending" results, there are more than a few worries about ethical and political issues (Burn-Murdoch 2012; Gillespie 2013). This has led some data scientists to promote a code of good behavior, "Doing Good with Analytics," that commits to assessing the ethical value of research before the process begins and to using it to bring about positive social change (D. Ross 2012). It has also prompted calls to democratize data science by making the new field more open and accessible to citizens (Harris 2013b).

Since private corporations control most of the research using big data, concerns have been raised about access to data because firms are reluctant to follow traditional social-science protocols for releasing evidence reported on in academic papers. The issue came to a head in 2012 when researchers with Google and Cambridge University refused to make available data for a conference paper on the popularity of YouTube in several countries. The chairman of the conference, a physicist who heads a social-science research group at HP, responded angrily and recommended that the conference should no longer accept papers from researchers who, whether for a commercial, security, or any other reason, refuse to share data. He followed that up with a letter to the prestigious science journal *Nature* declaring that big-data analysis, which was supposed to expand research horizons, is actually narrowing them because the private companies that own the data refuse to release it (Markoff 2012). On the other hand, a growing number of critical social-science scholars are developing tools to use commercial software and data generated by social media to advance alternative visions of society (Beer 2012).

Big data is also increasingly used in the humanities, shaking up traditional research approaches and stirring considerable debate (Hunter 2011). In the United States, the push to use big data in the liberal arts is led by the federal government's National Endowment for the Humanities (NEH). One of the largest funders of liberal-arts research in the United States, NEH is a federal agency founded in 1965. With an annual budget of about $170 million, the agency provides grants to cultural institutions such as libraries, universities, museums, public broadcasters, and individual scholars in order to strengthen teaching, research, and the institutional base of the humanities, including expanding access to educational and cultural resources. NEH created the Digital Humanities Initiative in 2006, and it was raised to the level of an Office of Digital Humanities (ODH) in 2008, a move that helped to legitimize use of the term *digital humanities* in the United States. With ODH support, scholars working in the field made their presence felt at the 2009 annual meeting of the Modern Language Association, what many consider a turning point in the field. Digital humanists apply computer science to the humanities, primarily by examining large data sets to carry out research that was difficult, if not impossible, to complete before computational methods were available to scholars working in such humanities fields as literature, history, and philosophy.

Some of the research, such as the ODH-funded Visual Page project, involves finding new ways to gather big data and analyze it: "All printed texts convey meaning through both linguistic and graphic signs, but existing tools for computational text analysis focus only on the linguistic content. The Visual Page will develop a prototype application to identify and analyze visual features in digitized Victorian books of poetry, such as margin space, line indentation, and typeface attributes" (U.S. National Endowment for the Humanities 2013). Other projects directly apply computational methods to analyze large data sets; one of these is an ODH-funded project on the life cycles of published works: "including not only scholarly and scientific literature, but also social networks, blogs, and other materials." The goal is to "identify which scholarly activities are indicative of emerging areas and identify datasets that should no longer be marginalized, but built into understandings and measurements of scholarship" (ibid.). Another funded project demonstrates why the grant program is called "digging into data": because it looked at "new ways of exploring the full text content of digital historical records ... using medieval charters which survive in abundance from the 12th to the 16th centuries and are one of the richest sources for studying the lives of people in the past. The new ChartEx tools will enable users to really dig into the content of these records, to recover their rich descriptions of places and people, and to go far beyond current digital catalogues which restrict searches to a few key facts about each document (the 'metadata')" (*Digging into Data Challenge* 2011).

The ODH program has succeeded in giving the humanities a significant push into quantitative research that takes advantage of cloud computing systems to examine large sets of data.[3] ODH has also attracted international attention and support. Its 2009 and 2011 "digging into big data" competitions received proposals from 150 research teams and funded 22 from the United States, United Kingdom, Canada, and the Netherlands. For 2013, support and sponsorship expanded across new research councils and government funding authorities, giving the program ten sponsors. This is significant because government support for the humanities, including research, teaching, and archiving, has declined to perilous levels in most Western societies, leaving cloud-based, big-data research one of the few areas where funding is on the rise (Delany 2013). Moreover, government research councils that have seen their budgets cut are devoting more of what little is left to funding computational research in the humanities. Defenders of the digital humanities support this shift because they believe it is bringing about a revolutionary transformation in all facets of humanities education and research. As the head of the NEH exclaimed, "A revolution has commenced where science and technology are melding with the humanities" (Leach 2011).

Not everyone in the humanities sees it this way, including Stanley Fish, one of the most distinguished literary and cultural-studies scholars of our time. For Fish, most supporters of the digital humanities advance a view that he considers "theological" because it promises freedom from the constrictions of a medium that is both linear and time-bound, which can only produce knowledge that is discrete, partial, and situated (i.e., for here and now, by this author, and for this audience). For its supporters, the digital humanities use the cloud and computational methods to provide a universe in which knowledge is fully available everywhere and to everyone. Through it, we all become nodes in a network of meaning production for a system that eliminates the spatial and temporal barriers between the person seeking knowledge and the object of cognition. Fish maintains that this is a state that most religions identify with the afterlife, when people cast off the shackles of mortality and all of its limitations to become one with the creator, the source of all knowledge. He admits that no one in the field speaks precisely in this way, but says they may as well because, for digital humanists, their mission affirms a future of "expanding, borderless collaboration in which all the infirmities of linearity will be removed" (Fish 2012a). He cites Fitzpatrick (2011), whose book *Planned Obsolescence* describes the limitations of traditional media and the social relations that arose with them, maintaining that in a world of new media "we need to think less about completed products and more about text in process; less about individual authorship and more about collaboration; less about originality and more about remix; less about ownership and more about sharing" (p. 83).

In his critique of what he considers the theology of the digital humanities, Fish is describing what I have called the digital sublime (Mosco 2004). At the very least, the digital humanities mythologize the online world by viewing it as means of transcending the banalities of everyday life, but even more so by helping to bring about the end of history, the end of geography, and the end of politics. In its extreme form, the digital humanities are clearly theological in that they draw inspiration from the writing of people like Teilhard de Chardin (1961), who envisioned mankind finding unity with God through the noosphere, the literal atmosphere of thought he believed was created by the growth of information. The work of Ray Kurzweil (2005) on informational immortality and the singularity marry Teilhard's theology with the digital world.

Fish also takes issue with the digital humanities on political grounds, particularly the goals of democratizing the humanities by breaking down the barriers that separate disciplines and the barriers separating scholars from the general public. What makes Fish's critique interesting is that he is not opposed to these goals per se, but he doubts that the digital humanities can reach them. For him they are more like mythic covers that justify the primary goal of gathering as much quantitative data as possible on literary texts and other works of popular culture to, at the very least, inspire new readings of texts and new assessments of the process and the context of their creation (Fish 2012b). The digital-humanities movement has sparked rigorous debate, with proponents making reference to the "backward" humanities and opponents using words like "diabolical" to describe Franco Moretti, one of its leading practitioners (Sunyer 2013).

There is nothing new in the principles behind big-data analytics. For many years social scientists have been working on large data sets to find relationships among seemingly unrelated variables. But the difference now is the concerted effort to make it the singularly most important tool in research and, for some, the magical alternative to the methods that have guided research in science as well as the humanities for centuries. Big data is not just a method; it is a myth, a sublime story about conjuring wisdom not from the flawed intelligence of humans, with all of our well-known limitations, but from the pure data stored in the cloud.

Proclaiming "the end of theory," Chris Anderson got the ball rolling in a 2008 *Wired* magazine article in which he stated, "the data deluge makes the scientific method obsolete" (Anderson 2008). For Anderson, big data marks nothing short of a revolution in what it means to know. This view is mythic because it envisions big data as a revolutionary development that does not just make science better, but ends science as we know it and replaces it with a new way of knowing. Like many myths, Anderson's tale imagines a new world where what was universally accepted yesterday is rejected and discarded today in favor of a simple alternative that solves the world's problems. Out with the scientific method, in with big-data correlations. Following an example of how Google is revolutionizing advertising, Anderson proclaimed, "The big target here isn't advertising, though. It's science." Or more precisely, it is the core of science embodied in an approach to knowledge. "The scientific method is built around testable hypotheses. These models, for the most part, are systems visualized in the minds of scientists. The models are then tested, and experiments confirm or falsify theoretical models of how the world works. This is the way science has worked for hundreds of years." It no longer has to work this way, but scientists have to give up their cherished notions. "Scientists are trained to recognize that correlation is not causation, that no conclusions should be drawn simply on the basis of a correlation between X and Y (it could just be a coincidence). Instead, you must understand the underlying mechanisms that connect the two. Once you have a model, you can connect the data sets with confidence. Data without a model is just noise. But faced with massive data, this approach to science—hypothesize, model, test—is becoming obsolete" (ibid.).

At their core, myths help us to cope with life's uncertainties, from the little banalities, such as what to have for breakfast, to the grand questions of how to find meaning and face mortality. They do not just offer an answer; they provide *the* answer, typically with convincing clarity, simplicity, and fervor. Big data is not just one among many instruments to understand and change the world; it is the essential one, and all others, including science, the method that has guided the modern world and its way of knowing, can be swept into the dustbin of history. Some understand this well. People like Chris Anderson and Ray Kurzweil are today's seers, who know the way that draws the curtain on an old age and foreshadows the new. Most myths are about endings, whether the end of history, of theory, or of science. They call on us to celebrate our good fortune to live at the end of an era and to begin to experience the new. For Anderson, today's visionary is Google because it is not just a successful company, a leading force in informational capitalism, but primarily because it is using the correlations it finds in mountains of big data to change what it means to know: "The new availability of huge amounts of data, along with the statistical tools to crunch these numbers, offers a whole new way of understanding the world. Correlation supersedes causation, and science can advance even without coherent models, unified theories, or really any mechanistic explanation at all. There's no reason to cling to our old ways. It's time to ask: What can science learn from Google?" (ibid.)

For some, the new visionary is the data scientist who magically conjures truth from mountains of seemingly unrelated information. According to one observer, "big data has created a mythical god called the data scientist: a lone-wolf, super-smart human with a solid foundation in computer science, modeling, statistics, analytics, math, and strong business acumen, coupled with the ability to communicate findings to both business and IT leaders in a way that can influence how an organization approaches a business challenge" (Walker 2013). One observer sees the data scientist as the successor to the iconic "Mad Men" of advertising (Steel 2012a). Myths matter. In this case the emergence of the data scientist as the latest mythical god is having a significant impact on higher education, where universities are scrambling to produce programs to train aspirants for what the *Harvard Business Review*, no stranger to hyperbolic excess, calls "the sexiest job in the 21st century" (Miller 2013). Despite budget constraints created in part by failed programs inspired by the dot-com bubble of the late 1990s and the financial bubble that greeted the new century, dozens of new programs have emerged at every level of higher education. Even the usually subdued *New York Times* has caught the fever. Declaring data scientists "the magicians of the Big Data era," the newspaper describes their many talents: "They crunch the data, use mathematical models to analyze it and create narratives or visualizations to explain it, then suggest how to use the information to make decisions" (ibid.). It is uncertain whether they can also bring home the bacon and fry it up in a pan, but the *Times* is satisfied to transmit, with no critical reflection, a promotional report by McKinsey that forecasts the millions of jobs that the demand for data scientists will create. It is remarkable that after the disastrous economic catastrophes brought about by near-rapturous faith in the IT of the late 1990s, and in the big-data algorithms that helped bring the West to the brink of a new Great Depression in 2008, educators continue to chase after the next new fad. This time will be different. Myths matter.[4]

A current exemplar of myth-building around big data is a 2013 book by a pair of knowledgeable analysts whose breathless prose begins with its title: *Big Data: A Revolution That Will Transform How We Live, Work, and Think*. One of the characteristics of a good myth is its ability to inoculate its story with what appears to be sober good sense in order to achieve a degree of legitimacy before plowing ahead with the tall tale. For the authors of *Big Data* this means putting some distance between them and Chris Anderson: "Big data may not spell the 'end of theory,' but it does fundamentally transform the way we make sense of the world" (Mayer-Schönberger and Cukier 2013, 72). Here, we are encouraged to question the implied hyperbole even as we adopt another, equally extraordinary claim. For the authors, "the IT revolution is all around us" and it is manifested not in the technology, but in information, which takes on seemingly magical powers to change the way we know the world (ibid., 77–78). This appears again when they turn to the method of choice in big-data analysis, finding correlations: "With correlations, there is no certainty, only probability. But if a correlation is strong, the likelihood of a link is high." They "demonstrate" this by asking us to observe the connection between Amazon's book suggestions and those books' appearance on people's shelves (ibid., 53). Undeterred by the absence of anything resembling evidence to support their contention, they plow forward: "By letting us identify a really good proxy for a phenomenon, correlations help us to capture the present and predict the future" (ibid., 53–54). What could be more mythical and sublime, more evidence of the conjurer's art, than the magic wand of correlation? Only this magic delivers more than rabbits from hats. It can tell us what is and what will be.

Because myths matter, it is important to provide some critical reflection on these claims. But it is also essential to understand the limits of any such critique, however telling. The cloud and big data are more than technical developments because their emergence has inspired a new mythology that puts a fresh face on the digital sublime, which, at the end of the last century, promised to end history, annihilate geography, and transform politics. Like all myths, they are full of magical conjurers who offer revolutionary transformations and happy endings that bid good-bye to the temporal, spatial, and social constraints that make up the banalities of everyday life and welcome a new world in the cloud. We can now know the past, represent the present, and predict the future like never before, with little of this contaminated by flawed human decision making. The data will speak for themselves or through data-science magicians. Like all myths, they cannot be fully judged based on their claims of truth, but rather, as the philosopher Alisdair MacIntyre (1970) concluded, only on whether they are living or dead. Myths live on if they continue to make life meaningful and if they continue to make socially and intellectually tolerable what otherwise might be experienced as painful and incoherent. Myths do not disappear when they are falsified—consider their persistence after the dot-com bust and the financial crash—as long they continue to energize people and feed their hopes and dreams. The cloud and big data do so by promising an endless supply of accessible information that will be used to solve the problems that afflict the world and make it possible to enjoy forms of perfection that have heretofore been little more than the stuff of dreams.

Big Data: A Critique of Digital Positivism

Big data gives priority to *quantitative* over qualitative data, arguing that the former provides the best opportunity for meaningful generalizations and that, when necessary, qualitative states can be rendered qualitatively. For example, a quantitative content analysis of search terms relating to flu provided Google with what it believed was a string of terms that correlated with flu outbreaks, thereby enabling researchers to predict, earlier than ever, the spread of flu. If, on the other hand, one chose to carry out a big-data analysis of a subjective state, say by associating positive Twitter posts about the Toyota Prius with sales of the car, then one might assign numerical values to capture the strength of responder posts. Or big data might run an analysis that combines the results of numerous customer-satisfaction surveys that assign a number to each possible response, such as a 5 for strong dislike or a 3 for simply disagreeing with a statement. After all, *strongly like or dislike* represents a more powerful attraction than just *like or dislike*. The measurement of quantity is not only central; it is absolutely essential to the transformative capacity of big data. As two of its proponents attest, "Just as the Internet radically changed the world by adding communications to computers, so too will big data change fundamental aspects of life by giving it a quantitative dimension it never had before" (Mayer-Schönberger and Cukier 2013, 12). There is much to be said for quantitative analysis. It renders complex behavior, as well as mental states, easy to process and analyze. It is no wonder that big-data specialists believe that "the more quantitative it is, the better" (Morozov 2013b, 232). The ease of analysis, the opportunity to draw broad generalizations and then to make predictions, provides a strong temptation to reduce all methodological approaches to quantitative ones. Indeed, the hot new profession of data scientist knows only quantitative approaches. Moreover, big data makes it possible to avoid the need to sample a population, and all of the risks associated with accurately representing a larger group, by examining results for an entire population.

The problems with relying solely or primarily on quantitative analysis are today more often than not ignored, but that is a mistake. Quantitative research provides a scientific gloss on behavioral or attitudinal data that is often far messier than the numbers make it appear. Social scientists are well aware of the limitations of working with data on reports of law-breaking behavior that are often massively skewed by the human limitations of witnesses, police, and the vagaries of plea-bargaining and trials. Nevertheless, big-data supporters and their corporate sponsors continue to press for what is euphemistically called "predictive policing" (Bachner

2013). Because quantitative research works best on data embodying little in the way of subjectivity, researchers tend to neglect questions that require their careful consideration. It is far easier to go for the low-hanging fruit of voter analysis (there is little subjectivity in the determination of whom one votes for), or of counting the frequency of search terms, than to examine, for example, how a young person becomes a racist. The latter involves an altogether different kind of methodology, which might make use of some quantitative data but also requires close observation and depth interviews—in other words, a careful qualitative study that aims to comprehend the rich subjectivity that makes up personal and inter-personal experiences. Big data deals with subjectivity to the extent that analysts can do the impossible—i.e., assign a precise numerical value to its various states. This is inherently flawed because subjective states such as happiness, depression, or satisfaction mean different things to different people, and assigning the same numerical value to the choice of this term simplifies to the point of absurdity. The same goes for other attitudinal terms such as like and dislike, agree and disagree, and their amplifiers, such as "strongly." What is the meaning of a number associated with these terms? How can one assign any meaning worth taking seriously to the numerical difference between disagree and strongly disagree?

It is uncertain which is worse: that big data treats problems through oversimplification or that it ignores those that require a careful treatment of subjectivity, including lengthy observation, depth interviews, and an appreciation for the social production of meaning. There is a difference, as the computer pioneer Jaron Lanier notes, between using big data to analyze weather or galaxy formation and using it to examine the emotional states of human beings, which are often contradictory and unreliable (Lanier 2013). Such an approach only feeds what Roman Kudryashov, drawing on Roland Barthes, refers to as the myth of the quantification of quality: "When language cannot handle the complexities of reality, it strives to economize the world: qualities become quantities, and once again, language goes beyond reality to judge it. Though language tries to be scientific about its descriptions here, it has attributed properties not belonging to the original object, and thus does not judge the object, but its properties" (Kudryashov 2010). As Barthes himself asserted, "A whole circuit of computable appearances establishes a quantitative equality between the cost of the ticket and the tears of an actor" (1982,

144). This comment takes us to *correlation*, the key technique for drawing quantitative conclusions through big-data analysis, whether it is the relationship of a ticket price to an actor's tears or between search terms and the spread of flu.

As a sociologist, I am very familiar with both the magic and the danger of the correlation. As a graduate student in the 1970s I can recall turning in punch cards and receiving printouts that appeared magical because they provided me with a series of correlations and confidence levels (measures of statistical significance) that, even armed with my statistics textbook, once took hours to complete. This gave me the first small taste of what a mainframe computer could do, but it was still within the realm of my own computational powers. More of a leap came in the 1980s when, with another colleague, I launched my own major research project based on a national survey of telephone workers in Canada (Mosco and Zureik 1987). For this, the variables multiplied exponentially and so were far beyond manual calculations. But there they were, hundreds of correlations that brought together demographic data on the workforce, everything from age to job category, with attitudes about the work, workmates, surveillance, and the technology that was taking over more and more of the labor process. This appeared to be even more magical because computers were now doing something that I could not even conceivably accomplish on my own. While not exactly the stuff of today's big-data studies, because we relied on a national sample rather than a complete population, it gave me the first feeling of what it was like to review a printout whose numbers appeared to speak to me. But it did not take long, especially because the senior member of our team was an experienced hand, to understand that much of what I was looking at was of our own construction. We set up and defined the variables, creating them out of our own theoretical vision that established what mattered most in our view—the impact of electronic surveillance on job satisfaction. As the popular (and very successful) data analyst Nate Silver explained, "The numbers have no way of speaking for themselves. We speak for them. We imbue them with meaning." Any other view is "badly mistaken" (Asay 2013). That became abundantly clear when I realized that most of what was spoken, whoever was doing the talking, was gibberish or, what Silver and others call *noise* (Silver 2012). That was primarily because most of the correlations we found, however strong, were spurious or irrelevant; that is, the relationship found between two variables either was created by one or more other variables or the correlations themselves were trivial. Rather than find a needle in a haystack, big data, as Nasim Talib (2012) and David Brooks (2013) have perceptively noted, often just leads to more haystacks. As Brooks (2013) put it, "As we acquire more data, we have the ability to find many, many more statistically significant correlations. Most of these correlations are spurious and deceive us when we're trying to understand a situation. Falsity grows exponentially the more data we collect. The haystack gets bigger, but the needle we are looking for is still buried deep inside."

Two of the best means of addressing a mass of correlations, most of which are spurious or trivial, employ strategies that tend to be ignored by big data, particularly by its biggest boosters: theory and history. Theory is the explanatory story that makes the most sense of the data. No story makes perfect sense because the complexity of the data and the world it represents can only be perfectly theorized by an explanation that is so general that it ceases to be useful. Rather, the goal is to find a theory that is both grounded in the data and makes reasonable sense. Some would argue that this requires the inclusion of another concept routinely eschewed by big-data enthusiasts: causality. It makes more sense to test data against a causal model than to expect data, however large and diverse the collection, to speak for itself. In fact, it is doubtful that the latter is possible because, in or outside the cloud, data is not an entity independent of human conception or contamination, but is created through human intelligence and purpose, with all of their limitations and biases. Nevertheless, the choice is not between causal theory or no theory at all. An intermediate position is built upon mutual constitution, which maintains that concepts and data, theory and evidence, construct or mutually constitute one another in an ongoing process of building an argument. Arguments are then tested against new data and alternative arguments.

There are other ways to constitute theory, but the point is that research of any consequence, including studies using large data sets, cannot do away with it. That is because the concepts expressed in the data presume a theoretical perspective. As Brooks explained, "data is never raw; it's always structured according to somebody's predispositions and values. The end result looks disinterested, but, in reality, there are value choices all the way through, from construction to interpretation" (ibid.). It may be ambiguous or clear, weak or strong, but by virtue of our naming what is collected, data does not speak for itself. Rather, we give it voice. Nevertheless, once we do so, data, if it is valuable, contains information that *can* speak to us, not by itself, but through the theoretical frame that helped bring it to life. This is the essence of mutual constitution. But it remains a message slow to get through to big-data enthusiasts. Five years after Chris Anderson proclaimed the end of theory, writers for *Wired* persist, "For science, it makes sense to see big data as a revolution. Algorithms will spot patterns and generate theories, so there's a decreasing need to worry about inventing a hypothesis first and then testing it with a sample of data" (Steadman 2013).

In addition to giving theory insufficient attention, big data tends to neglect context and history. That is partly because big data tends to examine behavior as a set of discrete events or data points. Again, Brooks offered insight: "Human decisions are not discrete events. They are embedded in sequences and contexts. The human brain has evolved to account for this reality. People are really good at telling stories that weave together multiple causes and multiple contexts. Data analysis is pretty bad at narrative and emergent thinking, and it cannot match the explanatory suppleness of even a mediocre novel" (Brooks 2013). The fear is that the seemingly magical combination of large data sets and massive computational power will lead people to replace narrative with correlation and, more importantly, to ask only or mainly those questions that big data can handle. In the real world of history, if not in the metaphorical one of needles and haystacks, context counts. It is not just the place where truth or solutions hide, but context actively gives shape and substance to truth. This conclusion is of more than "academic" value, as a study of communication technology used in urban development demonstrates. There are times when simple email among a group of community-minded individuals is more effective at bringing about the resolution to a complex practical issue than the most sophisticated big-data analysis (Applebaum 2013).

Big data is increasingly used in historical research, to the point that an entire specialty, cliodynamics, is increasingly applied to research like that carried out at the University of Toronto to date medieval manuscripts by analyzing language and phrasing (Tilahun, Feuerverger, and Gervers 2012). The specialty includes its own journal, *Cliodynamics: The Journal of Theoretical and Mathematical History*. The point is not that big data lacks usefulness in historical research, but rather that its use is limited and, unless this is clearly understood, it would be easy to extend the myth-making about the end of the scientific method and the end of theory and apply it to a putative end of history, or at least of historical research, as we have known it. This is especially tempting when the major source of funding for historical research is a government program to make history an arm of the digital humanities. Nor is it just a matter of taking large data sets and putting them in a historical context. Context and history are not discrete containers into which one can objectively insert data. They are fluid and require the experienced judgment of skilled professionals whose subjectivity is an asset that enriches what we know, not a liability to be set aside.

"At its core," according to two of its leading promoters, "big data is about *predictions*" (Mayer-Schönberger and Cukier 2013, 11; italics mine). It is hard to disagree with this conclusion and with the fact that it underscores both the promise and the danger of relying on large data sets. The ability to move beyond the random sample to the billions of data points that Google used to make predictions about the spread of the flu virus is certainly attractive and, for some, compelling and revolutionary. But keep in mind that even this project appears to have had a short predictive shelf life. After a few years of success, the Google model fell flat on its face in the 2012–2013 flu season, grossly overestimating the number of cases. It is hard to say precisely why this happened, but analysts point to the expansion of news-media coverage of the virus's spread in December and January, which led to far more Google searches using flu-related search terms than the company's algorithm expected. In addition, the spike in coverage took place during the holidays, when people have more time for both old and new media. It appears that people were searching more not because they had flu symptoms, but because the media stepped up its flu coverage at a time when people were paying more attention to media. Whatever the cause, the damage was done. As Google wiped the egg from its corporate face, it promised to improve its algorithm to make better predictions in the future (Butler 2013; Poe 2013). That a similar model was used for stock-market forecasting should cause concern about the consequences of overconfidence in big data for the economy (Waters 2013b). Nevertheless, economists are confident, to the point of exuberance, that big data will transform research and policy making (Einav and Levin 2013). One of the reasons for this enthusiasm is the potential analysts anticipate for using big data to better manage temporary, low-wage labor. As one report summed up, "It is rearranging how we allocate work—maybe to a state of permanent, temporary work, for the mostly nontechnical ranks of the work force" (Hardy 2013c).

The cloud and big data come with the vision of perfecting our knowledge of the world if we can collect more information, improve the sifting for correlations, and come up with just the right refinements in models and algorithms. But it may be that the world is so complex that the lofty aspirations of big-data enthusiasts are out of reach. Perhaps it would be better to at least supplement big-data studies with old-fashioned depth interviews on a carefully selected sample. But diversifying methods is possible only when analysts approach the problem with open minds and the skill to carry out research using multiple approaches, rather than with the view that we have discovered the key to a revolutionary transformation in how we acquire knowledge.

Given his considerable success in forecasting election results, one would not expect Nate Silver to take a critical view of big data. However, this is precisely the position he supports in all of his writing, but especially in *The Signal and the Noise* (2012), a carefully written overview of the potential and the problems of large-scale statistical analysis and prediction. For Silver, devotion to the statistical techniques and values of Bayesian analysis means committing to probabilities over certainties and recognizing that all research is infused with biases that we can recognize, if not eliminate, and then account for them. Assume, he maintains, that the complexity of the world puts certainty out of reach and one is likely to do a better job of approximating an accurate conclusion and make reasonable, if not always accurate, predictions. It is not the size of the data set, but, as has been the case for as long as people have carried out social research, the skill and humility of the researcher that most often determine success.

A good example of this point arose in 2013 when a doctoral student uncovered significant errors in an academic paper that has been used by government policy makers and corporate decision makers to support strong economic-austerity measures by public authorities around the world. The article "Growth in a Time of Debt" drew on several large data sets to ostensibly demonstrate that when the ratio of government debt to gross domestic product (GDP) exceeds 90 percent, the median rate of economic growth drops by 1 percent and the average growth rate by considerably more. The 90 percent threshold applied to both developed and emerging economies (Reinhart and Rogoff 2010). If one can speak of an academic finding going viral, this paper is a prime case in point. The authors, one an economist with the National Bureau of Economic Research in Washington, D.C., and the other at Harvard, achieved academic rock star status, including a lengthy *New York Times* profile with the breathless headline, "They Did Their Homework (800 Years of It)" (Rampell 2010). It was written and talked about in almost every major media outlet.[5] Another academic rock star, the historian Niall Ferguson, referred to it as "the law of finance" (Konczai 2013). More importantly, policy makers used the paper to promote rigid austerity measures because it appeared to demonstrate that cutting government spending would reverse economic decline and spur growth. This was a significant turn because, from the 1930s on, governments more or less believed that public spending, especially on infrastructure and public works, would spur growth, even if it meant taking on debt. The new research demonstrated something fundamentally different: once government debt reached the magic ratio of 90 percent of GDP, the economy shows sharply slower growth rates.

Governments, corporations, and conservative think tanks jumped on the findings to support, implement, and justify cuts in government spending even as their economies suffered from what some believed was inadequate spending. Even when governments continued to experience economic recession, double-dip and even triple-dip, their leaders held fast to the magic formula. Then in 2013, Thomas Herndon, a doctoral student at the University of Massachusetts who had not yet begun work on his own dissertation found significant errors in the original article's data, thereby calling into question its central findings. As a commentator described, "One of the core empirical points providing the intellectual foundation for the global move to austerity in the early 2010s was based on someone accidentally not updating a row formula in Excel" (Wise 2013). The student was simply trying to replicate the original results for an econometrics project and could not do so with publicly available documents, so he contacted the authors and asked for their spreadsheets, which they provided. He quickly spotted errors in data reporting on national growth rates and debt levels and published the results (Herndon, Ash, and Pollin 2013). Eventually the authors of the original piece admitted to the errors, but stood their ground on austerity policy.

As one might expect, the debate rages, with most governments continuing to practice austerity even as they change their underlying justification (Vina and Kennedy 2013). Nevertheless, the implications for big data are significant. Before the errors were detected, critics such as Nobel laureate Paul Krugman raised a concern familiar to big-data specialists. The Reinhart and Rogoff paper, Krugman complained, uses big data to draw conclusions based on correlations, not on causality: "All it does is look at a correlation between debt levels and growth. And since debt levels are not sharp extreme events, there's no good reason to believe that they're identifying a causal relationship. In fact, the case they highlight—the United States—practically screams spurious correlation: the years of high debt were also the years immediately following WWII, when the big thing happening in the economy was postwar demobilization, which naturally implied slower growth: Rosie the Riveter was going back to being a housewife" (Krugman 2010). In addition to identifying the limitations of correlational analysis, the case reveals that, by its nature, big data can create big problems. First, errors in entering data in key cells can create significant changes throughout the analysis, amplifying the consequences of the original errors. In this case, errors led to a powerful finding congenial to policy makers and corporate leaders predisposed to austerity, which turned out to be, at the very least, grossly exaggerated. Second, the size of the data sets makes it difficult for peer and other reviewers to catch errors. It is not common for reviewers to have access to original data inputs, and certainly not in the case of data sets with multiple variables spanning numerous nations and time periods. In this case, if it were not for the work of a highly motivated doctoral student, it is unlikely that the errors would have been caught, and the paper would have retained its stature as the intellectual cornerstone for pro-austerity policies. Big data can contain and mask big errors with big consequences. As one business educator concluded, "Don't get me wrong: Data is critical. But history suggests that it plays tricks on our ability to objectively understand all of the variables that are at play in the world. So be careful: Although many professionals tell you that the data is only one of many decision points, I have found that too many people rely too heavily on its information. But as we have seen, the data can lie!" (Langer 2013).

Cloud Culture

The technical criticisms directed at big data's singular reliance on quantification and correlation, and its neglect of theory, history, and context, can help to improve the approach, and perhaps research in general—certainly more than the all-too-common attempts to fetishize big data. But big data is more than just a methodological tool. It promotes a very specific way of knowing that, when connected to the global expansion of cloud computing, has significant implications. Specifically, cloud computing provides a powerful technological grounding to support big data's *digital positivism* or the specific belief that the data, suitably circumscribed by quantity, correlation, and algorithm, will, in fact, speak to us. The ability to process billions of data points in the cloud, in the time that it takes to read this sentence, helped to legitimize Google's flu-virus project, as it does so many other big-data projects. The cloud may be central to a myth but, in this as in so many other cases, myths matter. It is therefore important to critique the cloud as a cultural force because it is not just a method; it is a complete way of knowing that, if left without serious critical reflection, will crowd out other legitimate paths to understanding.

The cloud is an enormously powerful metaphor, arguably the most important developed in the short history of the IT world. As such, its significance far outweighs the accurate but banal roots of the term in the cloud network diagrams produced by telecommunications specialists. Naming it the cloud taps into a rich literary and discursive history that terms like cyberspace, Internet, and even the web fail to match. By its nature, culture resists essentialisms of all types, including the tendency in the digital world, now embodied in cloud computing, to reduce the cloud to an information repository and the foundation for the digital positivism of big-data analysis. There is more to the metaphor of the cloud than its crudely rendered image in the network diagrams that gave rise to the term *cloud computing*. Contrast this image, which looks as if drawn by a child, with the eerie, cloud-filled painting *The Empire of Light* by the icon of surrealism René Magritte. The painting features the bright blue of a daytime sky filled with puffy white clouds that oversee a row of houses in nighttime darkness. Unlike the cloud-computing diagram, which uses the image of the cloud to naturalize the technology, Magritte's jarring clash of row houses in darkness under the bright clouds and blue sky of daytime suggests that something is seriously awry in the clouds and on the ground.

Clouds are among the most evocative images in the history of culture because they have been a daily part of the lives of everyone who has ever lived. It is no surprise, therefore, that cloud gazing to search for symbols and signs, known as *nephelococcygia*, is an ancient art. Clouds are also richly evocative because they take on an almost infinite variety of designs, providing, for many, an early introduction to form and to what it means to transform one shape into another. The altocumulus fills the sky with giant cotton balls, the cirrocumulus with patches of rice, and the undulatus with celestial ripples of sand. These benign images disappear when an arcus formation signals the leading edge of an oncoming storm or when a tuba shoots out of dark clouds to create a water spout over a body of water (Pretor-Pinney 2011). Clouds are more than cultural evocations because they replenish the resource that is absolutely essential to sustain life, leading sorcerers and scientists over the millennia to apply their particular talents to conjure rain-bearing clouds. In this respect, the cloud is transcendent because it knows all time and all space, and oversees every form of organic life.

It is no wonder that clouds have a rich history in practically all cultures, and the West is certainly no exception. It is the perfect metaphor for today's computing, whose global network of 24/7 data centers linked to telecommunications systems and smart devices also transcends space and time and, just as real clouds produce rain, showers a resource that many consider absolutely essential for today's world: knowledge. Certainly a literalist might point to the vapor in the sky and the giant cement warehouses on earth and declare no connection between the two.[6] But that would miss the rich metaphorical links that give both a touch of the divine. We marvel at clouds in the sky because they are ever present and yet infinitely diverse. They are associated with sublime beneficence for the rain they bring and with sublime terror when they withhold it or bring destruction in the form of lightning, tornados, and floods. Their technological counterparts, the vast data factories in the fields, provide a cloud of knowing, a system of ubiquitous, infinite information that was once reserved for the divine and, since humankind's banishment from paradise, has been denied to all.

Even in their literal differences, the image of the cloud provides a gloss on computing. First, the clouds of vapor in the sky soften the hard-edged data center by giving cloud computing an ethereal quality. The cloud is the place of no place; the home of data stored and processed everywhere and nowhere. Moreover, the image of the cloud naturalizes computing, covering it with the aura of an organic process that transcends, to a degree, the physical presence of the data center as a blot on the landscape and an energy hog. Admittedly, there are dark clouds that can cause damage and we often wish the clouds would disperse to reveal the cherished blue sky. But we also know that these are all natural processes, part of the eternal cycle of nature, whose extension to the cloud makes computing appear natural as well. It is rare for clouds to inspire significant reprobation. Rather, there is a Cloud Appreciation Society, and, for those who prefer clouds to birds, a *Cloud Collectors Handbook* that enables people to chart and chronicle the varieties of clouds they have observed. Clouds are embraced by romantic poets like Shelley and Wordsworth for giving life, for contributing to nature's rhythmic cycles, and for pointing the way to the sublime visions that serve up a lifetime of rewards. What's not to like about the cloud?

There is more to the metaphor of the cloud than capturing the sublimity of cloud computing. In its rich history, the metaphor contains a critique that challenges utopian visions finding transcendence, if not the divine, in new technology. Considering its ubiquitous presence and persistence throughout time, it is no surprise to find the cloud in many expressions of the human imagination. The written word, music, and the visual arts would be much poorer without the metaphorical cloud. From the broad sweep of the cloud in culture, I have chosen three exemplars from vastly different periods in Western society to document antimonies between the metaphor and the information technology that would adopt it. It begins with *The Clouds*, a comedy written by Aristophanes that satirized intellectual life in fifth-century BC Greece. Next, we move to the fourteenth century AD and *The Cloud of Unknowing*, a spiritual guide to life written by an older monk to provide advice to a young man who has recently joined the monastery. Finally, I take up David Mitchell's masterful contemporary novel *Cloud Atlas*, which tells six interconnected stories that span human history across the world.

There are many other examples from the cultural history of the cloud that could have served as well. Clouds fill the natural and mythic imagery of Homer's *Iliad*, suggesting the duality of nature's pastoral beauty and the gods' interest in the dark clouds of war. Giotto's thirteenth-century fresco in the Basilica of Saint Francis of Assisi contains a devil hidden in the clouds, depicting the scene on earth and in heaven at the time of the saint's death. For the great artist, even a setting of celestial majesty includes a nod to the Prince of Darkness. The award-winning writer Annie Proulx titled her 2011 evocative "memoir of place" *Bird Cloud* because, on her first visit to the vast Wyoming wetland and prairie that would become her home, a bird-shaped cloud greeted her in the sky at dusk. For the writer, it was a sign to settle there and an intimation of the rich and seemingly ever-present bird life in the area. There are many other potential examples, and some will make a brief appearance, but the three I have chosen enjoy the advantage of covering a significant swathe of Western history, represent three different forms of the written word, and, more importantly, speak evocatively, if metaphorically, about the deeper significance and threats represented by cloud computing and big data. Others more expert than I can surely think of examples from music and the arts, and from outside the world of the Western humanities.[7]

The Wisdom of the Clouds

Even though it was panned by critics and forced into rewrites when first performed in 423 BC, it is hard to overestimate the importance of Aristophanes's *The Clouds* for literature, for the history of ideas, and for today's debates about what knowledge means in an information society. After 2,500 years, it remains a model for what Eve Smith calls "comedy as social conscience" (Smith 2013). Remarkably, the play accomplishes all of this through a satire that lampoons Socrates, one of the most venerated thinkers in the history of the world and, in the minds of some, a martyr to his beliefs. The plot centers on Strepsiades, a once-prosperous man now saddled with debts, who plans to get out from under them by sending his slacker son Pheidippides to the Thinkery, the fictitious school established by Socrates that teaches how to win an argument no matter how weak your position. Or as Strepsiades describes it to his son, "There they prove that we are coals enclosed on all sides under a vast snuffer, which is the sky. If well paid, these men also teach one how to gain lawsuits, whether they be just or not." The play turns the great philosopher into a Dale Carnegie, whose classic book on public relations, *How to Win Friends and Influence People*, became a marketing bible on publication in 1936. The Clouds is the name for the play's chorus, which rises out of the oceans to live in the heavens, surveying the world with a panoptic gaze and, when properly summoned, share its deep knowledge and clever rhetoric with earthly mortals. When Strepsiades's son proves more slacker than geek, Strepsiades decides to enroll himself in the Thinkery after consulting a student at the school who boasts about the research led by Socrates, including "How many times the length of its legs does a flea jump," which led to a new unit of measurement, the flea foot; the source of a gnat's buzz: its trumpet-shaped anus; and the sophisticated use of compasses to defeat a lizard that interrupted a "sublime thought" of the great philosopher who gazes up to the heavens just in time to receive one of the lizard's not-so-sublime droppings. Is this science or useless trivia? Whatever the answer, and it is clear where the playwright stands, the debate certainly resonates in a world characterized by an apparent glut of information (Andrejevic 2013).

Rather than flee the seemingly crazed Thinkery, Strepsiades is more convinced than ever that Socrates can rescue him, although it is unclear whether this is because he believes Socrates is a great thinker or such a masterful con man that he can convince people to praise his trivial research. It does not matter to the would-be student because he simply needs the rhetorical skill to win over debt-holders. At their first meeting Strepsiades meets Socrates, who summons the Clouds for counsel with sacrificial offerings and his signature oratorical skill: "Whether you be resting on the sacred summits of Olympus, crowned with hoar-frost, or tarrying in the gardens of Ocean, your father, forming sacred choruses with the Nymphs; whether you be gathering the waves of the Nile in golden vases or dwelling in the Maeotic marsh or on the snowy rocks of Mimas, hearken to my prayer and accept my offering." The summons is successful and the Cloud chorus immediately reveals its sardonic character by greeting Socrates as the "great high-priest of subtle nonsense." Chiding the philosopher for putting rhetoric ahead of knowledge, the chorus demonstrates its own rhetorical skill, promising the desperate Strepsiades, "Clients will be everlastingly besieging your door in crowds, burning to get at you, to explain their business to you and to consult you about their suits, which, in return for your ability, will bring you in great sums." Unfortunately for him, Strepsiades proves to be a poor student. Perhaps his age has given him too much experience, wisdom, and character to accept an education that values trivia and rhetoric. Or perhaps he is just not suited to the esoteric methods Socrates applies.

Ordered to a couch and covered in a blanket to encourage self-reflection, the bored old man instead decides to masturbate. Having failed to learn from Socrates, Strepsiades returns to his son, who, perhaps too young to care about whether he is offered wisdom or trivia, knowledge or rhetoric, agrees this time to be a model student. Socrates steps aside and instruction is taken over by two figures: one who stresses creating arguments based on knowledge, the other on manipulating people with rhetoric. The latter wins and, armed with the skills of a sharp talker, Pheidippides saves the day for his father by dismissing with his now-dazzling rhetoric those to whom his dad owes money. Unfortunately for Strepsiades, Socratic education makes his son arrogant to the point of beating his father and threatening his mother. He even manages to mount a convincing defense of his violence, what for Aristophanes is the true test of his successful transformation under the great philosopher. This leaves Dad to moan, "Oh! what madness! I had lost my reason when I threw over the gods through Socrates' seductive phrases." The Cloud chorus has little sympathy for Strepsiades: "Here is a perverse old man, who wants to cheat his creditors; but some mishap, which will speedily punish this rogue for his shameful schemings, cannot fail to overtake him from today. For a long time he has been burning to have his son know how to fight against all justice and right and to gain even the most iniquitous causes against his adversaries every one. I think this wish is going to be fulfilled. But mayhap, mayhap, will he soon wish his son were dumb rather!" The play ends with the old man climbing to the roof of the Thinkery to rip it apart and burn it down, getting in one last jab at the great philosopher. When someone demands to know what Strepsiades is up to, he answers, Socratically, "I am entering on a subtle argument with the beams of the house."

The Clouds is nearly 2,500 years old yet remains both hilarious and remarkably modern. When the Cloud chorus steps out of its role as a celestial source of wisdom to plead with the audience to "like" this new version of a play that first opened to weak reviews and then returns to character, one cannot help but think of the narrators in Thornton Wilder's *Our Town* and *The Skin of Our Teeth*, who move effortlessly through dramatic time and space. But for our purposes *The Clouds* speaks most powerfully across two and a half millennia to a world of new clouds that would also revise the meaning of knowledge. Consider their first words in response to Socrates's summons: "Eternal Clouds, let us appear; let us arise from the roaring depths of Ocean, our father; let us fly towards the lofty mountains, spread our damp wings over their forest-laden summits, whence we will dominate the distant valleys, the harvest fed by the sacred earth, the murmur of the divine streams and the resounding waves of the sea, which the unwearying orb lights up with its glittering beams. But let us shake off the rainy fogs, which hide our immortal beauty and sweep the earth from afar with our gaze." Aristophanes's metaphor of the chorus rising out of the oceans to become cloud-filled sky is appropriate to the modern cloud because it offers a way of envisioning through discourse the panoptic knowledge that is both information and means of surveillance looking out on the world and intervening to modify thought and behavior. Aristophanes sends a warning flare across the bow of cloud computing. There is no separating knowledge from power, ubiquitous information from ubiquitous surveillance.

For *The Clouds*, the key ontological tension is not between knowledge and data, but rather between reason and rhetoric. They are viewed as different because reason, what Aristophanes calls in the play "just discourse," advances, as its character states, "by presenting what is true." Rhetoric, on the other hand, described without subtlety as "unjust discourse," is a spin doctor, twisting the truth with skillfully constructed fabrications that carry the day. The Cloud chorus, it turns out, is of two minds, at first appearing to approve of the outcome, but later admitting that rhetoric was only permitted to win in order to teach Strepsiades a lesson: those seeking a shortcut to success will themselves be cut short. Here Aristophanes warns against the seductive power of dazzling language masquerading as the wisdom of the clouds. There is a fine line between reason and rhetoric, truth and spin, knowledge and publicity. The way of knowing established 2,500 years ago comes not in the form of the philosopher king—such a figure was just a Platonic aspiration. Rather it is the philosopher-trickster, the intellectual–spin doctor who dominates with knowledge and rhetoric both mutually constituting and mutually contaminating. In the Western way of knowing, there is no pure truth stored and processed in the cloud; there is just the ongoing struggle between reason and rhetoric, something that the contemporary philosopher-trickster Bruno Latour recognizes in his restaging of the debates between Socrates and the Sophists in the masterful *Pandora's Hope* (1999).

Before leaving the world of Aristophanes's Athens for a medieval monastery and *The Cloud of Unknowing*, it is worth noting two additional telling points of recognition. Today there is a great deal of attention paid to the myth of youth and new technology, which is made to mock and shame older men and women who are caricatured as laughably unskilled in the world of information technology. Instead, it is the young, unburdened by the weight of years, who are naturally adept at mastering smart devices and, unlike their elders, appreciate the wisdom of the cloud. I have elsewhere described this worship of youth in the history of technology, from stories of heroic young telegraph key operators through tales of the amateur radio boys whose bravery saved the day for sailors at sea and others in distress, to the garage-shop wizards of cyberspace who make their first billion before thirty and, as in the film *War Games*, save the world from nuclear holocaust (Mosco 2004). For those who buy into all or part of this myth, Aristophanes has a different tale to tell. Although no one is spared his satirical darts, the playwright saves some of his sharpest barbs for the young Pheidippides, who is transformed from a slacker, too lazy to help his family by attending the Thinkery, to a button-downed geek and slippery con artist. Sure, his father is no prize either, but at least Dad comes around to understand just how foolish he was. Armed with his new powers, Pheidippides is ready to take on the world to the point of justifying assaults on his parents: "How pleasant it is to know these clever new inventions and to be able to defy the established laws! When I thought only about horses, I was not able to string three words together without a mistake, but now that the master has altered and improved me and that I live in this world of subtle thought, of reasoning and of meditation, I count on being able to prove satisfactorily that I have done well to thrash my father." Perhaps, the play suggests, wisdom is wasted on the young. Finally, there is the Thinkery, a misnomer if there ever was one, a place of rank positivism (what is the relationship between the length of a flea's leg and its capacity to jump?) and rhetorical gobbledygook. Just because an institution bears the name of thought does not guarantee the delivery of wisdom. Two and a half millennia later, it is worth reminding ourselves that neither does the terabyte capacity of a data center.

Clouds Get in Our Way

Fourteenth-century residents of the British Isles lived in fear of the black shilling. This is a reference to the dark circular swelling that appeared in the armpit or groin signaling the presence of the bubonic plague and the likelihood that death was near. In the latter part of that century, half the population of England disappeared following the arrival of the circular disk, a stark reminder that the late medieval period meant far more than lords and ladies. As if the Black Plague were not enough, the country was in a constant state of war with France. In fact, the so-called Hundred Years' War lasted for more than a century. Small wonder that when a new poll tax was imposed on the peasantry, it responded with a social upheaval that swept through several countries and terrified the authorities. Out of this dark and tumultuous setting, an anonymous religious man (one suspects he was a priest or monk) produced a guide for a young monastery initiate called *The Cloud of Unknowing* (Anonymous 2009).

It was not unusual to find monasteries in pre-Reformation England, including several committed to a mysticism we tend to associate today with Eastern religious traditions like Buddhism. Out of this English monastic tradition and the upheavals of the time came the work of Walter Hilton, Julian of Norwich, and the anonymous author of a manuscript written in the colloquial Middle English of the time; that work reveals a way of knowing and a metaphor for the cloud that provides a distinct alternative to the digital positivism of big data and cloud computing. Their counterparts in continental Europe included a set of remarkable women, such as Gertrude the Great, Catherine of Siena, and Marguerite Porete. As cloud computing's way of knowing crowds out others and, indeed, takes on the characteristics of a singularity, or at least of the hegemonic discourse of digital positivism, it is essential to recall alternatives—at the very least, to consider what is being lost and to more fully comprehend the broader significance of today's cloud. For the author of *The Cloud of Unknowing*, that cloud is a metaphor for the everyday bits of data and experience that make it difficult to achieve genuine wisdom and for oneness with God. Such achievements are possible only by setting aside life's banalities and, through contemplation and meditation, concentrating the mind and spirit on the light beyond the cloud.

There is no masking the religious nature of *The Cloud of Unknowing*. Its purpose is to teach a young monk and the wider readership of the time how to reach God. Although it might appear unusual to those unfamiliar with the literature on the culture of information technology, as Franklin (2012) argues, "analogies with divine bodies persist with surprising regularity in analyses of digital technology" (445). Kevin Kelly, cofounder and former executive editor of *Wired* magazine, was not the first, or the last, when he declared in 2002 that "God is the Machine" in an article exploring "the transcendent power of digital computation" (2002). The emergence of the Internet sent gurus in search of its sublime origins and several, including former vice president Al Gore, the novelist Tom Wolfe, and web authorities like Erik Davis (1998) and Mark Dery (1996), found it in the work of the Jesuit priest Pierre Teilhard de Chardin. The United Nations sponsored a conference on his work and, in a characteristic burst of gushing enthusiasm, *Wired* magazine proclaimed that the Jesuit priest "saw the Net coming more than half a century before it arrived" (Kreisberg 1995). Teilhard's work remains popular today, particularly for his core concept of the *noosphere*, which he thought of as the mental space surrounding the earth in an atmosphere of thought (*noos* in ancient Greek means mind), and which has even received a contemporary spelling as the knowosphere (Revken 2012).

The Jesuit priest's work appeals to a sublime vision of transcendence through knowledge. Specifically, as Teilhard describes it in his major work *The Phenomenon of Man* (1961), in addition to the atmosphere surrounding our earth and making life as we know it possible, we are also encircled by a noosphere or sphere of thought that grows thicker and more powerful with the world's accelerating production of information. As the biologist and anthropologist David Sloan Wilson described, "As a new evolutionary process, however, our origin was almost as momentous as the origin of life. Teilhard called the human-created world the noosphere, which slowly spread like a skin over the planet, like the biological skin (the biosphere) that preceded it. He imagined 'grains of thought' coalescing at ever-larger scales until they became a single global consciousness that he called the Omega Point" (Revken 2012). For some early and current cyber-enthusiasts, Teilhard's work reaffirmed their commitment to progress through knowledge, to a vision of evolution that extended beyond Darwin to the realm of pure thought, and to their belief that the information age was more than a convenient marker for the latest step from the agricultural and industrial stages of human development. In their view, it was a watershed in human, organic, and cosmic evolution. More than a new means of production, the computer and other information technologies were keys to a posthuman world. Ours is not just an Age; it is a Mission.

Teilhard's popularity is both understandable and puzzling. One can certainly see the attraction to someone who believes with religious zeal that information technology is the key to progress. It is all the more significant that his major work appeared in the 1930s and '40s, well before the personal computer and the Internet.[8] Nevertheless, the Jesuit priest was steeped in controversy that remains today. His work as an archeologist was questioned as he was either a perpetrator or a victim of the hoax discovery of the Piltdown Man, one of many fraudulent "missing links" that appeared in the twentieth century. Moreover, his writing got him into continuous hot water with religious authorities who wondered what the noosphere, a term they knew to have come from the work of the nineteenth-century Russian scientist Vladimir Vernadsky, had to do with Catholicism or even Christianity. After all, Vernadsky was favored by Stalin, who awarded him the Stalin prize in science in 1943. And yet, Teilhard's work appears to preview so much of what comprises the cornerstone of current myths about the information age and now cloud computing. It speaks to those who see communication visionary Marshall McLuhan's (1989) image of information as the global nervous system of the human race, who view computer guru Ray Kurzweil's conception of a networked world approaching the dream of immortality in what he called the age of spiritual machines, and who see in these machines not just the instruments to create material abundance, but the key to salvation. Teilhard created the spiritual foundation for what might best be called *a cloud of knowing*, something that is conjured with each new IBM commercial hymn to its SmartCloud. Kurzweil inspired a quasi-religious reading of information technology with his arguments for a computerized version of immortality, as science develops the capacity to save the essence of an individual's intelligence and spirit in a storage device. Related to this is his work on the "singularity" or what amounts to a technological superintelligence, which Kurzweil believes is achievable in a few decades. It also bears a striking resemblance to Teilhard's religiously inspired noosphere (Kurzweil 2005).

The Cloud of Unknowing was meant as a spiritual guide to a life that aspires to oneness with God. But it can also be read as a secular text with the supernatural understood as a metaphor for the perfect machine, the perfect algorithm, or the wisdom derived from a rich understanding of knowledge and information made possible by technologies such as cloud computing. To my knowledge no one has addressed *The Cloud of Unknowing* through the lens of information technology. That is understandable because, unlike the clouds of Teilhard's noosphere or Kurzweil's singularity, those featured by the anonymous author of *The Cloud of Unknowing*, although substantially the same in content, are anything but the sublime gateway to cosmic evolution or the key to the age of spiritual machines. The cloud of that anonymous writing is associated with the data, facts, information, and details that comprise life's discursive banalities, what we might call big data stored in the cloud or the haystacks that surround the prized needles that data scientists discover. But for the fourteenth-century teacher, the clouds of information, so attractive today, only get in the way of life's purpose. For that work's author, life's purpose was to discover true knowledge of God; for a secular world it signifies how clouds of information get in the way of truth. For Teilhard, Kurzweil, and any defender of cloud computing and big data, the path to knowledge, if not to wisdom and the singularity, is to create more data, analyze it, and draw conclusions and predictions. For them more data and information lead to more knowledge, better predictions, and a better world.

For our fourteenth-century writer, pursuing the cloud is not the key to wisdom; it gets in the way of wisdom. Instead, he concludes, it is essential to systematically purge the banalities of life, including the many bits of data, information, and knowledge ("all created things, material and spiritual," 19) that literally cloud the truth. Given how difficult it is, even for people of the fourteenth century, to carry out this project, he describes the practices of contemplation and meditation that make it possible to overcome the cloud of unknowing: "Secular or religious, if your mind is inflated by pride or seduced by worldly pleasures, positions, and honors, or if you crave wealth, status, and the flattery of others, our God-given ability to reason is serving evil" (27). To know requires acts of unknowing. It is difficult for the modern mind, which is trained to view more as better, to grasp this perspective. For the secular-minded, the bigger the cloud (the data set or the haystack), the more likely we will solve the world's problems. For those who give support to what Noble (1997) called "the religion of technology," whether this means Kelly seeing God in the machine, Teilhard envisioning a noosphere, or Kurzweil anticipating an age of spiritual machines, the growth of the cloud is an essential part of human destiny, a step in the process of evolution. Given these views and others among technological enthusiasts, the religious nature of *The Cloud of Unknowing* appears to be less problematic than its epistemology or way of knowing by unknowing.

Nevertheless, the revival in the book's popularity and the interest in a range of religious and nonreligious meditation practices suggest that even its epistemology is not so far off the radar of contemporary thinking. The 2009 translation from the Middle English, with a long introductory essay in the edition used for this book, suggests that there is continuing interest in the work. A 1973 edition benefited from the rise of the 1960s counterculture and especially its interest in alternative ways of knowing, a point to which its introduction by the renowned religious scholar Huston Smith alludes. One of the most important novelists of our time, Don DeLillo, makes use of *The Cloud of Unknowing* in two of his best-known works. In 1985's *White Noise*, which traces the spread of a toxic cloud, he alludes to a child as "a cloud of unknowing" (290). Because children do not know death, they are open to more of the world than adults, who presumably see in life its inevitable demise. In the face of the inexplicable impact the "airborne toxic event" has brought to sunsets, people are reduced to a sublime feeling of childlike unknowing: "There is awe, it is all awe, it transcends previous categories of awe, but we don't know whether we are watching in wonder or dread, we don't know what we are watching or what it means, we don't know whether it is permanent, a level of experience to which we will gradually adjust, into which our uncertainty will eventually be absorbed, or just some atmospheric weirdness, soon to pass" (324–325). The sunset vision, brought about by technology run amok, brings a strange serenity, despite "men in Mylex suits … gathering their terrible data." DeLillo goes on, "No one plays a radio or speaks in a voice that is much above a whisper. Something golden falls, a softness delivered to the air" (325). More importantly, in his widely recognized masterpiece, 1998's *Underworld*, DeLillo uses the fourteenth-century book as the title and leitmotif for one of the six parts of his epic novel, having the main character Nick Shay describe its contents in the midst of lovemaking with a woman he has recently met. No amount of knowledge, Shay maintains, can comprehend the negation we call God. It is only by engaging in our own forms of unknowing that this begins to be possible. There are numerous other references from cultural icons, including Somerset Maugham (*The*

Razor's Edge), J. D. Salinger (*Franny and Zooey*), and Leonard Cohen (in his song "The Window").

The vision of knowing through unknowing appears in contemporary work that does not mention the book at all. Consider a 2012 essay by the well-known novelist Zadie Smith, in which she compares her broad knowledge of the written word with what is for her a sad lack of musical knowledge (2012). How, she wonders, did she go from an early experience of hating the work of folksinger Joni Mitchell only to come to love it many years later? Smith is baffled because she ultimately came to treat the folksinger's music as a sublime, rapturous experience, saying "it undid me completely," a feeling that she has not experienced in the work of her chosen profession. She concludes that it may have resulted from an experience of unknowing: "a certain kind of ignorance was the condition." Into this pure ignorance, this "non-knowledge," something sublime, perhaps an event, beyond or beneath the threshold of awareness, made the shift in her sensibility possible. She knows and loves Mitchell's work with an unexpected depth because she did not know it, or much of anything about music, before. Unlike her knowledge of fiction, which has accrued from years of incremental additions to her own cloud of consciousness, Smith's knowledge of music followed an epistemological break made possible not by small, consistent additions to a database, but by years of willful unknowing.[9]

It is unlikely that the writer of *The Cloud of Unknowing* will join the ranks of those who, like Teilhard, are hailed for predicting the Internet and now the cloud, well before their time. But perhaps he should, if only because the medieval teacher offered a genuine alternative to what would become a dominant way of knowing in the West that threatens to overwhelm challenges to the cloud, big data, and the digital positivism they promote.

An Atlas of Clouds

Aristophanes's play demonstrates that at one of the earliest points in Western literature, there was already serious concern about the arrogance that comes from excessive confidence in the ability to know the world through a narrow positivism and the ease with which we can make a fetish of information. For the unnamed author of *The Cloud of Unknowing*, the danger lies in being overwhelmed by information, the banal bits of data and discourse that literally cloud our vision and keep us from achieving transcendence. David Mitchell's 2004 novel *Cloud Atlas* begins with a seeming oxymoron and challenges basic conceptions of time, space, and information.

How can one even conceive of an atlas of clouds? After all, an atlas provides a map of relatively stable forms, like land masses and bodies of water. We think of an atlas as mapping the world, the nation, the universe, or perhaps the city, but not the masses of quick-moving vapor that dart about the sky and change shape in the blink of an eye. We do give them names and some people keep a record of common and rare forms, just as do birders. But there are far fewer people who "collect" clouds for a life list than those who go in search of feathered creatures, a testament to just how strange it is to capture clouds, by whatever means. Because of their inherent ambiguity, clouds lend themselves to subjectivity and so we are more likely to use poetry than an atlas to describe them. Of course there is a science of clouds on which many a weather forecast rises and falls. But we have tended to leave their description to those who conjure sublime images, such as William Wordsworth, who writes that after wandering "lonely as a cloud," the viewer comes upon a field of "golden daffodils" that forever appear in the "inward eye" to provide a source of pleasure in "blissful solitude." The key to a lifetime of such joy is, for the poet, to become a cloud. Or one thinks of Percy Bysshe Shelley, who in "The Cloud," a poem that generations of students were made to learn, presents the cloud as the key to a cyclical vision of time in nature. Mitchell's seemingly odd juxtaposition of the two words in his novel's title suggests a challenge: if one sees people not as data points to be captured in a network diagram or in a statistical regression analysis, but rather as ephemeral formations drifting or wandering through time and space, then what would a map of their lives, their cloud atlas, look like?

Mitchell's novel, which won numerous awards and nominations, was also adapted for the screen by the creators of *The Matrix* trilogy, to tepid reviews, perhaps evidence of how difficult it is to turn a novel whose author is primarily taken with the metaphor of the cloud into a film whose creators take their metaphors from the world of data. *Cloud Atlas* features six characters whose lives extend from the nineteenth century to the distant future, crisscrossing the world, but ending where they began, in the islands of the South Pacific. The characters are contained in discrete stories that proceed chronologically, the first five of which are broken off before ending. Each story references the previous one by having a character read about it as, for example, one person happens on the journal produced by the main character in an earlier story. The sixth story is the pivot point, and from that one, each story is completed in reverse chronological order, each tale nested within the others like a set of Russian dolls. Recalling Shelley's classic poem, Mitchell's history is cyclical. The linearity we appear to experience is little more than a comforting mirage.

The cloud and its atlas take three forms in the novel. The first is music, which, alongside poetry, is a familiar type of discourse for presenting clouds. One of the six characters, a young musician named Robert Frobisher, works on "The Cloud Atlas Sextet," which he completes just before committing suicide. The next main character to appear locates a rare recording of the piece in an old music shop. The sextet embodies the unity in difference that the six main characters represent and was produced while the young Frobisher was helping a well-known composer complete the major symphony, appropriately called *Eternal Recurrence*. Contemplating his plan to end his young life, Frobisher is resolute: "My head is a roman candle of invention. Lifetime's music arriving all at once. Boundaries between noise and sound are conventions, I see now. All boundaries are conventions, I see now, national ones too. One may transcend any convention, if only one can first conceive of doing so" (Mitchell 2004, 460). And so Frobisher transcends convention by conceiving an atlas of clouds, in musical form.

Frobisher's sextet is the cloud's way of speaking about the novel's protagonists, but each character is also connected to another, and thereby lives on in the flow of history, through a distinct form of communication, a second manifestation of the cloud. Adam Ewing leaves a personal diary, Luisa Rey is the character in a mystery potboiler, Timothy Cavendish lives on in a film made about his sad life, and Sonmi, a heroic cyborg, emerges in the future as a goddess whose totems are worshipped. The simple Zachry survives through the stories, some true, some not, that his children recall. Finally, as the world stands on the brink of self-inflicted destruction we encounter the orison, a small egg-shaped, holographic communication device that is several generations ahead of today's best-equipped smartphone. Not surprisingly, it appears magical to a community of people with little advanced technology, but none of its godlike powers can prevent the inevitable fall of the civilization that built it.

The third manifestation of the cloud and its atlas is through the metaphor of the soul. When Zachry asks a scientist, one of the few remaining in what was once an advanced civilization, how her people face death without belief in a soul, the scientist replies in Zachry's dialect, "our truth is terrorsome cold." Zachry finds it worse than cold: "Just that once I sorried for her. Souls cross the skies o' time … like clouds crossin' skies o' the world." And later, as Zachry and the scientist hide from attackers, "I watched clouds awobbly from the floor o' that kayak. Souls cross ages like clouds cross skies, an' tho' a cloud's shape nor hue, nor size don't stay the same, it's still a cloud an' so is a soul. Who can say where the cloud's blowed from or the soul'll be 'morrow? Only Sonmi, the east an' the west an' the compass an' the atlas, ya, only the atlas o' clouds" (Mitchell 2004, 308). As mysterious as clouds, the spirits of people live on across time and space and only a goddess or a spiritual atlas can tell us what they are and where they are going.

Like Aristophanes and *The Cloud of Unknowing*'s writer, David Mitchell is a cloud engineer who builds his clouds out of human imagination. Like the engineers who construct the systems that make up today's cloud computing, Mitchell's creations overcome the constraints of time and space to capture essential information and help us to process it in ways that advance our understanding of the human condition. Mitchell's cloud takes numerous forms, but they primarily embody a network of individuals who meet across time through the wide variety of media they leave behind, demonstrating that even as today's digital engineers work on the means of storing consciousness in complex systems, we already store consciousness in the devices that fill *Cloud Atlas*. The journal of a nineteenth-century lawyer, the musical score of an early twentieth-century composer, the detective story that describes the life of a struggling writer, the film that lampoons a British publisher's agent, and on into the future where we find the icon of a cyborg-turned-goddess, the computer device that brings time and space to this present moment, and the oral tales that a simple tribesman leaves his children, all form a cloud of consciousness. There are, of course, differences between the clouds shaped from the literary imagination and those that emerge from the no-less-imaginative worlds of science and technology. Clearly the former builds clouds out of fiction and is assessed for its capacity to create worlds that may or may not bear a close relationship to the world we know, whereas the latter create clouds of data and applications that are judged by their capacity to represent an empirical reality. But it is all too easy to dwell on simple differences; it is more important to consider the subtle ones that shed light on each enterprise, particularly by providing a cultural grounding from which to think about cloud computing.

For Mitchell, the cloud that counts is drawn from a rich pool of subjectivity, including emotional intelligence, that is constantly sensitive to the risk of reducing consciousness, character, spirit, or soul, to a few notable data points. *Cloud Atlas* is not just a story about the seeming universality of people preying on others, mainly for material gain, but also for the sheer pleasure of domination, and it is not just a tale about how people respond, sometimes successfully but often not, through struggle and resistance. If this were all that mattered, we would not need a cloud atlas because all clouds would be the same. Their richness and diversity emerge from the historical context in which each node in the network of clouds is immersed. This is often missed in big-data analysis, which addresses history by examining networks or even networks of networks over time, but does so through a process of extrapolation, typically from quantitative data. It is an approach that has difficulty with those key historical turns or slow, crescive changes that are vitally influential but hard to detect. To correct this problem requires imagination and experience as well as human or machine intelligence.

Making matters more complex are the subjective categories and interpretations of those, including the novelist and the reader, who provide descriptions and assessments. The classic description of the communication process, Shannon and Weaver's mathematical model (1949), distinguishes transmitter from receiver, information source from destination, and signal from noise. When it is relatively easy to identify each of these, primarily when each step in the process is mechanized, the model makes some sense. But for most forms of human communication, the terms are far more ambiguous than it might at first appear. "Boundaries between noise and sound are conventions," declares Frobisher in Mitchell's novel, and all conventions can and should be transcended. As Nate Silver (2012), one of big data's best-known champions, understands, one cannot simply announce a distinction between signal and noise because they are both ambiguous and relative to the subjective expectations of those connected to the communication network. Just as modern physics challenges the existence of an independent observer operating outside the system under study, meaning that relativity is universal, no one, neither the novelist nor the data analyst, resides outside the social network of human actors. Information sources can also be destinations, transmitters can simultaneously receive, and what is noise for some is sweet music or effective communication for others. Moreover, writers and researchers are also communicators with stakes in the objects under their particular microscopes.

Finally, there is the medium of interpretation itself, demonstrated by the stark difference between *Cloud Atlas* the novel and *Cloud Atlas* the film. One does not have to travel as far down the deterministic road as McLuhan did to agree that the medium, whether it is a novel, film, or research report, has an impact on the message communicated. The novel creates room for complexity, nuance, and the reader's imagination that film, however visually stunning, is more challenged to replicate. The research report provides a concise snapshot of enormous quantities of data that neither the novel nor the film can match. But in doing so, the report makes assumptions about definitions and choices and, more often than not, pays the price for its concision by repressing the complexity and subjectivity of the objects under study. Nor does the report take into account the complexity of its formation—specifically how, as the science scholar Bruno Latour (2009) has demonstrated, the scientific process makes its way to completion through multiple modes of expression and representation.

At the very least, Mitchell's atlas of clouds reminds us that there are legitimate alternative ways of knowing and of communicating knowledge alongside those enshrined in clouds of big data accessed through digital positivism. However, the latter is increasingly crowding out the former as advances in computational capability and data analysis are applied to more of what used to be the humanities and the social sciences. The spread of the digital humanities, their access to funding, and their support from university leaders who desperately need the resources that big data in the humanities can attract make it more difficult for those who defend the kind of detailed, qualitative understandings that humanities scholars have deployed for centuries.

Coda: Clouds Are in the Air

The cloud metaphor has always played a role in our literary and artistic traditions. But I cannot help but think that this is a time when the image of the cloud holds a particularly important cultural prominence. Perhaps it is the debate over climate change. After all, cloud cover is a major uncertainty in forecasting future climate. Perhaps it is the media's fascination with weather coverage, especially when natural disaster strikes. It may also have to do with growing awareness of cloud computing. That the metaphorical cloud, as well as the literal one, is in the air was evident on a 2012 trip to New York City where, on a visit to the Metropolitan Museum of Art, I observed a modern classic of cloud culture and one aspiring to join that category. The first was an exhibition of Andy Warhol's *Silver Clouds*, comprising a room full of helium-filled metal "pillows" floating gently, like fair-weather clouds on a spring day. Warhol began work on his clouds after the scientist he worked with, Billy Klüver of Bell Labs, convinced Warhol that his original idea, floating lightbulbs, would not work. Rather than drop the project, Warhol reportedly responded immediately with, "Let's make clouds" ("The Warhol: Silver Clouds" 2010). The result was one of the great modern collaborations between an artist and an engineer, a work of art whose pieces float through a room and gently bump up against one another and their observers. The metallic exterior creates an initial surprise because metal objects are not supposed to float on air. This feeling quickly gives way to a sense of random movement that has been captured formally by dance companies after the 1968 success of Merce Cunningham's ensemble dressed in costumes designed by Warhol's artist friend Jasper Johns. But it is also expressed informally, as any observer of a *Silver Cloud* installation notices when normally stationary museum-goers cannot help but dance their way, however awkwardly, around the cloud-filled room.

That same day took me up to the rooftop garden of the Met, where more artistic clouds attracted large crowds. This time it was Tomás Saraceno's installation *Cloud City*, a collection of large, connected modules built with reflective and transparent material that rise from the ground and invite observers to climb among them.[10] The sight of groups of us climbing through a network of clouds, reflecting our images many times over, as we rose above the city, was beautiful, particularly because we were surrounded by the city's buildings and by Central Park, but also frightening, because the network of people nested in reflective and transparent surfaces created the sensation of life inside an information-processing device. But that may have been only because I have been thinking a lot about another type of cloud.

Cloud computing itself is becoming the object of conscious artistic expression, most notably in the *Clouding Green* collection created by Tamiko Thiel (2012), one of a remarkable group of contemporary artists who give life to the art-science movement. With degrees in product design engineering (Stanford) and mechanical engineering (MIT), Thiel works on multi-dimensional, augmented-reality projects that create dramatic narratives of social and cultural significance. *Clouding Green* uses technology to present a visual expression of the share of data-center emissions taken up by renewable energy sources. Using the Greenpeace (2012) report "How Clean Is Your Cloud?" she provides a visually stunning presentation of color-coded clouds sweeping across the skies over corporate cloud data centers. In doing so, Thiel builds a bridge across the divide between cloud computing and cloud culture with the goal of creating both art and environmental awareness. In the hands of an artist, clouds of data come alive with the emotional resonance needed to energize an informed response. This convergence of technology, art, and politics renews the hope that dark clouds are not the only ones on our collective horizon.

Notes

Chapter 2

1. For an example of how Apple wielded this power to protect its iTunes service, see Bott 2013.

2. The consequences of a cloud company's bankruptcy can be catastrophic for customers, as some learned when the promising cloud provider Nirvanix disappeared in 2013 (Kepes 2013).

3. One path is to pursue strategic alliances with cloud companies that do not have the burden of legacy systems. In November 2013, HP took this approach by teaming with Salesforce to put dedicated HP computer servers, data storage, and networking into Salesforce's cloud-computing facilities (Kolakowski 2013).

4. On the ideology of "openness" see Morozov 2013a.

5. VMware disrupted the traditional server market by developing software that allows servers to do the work of multiple machines, enabling complex tasks to be shared over several servers.

6. Not known for excessive modesty, Ellison has now become a big cloud booster: "I don't accept the notion I didn't get the cloud. I think I invented it" (Waters 2012).

7. The U.K. is also investing heavily in its capacity to launch cyber-attacks. In fact, in 2013 it became the first nation to formally announce that it was developing an offensive cyberwarfare capability (Fung 2013).

Chapter 3

1. Although this simpler version of myth can be useful; see Landa 2013.

2. At the time of writing, this ad is available to watch at www.youtube.com /watch?v=MaA9l2H8BM8.

3. The quotation appeared in the comments section of a posting of the advertisement on YouTube, which was later taken down. For a time, the video was unavailable online until it reappeared on YouTube. The advertisement was so controversial that it inspired a satire: www.youtube.com/watch ?feature=player_embedded&v=buYxMvqkDfs.

4. Apple has also succeeded at lobbying the federal government. The $2.5 million it spent lobbying Washington, D.C., from 2012 to 2013 paid off when President Obama took the unusual step of overturning a U.S. International Trade Commission patent-infringement ruling against Apple (Kirchgaessner 2013).

5. He is not alone in this view. See Parry 2013.

6. In 2013, an entire school was set up with what appears to be the primary goal of generating enthusiasm for information technology. Draper University of Heroes, based in Silicon Valley and just down the road from Facebook headquarters, teaches aspiring entrepreneurs "the tech world's own brand of magical thinking." Students fork over $9,500 to spend two months chanting under posters of Bill Gates and other IT luminaries, learning a little bit of coding and a lot of ways to worship at the altar of the cloud, big data, and all that makes up IT. According to one description, "it's really an eight-week infomercial for the culture of Silicon Valley. Its goal is to infect students with the exuberance of tech and make them brave enough to leave a traditional career path for a stint in start-up land" (Roose 2013).

Chapter 4

1. Google's Project Loon, which operates through a network of solar-powered balloons to deliver Wi-Fi services to underserved areas, is a small case of a cloud system that actually uses cloud-like objects. Nevertheless, it is, for some, the confusing exception (Meehan 2013).

2. See www.OVH.com.

3. For media scholar Sean Cubitt, "The cloud is not weightless: it is a heavy industry. Add in the metals and plastics, the hydro dams, the thousands of miles of cables, the satellites and their rocket launches, and the millions of tons of electronic gadgets we use to access our movies—and the cloud looks a little less fluffy" (2013).

4. Other considerations, including a business-friendly tax code, enabled the company to pay no federal or state income tax on those earnings. In fact, it received a refund of $429 million (Citizens for Tax Justice 2013).

5. It is also not very comforting to hear Google reject claims to privacy, as when its filing in a privacy case declared that "a person has no legitimate expectation of privacy in information he voluntarily turns over to third parties" (Szoldra 2013).

6. The company is also trying to move up the IT food chain by setting up one of the world's largest cloud-computing research and development centers in Taiwan (*CioL* 2013).

7. Consider a 2013 conference announcement on libraries: "It is predicted that within five years, all library collections, systems and services will be driven into the

cloud. This conference will be an attempt to explore how cloud computing could be applied for library applications" (*Daily Pioneer* 2013).

8. See http://microwork-dev.ucsd.edu/.

Chapter 5

1. https://en.wikipedia.org/wiki/Big_data.

2. Walter Binney left the NSA in 2001 but stayed in contact with NSA employees. He left once the agency started its warrantless wiretap program. Binney explains, "They violated the Constitution setting it up. But they didn't care. They were going to do it anyway, and they were going to crucify anyone who stood in the way. When they started violating the Constitution, I couldn't stay" (Bamford 2012).

3. See, for example, Tilahun, Feuerverger, and Gervers 2012.

4. Not every expert and commentator agrees with the myth. In a 2013 address to a conference session titled "Data Scientist: The Sexiest Job of the 21st Century," the chief technology officer for President Obama's 2012 campaign argued that "data scientist as a profession is largely a fad" (Parry 2013).

5. See www.reinhartandrogoff.com/related-research/growth-in-a-time-of -debt-featured-in.

6. The sight of a data center tempts me to think about another popular Magritte painting, this one of a pipe (*The Treachery of Images* or *Ceci n'est pas une pipe*—This is not a pipe). I would caption the image of the data center's dull banality *Ceci n'est pas un nuage*—This is not a cloud.

7. Frankly, I feel blessed to have received a rich education in the humanities well before the field required the adjective "digital" for its legitimacy and perhaps for its survival.

8. I can recall reading his work for the first time as a university student in the 1960s and feeling the surge of possibility in knowing that by cultivating the mind we would be participating in a global process of advancing the human race closer to its cosmic destiny at the Omega Point.

9. It is only slightly ironic that Joni Mitchell is well known for singing about clouds in the song "Both Sides, Now" and especially for its lyric "But clouds got in my way."

10. www.metmuseum.org/saraceno.

References

Abdul, Salam. 2013. "What John Smith Thinks of Cloud Computing: A Big 'Ol Warehouse." *Cloud Tweaks*. www.cloudtweaks.com/2013/01/what-john-smith -thinks-of-cloud-computing-a-big-ol-warehouse.

Acaroglu, Leyla. 2013. "Where Do Old Cellphones Go to Die?" *New York Times*. www.nytimes.com/2013/05/05/opinion/sunday/where-do-old-cellphones -go-to-die.html.

Anderson, Chris. 2008. "The End of Theory: The Data Deluge Makes the Scientific Method Obsolete." *Wired*. www.wired.com/science/discoveries/magazine /16-07/pb_theory.

Andrejevic, Mark. 2013. *Infoglut: How Too Much Information Is Changing the Way We Think and Know*. New York: Routledge.

Anonymous. 2009. *The Cloud of Unknowing*. Edited and translated by Carmen Acevedo Butcher. Boston: Shambala.

Ante, Spencer. 2012. "IBM and the Cloud: Danger and Opportunity." *Wall Street Journal*. http://blogs.wsj.com/corporate-intelligence/2012/10/17/ibm-and -the-cloud-danger-and-opportunity.

Apple. 2011. "Apple iCloud Commercial." YouTube. www.youtube.com/watch ?v=YWZTMyjmcnU.

———. 2012. "Apple TV Ad iCloud Harmony." YouTube. www.youtube.com/watch ?v=YWZTMyjmcnU.

Applebaum, Alec. 2013. "Techs in the City." *New York Times*. www.nytimes.com /2013/06/02/opinion/sunday/the-limits-of-big-data-in-the-big-city.html.

Asay, Matt. 2013. "Nate Silver Gets Real about Big Data." *ReadWriteEnterprise*. http://readwrite.com/2013/03/29/nate-silver-gets-real-about-big-data.

Babcock, Charles. 2013a. "Amazon Again Beats IBM for CIA Cloud Contract." *InformationWeek*. www.informationweek.com/cloud/infrastructure-as-a-service /amazon-again-beats-ibm-for-cia-cloud-contract/d/d-id/1112211.

———. 2013b. "Amazon, Telcos Will Battle for Cloud Customers." *Information-Week*. www.informationweek.com/cloud-computing/infrastructure/amazon -telcos-will-battle-for-cloud-cust/240150631.

Bachman, Katy. 2013. "Is Facebook About to Run into Privacy Issues Again?" *Adweek*. www.adweek.com/news/technology/facebook-about-run -privacy-issues-again-147491.

Bachner, Jennifer. 2013. *Predictive Policing: Preventing Crime with Data and Analytics*. Washington, DC: IBM Center for the Business of Govern-ment. www.businessofgovernment.org/content/about-center-business -government-connecting-research-practice.

Bamford, James. 2012. "The NSA Is Building the Country's Biggest Spy Center (Watch What You Say)." *Wired*. www.wired.com/threatlevel/2012/03/ff _nsadatacenter/all.

———. 2013. "They Know Much More Than We Think." *New York Review of Books*. www.nybooks.com/articles/archives/2013/aug/15/nsa-they-know -much-more-you-think.

Barr, Alistair. 2013. "Amazon vs. IBM: Big Blue Meets Match in Battle for the Cloud." Reuters Canada. http://ca.reuters.com/article/businessNews /idCABRE96K04B20130721.

Barrett, Brian. 2012. "Should the Internet Be a Utility?" *Gizmodo*. http://gizmodo .com/5972173/should-the-internet-be-a-utility.

Barthes, Roland. 1979. *Mythologies*. Translated by A. Lavers. New York: Hill and Wang.

———. 1982. *A Barthes Reader*. Edited by Susan Sontag. New York: Hill and Wang.

Barton, Mike. 2012. "Greenpeace Cloud Protest: Do Amazon, Microsoft Deserve the Doghouse?" *Wired*. www.wired.com/insights/2012/04/greenpeace -cloud-protest.

Basulto, Dominic. 2013. "Is This the Year Everybody Gets Hacked?" *Washington Post*. www.washingtonpost.com/blogs/innovations/post/is-this-the-year-everybody -gets-hacked/2013/02/21/eeb88fd4-7c2f-11e2-9073-e9dda4ac6a66_blog .html.

Bauman, Zygmunt. 2000. *Liquid Modernity*. Cambridge, UK: Polity.

Beer, David. 2012. "Using Social Media Data Aggregators to Do Social Research." *Sociological Research* Online. www.socresonline.org.uk/17/3/10.html.

Beidel, Eric. 2012. "Flood of Data Puts Air Force's Drone Growth on Hold." *National Defense*. www.nationaldefensemagazine.org/blog/Lists/Posts/Post .aspx?ID=738.

Bernnat, Rainer, Wolfgang Zink, Nicolai Bieber, and Joachim Strach. 2012. "Stan-dardizing the Cloud: A Call to Action." Booz & Co. www.booz.com/media /uploads/BoozCo_Standardizing-the-Cloud.pdf.

Bilton, Nick, and Claire Cain Miller. 2013. "How Pay-per-Gaze Advertising Could Work for Google Glass." *New York Times*. http://bits.blogs.nytimes .com/2013/08/20/google-patents-real-world-pay-per-gaze-advertising.

Bott, Ed. 2013. "How Apple Used Its Money and Muscle to Kill an iTunes Competitor." *ZDNet.* http://anteyekon4myst.sharedby.co/share/eP3mAq.

Bourne, James. 2013. "Cloud Computing Saves Energy on Huge Scale, Says New Study—but How?" *Cloud Tech.* www.cloudcomputing-news.net/news/2013/jun/12/cloud-computing-saves-energy-huge-scale-says-new-study-how.

Boyd, Danah, and Kate Crawford. 2012. "Critical Questions for Big Data." *Information, Communication and Society* 15, no. 5: 662–679.

Bradshaw, Tim. 2012. "Apple: Innovator's Dilemma." *Financial Times.* www.ft.com/intl/cms/s/2/b558911a-4ac7-11e2-9650-00144feab49a.html.

———. 2013. "Apple Says Child Labour Found at Suppliers." *Financial Times.* www.ft.com/intl/cms/s/0/8af2a286-6754-11e2-8b67-00144feab49a.html.

Bradshaw, Tim, and Emily Steel. 2013. "Hacked PCs Falsify Billions of Ad Clicks." *Financial Times.* www.ft.com/intl/cms/s/0/ab60c728-908f-11e2-a456-00144feabdc0.html.

Bradsher, Keith, and David Barboza. 2013. "H.P. Directs Its Supplies in China to Limit Student Labor." *New York Times.* www.nytimes.com/2013/02/08/business/global/hewlett-packard-joins-push-to-limit-use-of-student-labor-in-china.html.

Brannen, Kate. 2013. "Wanted: Geeks to Help Fight Pentagon Cyberwar." *Politico.* www.politico.com/story/2013/01/wanted-geeks-to-help-fight-pentagons-cyberwar-86946.html.

Brian, Matt. 2013. "Thousands of Accounts Found to Host Unsecured Passwords, Photos, and Other Files on Amazon's Cloud." *Verge.* www.theverge.com/2013/3/27/4152964/researcher-exposes-data-businesses-amazon-s3.

Briscoe, Gerard, and Alexandros Marinos. 2009. "Community Cloud Computing." First International Conference on Cloud Computing, Beijing, China. LSE Research Online. http://eprints.lse.ac.uk/26516/1/community_cloud_computing_%28LSERO_version%29.pdf.

Brooks, David. 2013. "What Data Can't Do." *New York Times.* www.nytimes.com/2013/02/19/opinion/brooks-what-data-cant-do.html.

Bryant, Chris. 2013. "European Data Protection under a Cloud." *Financial Times.* www.ft.com/intl/cms/s/0/dbee868a-f43c-11e2-8459-00144feabdc0.html.

Budden, Robert. 2013. "Ads on Facebook Drop after Appearing Next to Offensive Posts." *Financial Times.* www.ft.com/intl/cms/s/0/d1e74ee8-c7ae-11e2-be27-00144feab7de.html.

Bump, Philip. 2013. "Update: Now We Know Why Googling 'Pressure Cookers' Gets a Visit from Cops." *Atlantic Wire.* www.theatlanticwire.com/national/2013/08/government-knocking-doors-because-google-searches/67864.

Bundy, Todd, and Michael Haley. 2012. "China's Cloud Cities." *OSP.* www.ospmag.com/issue/article/Chinas-Cloud-Cities.

Burke, Edmund. 1998. *Philosophical Enquiry into the Origin of Our Ideas of the Sublime and Beautiful.* New York: Penguin (original work published 1756).

Burn-Murdoch, John. 2012. "Big Data: What Is It and How Can It Help?" *Guardian*. www.guardian.co.uk/news/datablog/2012/oct/26/big-data-what-is-it-examples.

Butler, Brandon. 2012a. "Gartner: 1/3 of Consumer Data Will Be Stored in the Cloud by '16." *Network World*. www.networkworld.com/news/2012/062512-gartner-cloud-260450.html.

———. 2012b. "Gartner: Cloud Putting Crimp in Traditional Software, Hardware Sales." *Network World*. www.networkworld.com/news/2012/071312-gartner-cloud-260882.html.

———. 2013a. "Cost Battle: Cloud Computing vs. In-House IT." *Network World*. www.networkworld.com/news/2013/031813-cloud-cost-267615.html.

———. 2013b. "What GE's Cloud Computing Foray Means for Big Data." *Network World*. www.networkworld.com/news/2013/061913-ge-cloud-271011.html.

Butler, Declan. 2013. "When Google Got Flu Wrong." *Nature*. www.nature.com/news/when-google-got-flu-wrong-1.12413.

Calo, Ryan. 2013. "The Catch-22 That Prevents Us from Truly Scrutinizing the Surveillance State." *Atlantic*. www.theatlantic.com/technology/archive/2013/03/the-catch-22-that-prevents-us-from-truly-scrutinizing-the-surveillance-state/273738.

Cassidy, John. 2013. "Bezos and the *Washington Post*: A Skeptical View." *New Yorker*. www.newyorker.com/online/blogs/johncassidy/2013/08/bezos-and-the-washington-post-a-skeptical-view.html.

Castle, Stephen. 2013. "Report of U.S. Spying Angers European Allies." *New York Times*. www.nytimes.com/2013/07/01/world/europe/europeans-angered-by-report-of-us-spying.html.

Center for Energy-Efficient Telecommunications. 2013. *The Power of Wireless Cloud*. Melbourne, Australia: University of Melbourne. www.ceet.unimelb.edu.au/pdfs/ceet_white_paper_wireless_cloud.pdf.

Chappuis, Bertil. 2012. "Cloudpreneurs." *Techonomy*. http://techonomy.com/conf/12-tucson/entrepreneurship-2/cloudpreneurs.

Chatter.com. 2011a. "Halftime Ad 1 with wil.i.am." YouTube. www.youtube.com/watch?v=tdqoQ0zL7GQ.

———. 2011b. "Halftime Ad 2." YouTube. www.youtube.com/watch?v=tcjAD-_H_rk.

Chen, Brian X. 2012. "'The Cloud' Challenges Amazon." *New York Times*. www.nytimes.com/2012/12/27/technology/latest-netflix-disruption-highlights-challenges-of-cloud-computing.html.

Chief Information Officer, Department of Defense. 2012. *Cloud Computing Strategy*. www.defense.gov/news/dodcloudcomputingstrategy.pdf.

Chou, Timothy. 2012. "Marco Polo 2.0: Report from China." *CFO*. www3.cfo.com/article/2012/12/the-cloud_china-cloud-services-companies-strategies.

Chronicle of Higher Education. 2013. "Major Players in the MOOC Universe." http://chronicle.com/article/Major-Players-in-the%20MOOC/138817.

CioL. 2013. "Foxconn Plans to Establish Cloud Computing R&D Center in Southern Taiwan." www.ciol.com/ciol/news/193445/foxconn-plans-establish-cloud-computing-r-d-center-southern-taiwan.

Cisco. 2013. "Cisco Global Cloud Index: Forecast and Methodology, 2012–2017." www.cisco.com/en/US/solutions/collateral/ns341/ns525/ns537/ns705/ns1175/Cloud_Index_White_Paper.pdf.

Citizens for Tax Justice. 2013. "Facebook's Multi-Billion Dollar Tax Break: Executive-Pay Tax Break Slashes Income Taxes on Facebook—and Other Fortune 500 Companies." http://ctj.org/ctjreports/2013/02/facebooks_multi-billion_dollar_tax_break_executive-pay_tax_break_slashes_income_taxes_on_facebook--.php.

Clancy, Heather. 2012. "Greenpeace Re-grades Apple in Green Data Center Report." *ZDNet.* www.zdnet.com/greenpeace-re-grades-apple-in-green-data-center-report-7000000805.

Clark, Jack. 2012a. "Cloud Computing's Utility Future Gets Closer." *ZDNet.* www.zdnet.com/cloud-computings-utility-future-gets-closer-7000007256.

———. 2012b. "How Google Compute Engine Hopes to Sidestep AWS Failures." *ZDNet.* www.zdnet.com/google-compute-engine-hopes-to-sidestep-aws-failures-7000001379.

Clement, Andrew. 2013. "IXmaps—Tracking Your Personal Data through the NSA's Warrantless Wiretapping Sites." Paper presented at the 2013 IEEE International Symposium on Science and Technology, June 27–29, Toronto.

Clifford, Stephanie, and Jessica Silver-Greenberg. 2013. "Retailers Track Employee Thefts in Vast Databases." *New York Times.* www.nytimes.com/2013/04/03/business/retailers-use-databases-to-track-worker-thefts.html.

Cloud Expo. 2013. "Enterprise IT's Two Biggest Game Changers under One Roof—Cloud Computing and Big Data." www.cloudcomputingexpo.com.

Cloud Tweaks. 2012. "Cloud Predictions for the New Year." http://us2.campaign-archive2.com/?u=04809abc68958c8c94da79e96&id=36235497ec&e=0eda32265e.

———. 2013. "Do Cloud Companies Know How to Market Themselves?" http://us2.campaign-archive2.com/?u=04809abc68958c8c94da79e96&id=183a823c77&e=0eda32265e.

Cohen, Julie E. 2013. "What Privacy Is For." *Harvard Law Review* 126: 1904–1933. www.harvardlawreview.org/media/pdf/vol126_cohen.pdf.

Cohen, Reuven. 2012. "How Cloud Computing Helped Obama Win the Presidential Election." *Forbes.* www.forbes.com/sites/reuvencohen/2012/11/15/how-cloud-computing-helped-obama-win-the-presidential-election.

———. 2013. "Cloud Computing at the Hotel California: Check-In and Never Leave!" *Forbes.* www.forbes.com/sites/reuvencohen/2013/05/02/cloud-computing-at-the-hotel-california-check-in-and-never-leave.

Columbus, Louis. 2012a. "Cloud Computing and Enterprise Software Forecast Update, 2012." *Forbes.* www.forbes.com/sites/louiscolumbus/2012/11/08/cloud-computing-and-enterprise-software-forecast-update-2012.

———. 2012b. "Roundup of Cloud Computing Forecasts and Cloud Computing Estimates, 2012." Software Strategies Blog. http://softwarestrategiesblog.com/2012/01/17/roundup-of-cloud-computing-forecasts-and-market-estimates-2012.

Crawford, Susan. 2012. "US Internet Users Pay More for Slower Service." *Bloomberg.* www.bloomberg.com/news/2012-12-27/u-s-internet-users-pay-more-for-slower-service.html.

CRM Software Blog editors. 2011. "6 Reasons Why Salesforce.com Is Worried about Microsoft CRM." CRM Software Blog. www.crmsoftwareblog.com/2011/09/6-reasons-why-salesforce-com-is-worried-about-microsoft-crm.

Crovitz, L. Gordon. 2013. "Silicon Valley's 'Suicide Impulse.'" *Wall Street Journal.* http://online.wsj.com/article/SB10001424127887323539804578266290231304934.html.

Cubitt, Sean. 2013. "How to Weigh a Cloud." *The Conversation.* http://theconversation.com/how-to-weigh-a-cloud-19581.

Cushing, Ellen. 2013. "Amazon Mechanical Turk: The Digital Sweatshop." *UTNE Reader.* www.utne.com/science-technology/amazon-mechanical-turk-zm0z13jfzlin.aspx.

Daily Pioneer. 2013. "Meet on Cloud Computing." http://archive.dailypioneer.com/avenues/127319-meet-on-cloud-computing-.html.

Dalwadi, Manish. 2012. "Enterprise Cloud Computing: The War for Enterprise Software." Center for Digital Strategies, Tuck School of Business at Dartmouth. http://digitalstrategies.tuck.dartmouth.edu/assets/images/Enterprise_Cloud_Final_Manish_Dalwadi.pdf.

Darrow, Barb. 2013. "If PRISM Doesn't Freak You Out about Cloud Computing, Maybe It Should, Says Privacy Expert." *Gigaom.* http://gigaom.com/2013/06/28/if-prism-doesnt-freak-you-out-about-cloud-computing-maybe-it-should-says-privacy-expert.

Data Center Journal. 2013. "Industry Perspective: Energy Efficiency and Renewable Sources for the Data Center." www.datacenterjournal.com/facilities/industry-perspective-energy-efficiency-and-renewable-sources-for-the-data-center.

Davenport, Thomas H., Paul Barth, and Randy Bean. 2012. "How 'Big Data' Is Different." *MIT Sloan Management Review.* http://sloanreview.mit.edu/article/how-big-data-is-different.

Davis, Erik. 1998. *Techgnosis: Myth, Magic and Mysticism in the Age of Information.* New York: Harmony.

Deibert, Ronald J. 2013. *Black Code: Inside the Battle for Cyberspace.* New York: Random House.

Delany, Ella. 2013. "Humanities Studies under Strain around the World." *New York Times*. www.nytimes.com/2013/12/02/us/humanities-studies-under-strain -around-the-globe.html.

DeLillo, Don. 1985. *White Noise*. New York: Viking.

Deloitte. 2009. "Cloud Computing: Forecasting Change." www.deloitte.com/assets /Dcom-Netherlands/Local%20Assets/Documents/EN/Services/Consulting /nl_en_consulting_cloud_computing_security_privacy_and_trust.pdf.

Dembosky, April. 2013a. "Facebook Buys Ad-Serving Platform." *Financial Times*. www.ft.com/intl/cms/s/0/5de42176-81ed-11e2-b050-00144feabdc0.html.

———. 2013b. "Facebook Spending on Lobbying Soars." *Financial Times*. www.ft .com/intl/cms/s/0/cfaf0c78-65b2-11e2-a17b-00144feab49a.html.

Dembosky, April, and James Fontanella-Khan. 2013. "US Tech Groups Criticized for EU Lobbying." *Financial Times*. www.ft.com/intl/cms/s/0/e29a717e -6df0-11e2-983d-00144feab49a.html.

Dery, Mark. 1996. "Industrial Memory." *21c*. www.21cmagazine.com/Mark-Dery -Industrial-Memory.

Digging into Data Challenge. 2011. "ChartEx." www.diggingintodata.org/Home /AwardRecipientsRound22011/tabid/185/Default.aspx.

Dignan, Larry. 2011a. "Analytics in 40 Years: Machines Will Kick Human Managers to the Curb." *ZDNet*. www.zdnet.com/blog/btl/analytics-in -40-years-machines-will-kick-human-managers-to-the-curb/61092.

———. 2011b. "Cloud Computing's Real Creative Destruction May Be the IT Workforce." *ZDNet*. www.zdnet.com/blog/btl/cloud-computings-real -creative-destruction-may-be-the-it-workforce/61581.

Duhigg, Charles, and David Barboza. 2012. "In China, Human Costs Are Built into an iPad." *New York Times*. www.nytimes.com/2012/01/26/business /ieconomy-apples-ipad-and-the-human-costs-for-workers-in-china.html.

Dutta, Soumitra, and Beñat Bilbao-Osorio. 2012. *Global Information Technology Report 2012: Living in a Hyperconnected World*. Geneva: World Economic Forum.

Dyer-Witheford, Nick. 2013. "Red Plenty Platforms." *Culture Machine* 14: 1–27.

Eckel, Erik. 2012. "Why Businesses Shouldn't Trust Apple's Cloud Services." *TechRepublic*. www.techrepublic.com/blog/mac/why-businesses -shouldnt-trust-apples-cloud-services/2262.

Edwards, Jim. 2013. "Liberal Groups Begin Facebook Ad Boycott over Zuckerberg's Big Oil Lobbying." *Business Insider*. www.businessinsider.com /facebook-ad-boycott-over-fwdus-oil-lobbying-2013-5.

Eggers, David. 2013. *The Circle: A Novel*. New York: Knopf.

Einav, Liran, and Jonathan D. Levin. 2013. "The Data Revolution and Economic Analysis." Working Paper 19035, National Bureau of Economic Research, Cambridge, MA. www.nber.org/papers/w19035.

Elowitz, Ben. 2013. "In Media, Big Data Is Booming but Big Results Are Lacking." *All Things D.* http://allthingsd.com/20130520/in-media-big-data-is-booming-but-big-results-are-lacking.

Erl, Thomas, Ricardo Puttini, and Zaigham Mahmood. 2013. *Cloud Computing: Concepts, Technology and Architecture.* Upper Saddle River, NJ: Prentice Hall.

Evans-Pritchard, Ambrose. 2012. "High Tech Expansion Drives China's Second Boom in the Hinterland." *Telegraph.* www.telegraph.co.uk/finance/comment/9701910/Hi-tech-expansion-drives-Chinas-second-boom-in-the-hinterland.html.

Ewing, Jack. 2013. "Amazon's Labor Relations under Scrutiny in Germany." *New York Times.* www.nytimes.com/2013/03/04/business/global/amazons-labor-relations-under-scrutiny-in-germany.html?pagewanted=all&_r=0&gwh=FCF0A5D17B34AF08B45C6563A3889C3E&gwt=pay.

Fingas, Jon. 2013. "Strategy Analytics: iCloud, Dropbox and Amazon Top Cloud Media in the US." *Engadget.* www.engadget.com/2013/03/21/strategy-analytics-cloud-media-market-share.

Finkle, Jim. 2012. "Amazon-Netflix Christmas Outage and the Costly Risks of 'Cloud' Reliance." *Globe and Mail.* www.theglobeandmail.com/report-on-business/international-business/us-business/amazon-netflix-christmas-outage-and-the-costly-risks-of-cloud-reliance/article6736744.

———. 2013. "White House Will Soon Revive Cybersecurity Legislation." *Reuters.* www.reuters.com/article/2013/02/26/us-cybersecurity-obama-idUSBRE91P02120130226.

Fish, Stanley. 2012a. "The Digital Humanities and the Transcending of Morality." *New York Times.* http://opinionator.blogs.nytimes.com/2012/01/09/the-digital-humanities-and-the-transcending-of-mortality.

———. 2012b. "Mind Your P's and B's: The Digital Humanities and Interpretation." *New York Times.* http://opinionator.blogs.nytimes.com/2012/01/23/mind-your-ps-and-bs-the-digital-humanities-and-interpretation.

Fitzpatrick, Katharine. 2011. *Planned Obsolescence: Publishing, Technology, and the Future of the Academy.* New York: New York University Press.

Foley, John. 2012. "10 Developments Show Government Cloud Maturing." *Information Week.* www.informationweek.com/government/cloud-saas/10-developments-show-government-cloud-ma/240002578?itc=edit_in_body_cross.

Fontanella-Kahn, James, and Bede McCarthy. 2013. "Brussels to Soften Data Protection Rules." *Financial Times.* www.ft.com/intl/cms/s/0/dbf20262-8685-11e2-b907-00144feabdc0.html.

Forbes. 2012. "Americans Still Unclear about Cloud Computing." www.forbes.com/sites/thesba/2012/11/13/americans-still-unclear-about-cloud-computing.

Fox, Justin. 2013. "The Web's New Monopolists." *Atlantic.* www.theatlantic.com/magazine/archive/2013/01/the-webs-new-monopolists/309197.

Franck, Lewis. 2013. "4 Non-obvious Costs of Cloud Downtime." *Cloud Tech*. www.cloudcomputing-news.net/blog-hub/2013/feb/05/4-non -obvious-costs-of-cloud-downtime.

Franklin, Seb. 2012. "Cloud Control, or the Network as Medium." *Cultural Politics* 8, no. 3: 443–464.

Freeland, Chrystia. 2013. "When Work and Wages Come Apart." *New York Times*. www.nytimes.com/2013/02/22/us/22iht-letter22.html.

Fung, Brian. 2013. "How Britain's New Cyberarmy Could Reshape the Laws of War." *Washington Post*. www.washingtonpost.com/blogs/the-switch /wp/2013/09/30/how-britains-new-cyberarmy-could-reshape-the-laws-of -war.

Gallagher, Ryan. 2013. "Software That Tracks People on Social Media Created by Defence Firm." *Guardian*. www.guardian.co.uk/world/2013/feb/10 /software-tracks-social-media-defence.

Gallagher, Sean. 2012. "How Team Obama's Tech Efficiency Left Romney IT in the Dust." *Ars Technica*. http://arstechnica.com/information-technology/2012/11 /how-team-obamas-tech-efficiency-left-romney-it-in-dust.

Gangireddy, Geetha. 2012. "Making the Most of Cloud Computing in the Military and Department of Defense." *Blackboard Blogs*. http:// blog.blackboard.com/professional-education/making-the-most-of-cloud -computing-in-the-military-department-of-defense.

Gapper, John. 2013a. "Bosses Are Reining in Staff Because They Can." *Financial Times*. www.ft.com/intl/cms/s/0/90300088-80cf-11e2-9c5b-00144feabdc0 .html.

———. 2013b. "Google Is the General Electric of the 21st Century." *Financial Times*. www.ft.com/intl/cms/s/0/e57abef0-cd0c-11e2-90e8-00144feab7de.html.

Gartner. 2013. "About Gartner." www.gartner.com/technology/about.jsp.

Gates, Bill. 1995. *The Road Ahead*. New York: Viking.

Gerovitch, Slava. 2010. "The Cybernetic Scare and the Origins of the Internet." *Baltic Worlds*. http://balticworlds.com/the-cybernetics-scare -and-the-origins-of-the-internet.

Gillespie, Tarleton. 2013. "Can an Algorithm Be Wrong?" *Limn*. http://limn.it /can-an-algorithm-be-wrong.

Gilmoor, Dan. 2013. "Embrace the Cloud Computing Revolution with Caution." *Guardian*. www.guardian.co.uk/commentisfree/2013/mar/05 /cloud-data-revolution-google-chromebook-pixel.

Ginsberg, Jeremy, Matthew H. Mohebbi, Rajan S. Patel, Lynnette Brammer, Mark S. Smolinski, and Larry Brilliant. 2009. "Detecting Influenza Epidemics Using Search Engine Query Data." *Nature* 457: 1012–1014.

Giridharadas, Anand. 2013a. "Reality Crashes the Technocrats' Party." *New York Times*. www.nytimes.com/2011/03/26/us/26iht-currents26.html.

———. 2013b. "What the Facebook Search Engine Tells Us." *New York Times*. www.nytimes.com/2013/02/23/us/23iht-letter23.html.

Glanz, James. 2012a. "Data Barns in a Farm Town, Gobbling Power and Flexing Muscle." *New York Times*. www.nytimes.com/2012/09/24/technology/data-centers-in-rural-washington-state-gobble-power.html.

———. 2012b. "Power, Pollution, and the Internet." *New York Times*. www.nytimes.com/2012/09/23/technology/data-centers-waste-vast-amounts-of-energy-belying-industry-image.html.

———. 2013. "Landlords Double as Energy Brokers." *New York Times*. www.nytimes.com/2013/05/14/technology/north-jersey-data-center-industry-blurs-utility-real-estate-boundaries.html.

Glanz, James, and Eric Lipton. 2004. *The Rise and Fall of the World Trade Center*. New York: Times Books.

Globe Investor. 2012. "Competition Chatter around U.S. Telcos Gets Louder." www.theglobeandmail.com/globe-investor/news-sources/?date=20121231&archive=rtgam&slug=escenic_6804996.

Glover, Tony. 2013. "Cloudy Outlook for Blue Sky Computing in the Middle East." *National*. www.thenational.ae/business/industry-insights/technology/cloudy-outlook-for-blue-sky-computing-in-the-middle-east.

Gold, Matthew K. 2012. *Debates in the Digital Humanities*. Minneapolis: University of Minnesota Press.

Goldberg, Michael. 2013. "Cloud Computing Experts Detail Big Privacy and Security Risks." *DataInformed*. http://data-informed.com/cloud-computing-experts-detail-big-data-security-and-privacy-risks.

Goldner, Matt. 2010. *Winds of Change: Libraries and Cloud Computing*. Dublin, OH: Online Computer Library Center.

Gonsalves, Antone. 2013. "The Nine Top Threats Facing Cloud Computing." *ReadWriteEnterprise*. http://readwrite.com/2013/03/04/9-top-threats-from-cloud-computing.

Gordon, Michael. 2013. "2 Americans Advised Not to Visit North Korea." *New York Times*. www.nytimes.com/2013/01/04/world/asia/bill-richardson-and-googles-eric-schmidt-are-advised-not-to-visit-north-korea.html.

Gordon, Robert J. 2000. "Does the 'New Economy' Measure Up to the Great Inventions of the Past?" *Journal of Economic Perspectives* 14, no. 4: 49–74.

Greenhouse, Steven. 2013. "Tackling Concerns of Independent Workers." *New York Times*. www.nytimes.com/2013/03/24/business/freelancers-union-tackles-concerns-of-independent-workers.html.

Greenpeace International. 2010. "Making IT Green: Cloud Computing and Its Contribution to Climate Change." www.greenpeace.org/international/Global/international/planet-2/report/2010/3/make-it-green-cloud-computing.pdf.

———. 2011. "How Dirty Is Your Data? A Look at the Energy Choices That Power Cloud Computing." www.greenpeace.org/international/Global/international/publications/climate/2011/Cool%20IT/dirty-data-report-greenpeace.pdf.

————. 2012. "How Clean Is Your Cloud?" www.greenpeace.org/international /Global/international/publications/climate/2012/iCoal/HowCleanisYour Cloud.pdf.

Greenwald, Glenn. 2013. "Liberal Icon Frank Church on the NSA." *Guardian*. www.guardian.co.uk/commentisfree/2013/jun/25/frank-church-liberal-icon.

Gross, Grant. 2013. "Ovum: Big Data Collection Clashing with Privacy Concerns." *InfoWorld*. www.infoworld.com/d/big-data/ovum-big-data-collection -colliding-privacy-concerns-212397.

Groucutt, Peter. 2013. "Cloud Computing Is Becoming a Utility." *Real Business*. http:// realbusiness.co.uk/article/24508-cloud-computing-is-becoming-a-utility-.

Hanna, Sheree. 2013. "Cloud Computing—Where Does Your Data Go When the Service Dies?" *African Business Review*. www.africanbusinessreview.co.za /business_leaders/cloud-computing-where-does-your-data-go-when-the -service-dies.

Hardy, Quentin. 2012a. "Active in Cloud, Amazon Reshapes Computing." *New York Times*. www.nytimes.com/2012/08/28/technology/active-in-cloud-amazon -reshapes-computing.html.

————. 2012b. "Google Apps Challenging Microsoft in Business." *New York Times*. www.nytimes.com/2012/12/26/technology/google-apps-moving-onto -microsofts-business-turf.html.

————. 2012c. "Intel's Schooling from the 'Big Four' Cloud Customers." *New York Times*. http://bits.blogs.nytimes.com/2012/12/05/intels-schooling -from-cloud-customers.

————. 2013a "Amazon Bares Its Computers." *New York Times*. http://bits.blogs .nytimes.com/2013/11/15/amazon-bares-its-computers.

————. 2013b. "Declaring This a Year for Fixing and Rebuilding, H.P. Posts Lower Profit." *New York Times*. www.nytimes.com/2013/02/22/technology/hp -reports-decline-in-revenue-and-profit.html.

————. 2013c. "Elance Pairs Hunt for Temp Work with Cloud Computing." *New York Times*. http://bits.blogs.nytimes.com/2013/09/24/elance -pairs-hunt-for-temp-work-with-cloud-computing.

————. 2013d. "Google: Let a Billion Supercomputers Bloom." *New York Times*. http://bits.blogs.nytimes.com/2013/05/21/google-let-a-billion -supercomputers-bloom.

————. 2013e. "I.B.M. Inflates Its Cloud." *New York Times*. http://bits.blogs .nytimes.com/2013/06/18/i-b-m-inflates-its-cloud.

————. 2013f. "Intel Tries to Secure Its Footing beyond PCs." *New York Times*. www.nytimes.com/2013/04/15/technology/intel-tries-to-find-a-foothold -beyond-pcs.html?pagewanted=all&_r=0.

————. 2013g. "Intel's Extensive Makeover." *New York Times*. http://bits.blogs .nytimes.com/2013/09/10/intels-extensive-makeover.

————. 2013h. "Oracle and Salesforce: A Data Sharing Deal." *New York Times*. http:// bits.blogs.nytimes.com/2013/06/21/oracle-and-salesforce-a-data-sharing-deal.

————. 2013i. "Why Big Data Is Not Truth." *New York Times.* http://bits.blogs .nytimes.com/2013/06/01/why-big-data-is-not-truth.

Harpreet. 2013. "Huawei to Offer Cloud Storage to CERN." *Tools Journal.* www .toolsjournal.com/cloud-articles/item/1272-huawei-to-offer-cloud-storage -to-cern.

Harris, Derrick. 2013a. "Researchers Create Cloud-Based Brain for Robots." *Gigaom.* http://gigaom.com/2013/03/11/researchers-create-cloud-based -brain-for-robots.

————. 2013b. "We Need a Data Democracy, Not a Data Dictatorship." *Gigaom.* http://gigaom.com/2013/04/07/we-need-a-data-democracy -not-a-benevolent-data-dictatorship.

Hartzog, Woodrow, and Evan Selinger. 2013. "Obscurity: A Better Way to Think about Your Data Than 'Privacy.'" *Atlantic.* www.theatlantic.com /technology/archive/2013/01/obscurity-a-better-way-to-think-about-your -data-than-privacy/267283.

Hayles, N. Katherine. 1999. *How We Became Posthuman: Virtual Bodies in Cybernetics, Literature, and Informatics.* Chicago: University of Chicago Press.

Herndon, Thomas, Michael Ash, and Robert Pollin. 2013. "Does High Public Debt Consistently Stifle Economic Growth? A Critique of Reinhart and Rogoff." University of Massachusetts Amherst, Political Economy Research Institute. www.peri.umass.edu/236/hash/31e2ff374b6377b2ddec04deaa6388b1 /publication/566.

Hickey, Andrew R. 2012. "Verizon Relies on Cloud Services for Future Growth." *CRN.* www.crn.com/news/cloud/232500629/verizon-relies-on-cloud-services -for-future-growth.htm.

Hill, Kashmir. 2013. "Surprise Visitors Are Unwelcome at the NSA's Unfinished Utah Spy Center (Especially When They Take Photos)." *Forbes.* www.forbes .com/sites/kashmirhill/2013/03/04/nsa-utah-data-center-visit.

Hille, Katharin, and Daniel Thomas. 2013. "China Blames U.S. Hackers for Attacks." *Financial Times.* www.ft.com/intl/cms/s/0/8203676e-818f-11e2 -904c-00144feabdc0.html.

Hodson, Hal. 2013. "Crowdsourcing Grows Up as Online Workers Unite." *New Scientist.* www.newscientist.com/article/mg21729036.200-crowdsourcing -grows-up-as-online-workers-unite.html.

Hoover, J. Nicholas. 2012. "6 Ways Amazon Helped Obama Win." *InformationWeek.* www.informationweek.com/government/cloud-saas/6-ways -amazon-cloud-helped-obama-win/240142268.

————. 2013. "Military Plans Exabyte Storage Cloud." *InformationWeek.* www.informationweek.com/government/cloud-saas/military-plans-multi -exabyte-storage-clo/240152481.

Horn, Leslie. 2011. "Facebook Picks Sweden for First Data Center Outside U.S." *PC.* www.pcmag.com/article2/0,2817,2395378,00.asp.

Houlder, Vanessa. 2013. "Google Accused of Devious and Unethical Behaviour." *Financial Times.* www.ft.com/intl/cms/s/0/d1193b70-be2b-11e2-bb35 -00144feab7de.html.

Hunnius, Gerry, G. David Garson, and John Case, eds. 1973. *Workers' Control: A Reader on Labour and Social Change.* New York: Random.

Hunter, Andrea. 2011. *The Digital Humanities: Third Culture and Democratization of the Humanities.* PhD diss., Queen's University, Kingston, Ontario, Canada.

IBM. 2012a. "All in the Cloud." YouTube. www.youtube.com/watch?v=q_d7Io_rr2s.

———. 2012b. "IBM Advertisement." *New Yorker,* November 19, 23.

———. 2013. "IBM Advertisement." *New Yorker,* April 8, 11.

Investor's Business Daily. 2013. "Cloud Computing Users Are Losing Data, Symantec Finds." http://finance.yahoo.com/news/cloud-computing-users-losing-data -205500612.html.

Ipeirotis, Panos. 2013. "Mechanical Turk: Now with 40.92% Spam." *A Computer Scientist in a Business School.* www.behind-the-enemy-lines.com/2010/12 /mechanical-turk-now-with-4092-spam.html.

Isaacson, Walter. 2011. *Steve Jobs.* New York: Simon and Schuster.

Jacob, Rahul. 2013. "Better Workplaces Require Better Consumers." *Financial Times.* www.ft.com/intl/cms/s/0/94215ed0-97d6-11e2-b7ef-00144feabdc0.html.

Jenkins, Patrick. 2013. "HSBC Set to Cut Thousands of Jobs." *Financial Times.* www.ft.com/intl/cms/s/0/8d7afe12-8cd0-11e2-8ee0-00144feabdc0.html.

John, James. 2013. "Cloud Computing for Government Is Not Just a Cost Cutter." *Information Daily.* www.theinformationdaily.com/2013/02/01 /cloud-computing-for-government-is-not-just-a-cost-cutter.

Jokinen, Pekka, Pentti Malaska, and Jari Kaivo-oja. 1998. "The Environment in an 'Information Society': A Transition Stage towards More Sustainable Development?" *Futures* 30, no. 6: 485–498.

Kaminska, Izabella. 2013. "What Google Reader Tells Us about Banking and Nationalisation." *Financial Times.* http://ftalphaville.ft.com/2013/03/25/1438422 /what-google-reader-tells-us-about-banking-and-nationalisation.

Kanter, James. 2013. "European Regulators Fine Microsoft, Then Promise to Do Better." *New York Times.* www.nytimes.com/2013/03/07/technology/eu-fines -microsoft-over-browser.html.

Kelly, Kevin. 2002. "God Is the Machine." *Wired,* December, 180–185.

———. 2010. *What Technology Wants.* New York: Penguin.

Kenealy, Chris. 2013. "Five Different Ways to Sell Cloud Computing to Anyone." *Cloud Tweaks.* www.cloudtweaks.com/2013/03/five-different-ways-to -sell-cloud-computing-to-anyone.

Kepes, Ben. 2013. "A Nirvanix Post-Mortem—Why There's No Replacement for Due Diligence." *Forbes.* www.forbes.com/sites/benkepes/2013/09/28/a-nirvanix -post-mortem-why-theres-no-replacement-for-due-diligence.

Kerner, Sean Michael. 2013. "30 Years of TCP/IP Dominance Began with a Deadline." InternetNews.com. www.internetnews.com/blog/skerner/30-years-of-tcpip -dominance-began-with-a-deadline.html.

Kerr, Dara. 2012. "Microsoft to Google: You're Not 'Serious' about Business Apps." *CNET*. http://news.cnet.com/8301-1023_3-57561046-93/microsoft -to-google-youre-not-serious-about-business-apps.

———. 2013. "NASA Falls Short on Its Cloud Computing Security." *CNET*. http://news.cnet.com/8301-1009_3-57596053-83/nasa-falls-short-on-its -cloudcomputing-security.

Kirchgaessner, Stephanie. 2013. "Obama Patent Move Caps New Apple March on Washington." *Financial Times*. www.ft.com/intl/cms/s/0/b84f5a88-ff77 -11e2-b990-00144feab7de.html.

Kirilov, Kiril. 2011. "Cloud Computing Market Will Top $241 Billion in 2020." *Cloud Tweaks*. www.cloudtweaks.com/2011/04/cloud -computing-market-will-top-241-billion-in-2020.

Kisker, Holger. 2011. "10 Cloud Predictions for 2012." *Forrester*. http://blogs .forrester.com/holger_kisker/11-12-13-10_cloud_predictions_for_2012.

Ko, Carol. 2012. "How to Sell Cloud Computing to CIOs and CFOs." *Asia Cloud Forum*. www.asiacloudforum.com/content/how-sell-cloud-computing-cios-and-cfos.

Kolakowski, Nick. 2013. "Salesforce, HP Teaming Up to Sell 'Superpods.'" *Slashdot*. http://slashdot.org/topic/cloud/salesforce-hp-teaming-up-to-sell-superpods/.

Konczai, Mike. 2013. "Reinhart-Rogoff a Week Later: Why Does This Matter?" *Next New Deal*. www.nextnewdeal.net/rortybomb/reinhart-rogoff -week-later-why-does-matter.

Kreisberg, Jennifer Cobb. 1995. "A Globe, Clothing Itself with a Brain." *Wired*. www.wired.com/wired/archive/3.06/teilhard.html.

Krugman, Paul. 2010. "Notes on Rogoff (Wonkish)." *New York Times*. http:// krugman.blogs.nytimes.com/2010/07/21/notes-on-rogoff-wonkish.

———. 2013. "Is There Any Point to Economic Analysis?" *New York Times*. http:// krugman.blogs.nytimes.com/2010/07/21/notes-on-rogoff-wonkish.

Kudryashov, Roman. 2010. "Roland Barthes: Myth Today." *What Are These Ideas?* http://whataretheseideas.com/roland-barthes-myth-today.

Kurzweil, Ray. 2005. *The Singularity Is Near*. New York: Viking.

Lam, Lana. 2013. "Edward Snowden: U.S. Government Has Been Hacking Hong Kong and China for Years." *South China Morning Post*. www.scmp .com/news/hong-kong/article/1259508/edward-snowden-us-government -has-been-hacking-hong-kong-and-china.

Landa, Heinan. 2013. "Top 4 Myths of Cloud Computing." *TechFlash*. www .bizjournals.com/washington/blog/techflash/2013/01/top-4-myths-of-cloud -computing.html.

Langer, Art. 2013. "It's Not Just the Data, Stupid." *Wall Street Journal*. http:// mobile.blogs.wsj.com/cio/2013/02/19/its-not-just-the-data-stupid.

Lanier, Jaron. 2013. *Who Owns the Future?* New York: Simon and Schuster.

Latour, Bruno. 1999. *Pandora's Hope: Essays on the Reality of Science Studies.* Cambridge, MA: Harvard University Press.

Leach, Jim. 2011. "The Revolutionary Implications of the Digital Humanities." Speech to 5th Annual Conference of HASTAC, University of Michigan. National Endowment for the Humanities. www.neh.gov/about/chairman/speeches/the-civilizing-implications-the-digital-humanities.

Lee, Edmund. 2012. "Apple's iTunes Would Be One of World's Biggest Media Companies." *Techblog.* http://go.bloomberg.com/tech-blog/2012-12-03-apple%E2%80%99s-itunes-would-be-one-of-world%E2%80%99s-biggest-media-companies.

Lee, Justin. 2013a. "China Cloud Program to Invest $360B to More Than Double Data Center Capacity." *Web Host Industry Review.* www.thewhir.com/web-hosting-news/china-cloud-program-to-invest-360b-to-more-than-double-data-center-capacity.

———. 2013b. "Public Cloud Services Spending to Reach $47.4 Billion in 2013: IDC Report." *Web Host Industry Review.* www.thewhir.com/web-hosting-news/public-cloud-services-spending-to-reach-47-4b-in-2013-idc-report.

Lee, Timothy B. 2013. "These Tech Companies Are Spending Millions on High-Priced Lobbyists." *Washington Post.* www.washingtonpost.com/blogs/wonkblog/wp/2013/07/02/these-tech-companies-are-spending-millions-on-high-priced-lobbyists.

Lessin, Jessica E. 2012. "Google's Explainer-in-Chief Can't Explain Apple." *Wall Street Journal.* http://online.wsj.com/article/SB10001424127887323717004578159481472653460.html.

Lewin, Tamar. 2013. "Online Classes Fuel a Campus Debate." *New York Times.* www.nytimes.com/2013/06/20/education/online-classes-fuel-a-campus-debate.html.

Linthicum, David. 2012. "Cloud Computing in 2013: Two Warnings." *InfoWorld.* www.infoworld.com/d/cloud-computing/cloud-computing-in-2013-two-warnings-208759.

———. 2013a. "Everyone Has Heard of the Cloud, but Few Know What It Is." *InfoWorld.* www.infoworld.com/d/cloud-computing/everyone-has-heard-of-the-cloud-few-know-what-it-210818.

———. 2013b. "Hey, HR, Get Off My Cloud." *InfoWorld.* www.infoworld.com/d/cloud-computing/hey-hr-get-of-my-cloud-218413.

———. 2013c. "The Proof Is In: Amazon Fully Controls the Cloud." *InfoWorld.* www.infoworld.com/d/cloud-computing/the-proof-in-amazon-fully-controls-the-cloud-222641.

———. 2013d. "Thanks NSA, You're Killing the Cloud." *Cloud Computing.* www.infoworld.com/d/cloud-computing/thanks-nsa-youre-killing-the-cloud-220434.

———. 2013e. "What Will 'Cloud Computing' Mean in 10 Years?" *InfoWorld*. www.infoworld.com/d/cloud-computing/what-will-cloud-computing-mean -in-10-years-219497.

Liptak, Adam. 2013. "Justices Turn Back Challenge to Broader US Eavesdropping." *New York Times*. www.nytimes.com/2013/02/27/us/politics/supreme-court -rejects-challenge-to-fisa-surveillance-law.html.

Lohr, Steve. 2013a. "Big Data Sleuthing, 1960s Style." *New York Times*. http://bits .blogs.nytimes.com/2013/06/10/big-data-intelligence-sleuthing-1960s-style.

———. 2013b. "Big Data Trying to Build Better Workers." *New York Times*. www .nytimes.com/2013/04/21/technology/big-data-trying-to-build-better -workers.html.

———. 2013c. "McKinsey: The $33 Trillion Technology Advantage." *New York Times*. http://bits.blogs.nytimes.com/2013/05/22/mckinsey-the-33-trillion -technology-payoff.

Luce, Edward. 2013. "Data Intelligence Complex Is the Real Issue." *Financial Times*. www.ft.com/intl/cms/s/0/a1dd626c-cf80-11e2-be7b-00144feab7de.html.

Luckerson, Victor. 2013. "PRISM by the Numbers: A Guide to the Govern-ment's Secret Internet Data-Mining Program." *Time*. http://newsfeed.time .com/2013/06/06/prism-by-the-numbers-a-guide-to-the-governments-secret -internet-data-mining-program.

Lynch, Michael P. 2013. "Privacy and the Threat to the Self." *New York Times*. http://opinionator.blogs.nytimes.com/2013/06/22/privacy-and-the-threat -to-the-self.

MacIntyre, Alisdair. 1970. *Sociological Theory and Philosophical Analysis*. New York: Macmillan.

MacLeod, Ian. 2013. "Cloud E-data Law Puts Users at Risk; Canadians' Private Info Open to U.S. Eyes via Computing Service." *Ottawa Citizen*, February 2, A1.

Makower, Joel. 2012. "How Do You Measure the Cloud's Environmental Impact?" *GreenBiz.com*. www.greenbiz.com/blog/2012/04/14/how-do -you-measure-environmental-impact-cloud.

Manjoo, Farhad. 2013. "Facebook Follows You to the Supermarket." *Slate*. www .slate.com/articles/technology/technology/2013/03/facebook_advertisement _studies_their_ads_are_more_like_tv_ads_than_google.html.

Market Watch. 2013. "Cloud Security Alliance Warns Providers of 'The Notori-ous Nine' Cloud Computing Top Threats in 2013." www.marketwatch.com /story/cloud-security-alliance-warns-providers-of-the-notorious-nine-cloud -computing-top-threats-in-2013-2013-02-25.

Markoff, John. 2012. "Troves of Personal Data, Forbidden to Researchers." *New York Times*. www.nytimes.com/2012/05/22/science/big-data-troves-stay -forbidden-to-social-scientists.html.

Marlow, Iain. 2013. "Huawei Canada's Sean Yang." *Globe and Mail*. www .theglobeandmail.com/report-on-business/careers/careers-leadership/huawei -canadas-sean-yang-dismissing-suspicion-over-dim-sum/article6957873.

Marshall, Alex. 2013. "Should the Public or Private Sector Control Broadband?" *Government Technology*. http://m.benton.org/node/148781?utm_campaign=Newsletters&utm_source=sendgrid&utm_medium=email.

Marshall, Bob. 2012. "IBM's 'Smarter Planet' TV Campaign Gets a Makeover." *Agency Spy*. www.mediabistro.com/agencyspy/ibms-smarter-planet-tv-campaign-gets-a-makeover_b28274.

Marx, Leo. 1964. *The Machine in the Garden: Technology and the Pastoral Ideal in America*. New York: Oxford University Press.

Mathias, Craig. 2012. "The Huawei Controversy—The Rest of the Argument." *Nearpoints*. www.networkworld.com/community/blog/huawei-controversy-%E2%80%93-rest-argument.

Maxwell, Richard, and Toby Miller. 2012a. *Greening the Media*. New York: Oxford.

———. 2012b. "Greening Starts with Us." *New York Times*. www.nytimes.com/roomfordebate/2012/09/23/informations-environmental-cost/greening-starts-with-ourselves.

Mayer-Schönberger, Viktor, and Kenneth Cukier. 2013. *Big Data: A Revolution That Will Transform How We Live, Work, and Think*. New York: Houghton-Mifflin.

Mazzucato, Mariana. 2013. *The Entrepreneurial State: Debunking Public vs. Private Sector*. London: Anthem Press.

McCall, Jay. 2012. "Avoid the Cloud Services Piecemeal Trap." *Business Solutions*. www.bsminfo.com/blog/bsm-blog.

McCarthy, Bede. 2013. "Staff Undermines Cybersecurity Efforts." *Financial Times*. www.ft.com/intl/cms/s/0/01f936e6-a365-11e2-ac00-00144feabdc0.html.

McChesney, Robert W. 2013. *Digital Disconnect: How Capitalism Is Turning the Internet against Democracy*. New York: New Press.

McDuling, John. 2013. "Why Is the World's Biggest Seed Company Betting Nearly $1 Billion on a Big Data Startup?" *Quartz*. http://qz.com/130946/why-is-the-worlds-biggest-seed-company-betting-nearly-1-billion-on-a-big-data-startup/.

McFedries, Paul. 2012. *Cloud Computing: Beyond the Hype*. San Francisco: HP Press.

McKendrick, Joe. 2013a. "10 Quotes on Cloud Computing That Really Say It All." *Forbes*. www.forbes.com/sites/joemckendrick/2013/03/24/10-quotes-on-cloud-computing-that-really-say-it-all.

———. 2013b. "Cloud Computing Market May Become an Oligopoly of High Volume Vendors." *Forbes*. www.forbes.com/sites/joemckendrick/2013/07/11/cloud-computing-market-may-become-an-oligopoly-of-high-volume-vendors.

———. 2013c. "In the Rush to Cloud Computing, Here's One Question Not Enough People Are Asking." *Forbes*. www.forbes.com/sites/joemckendrick/2013/02/19/in-the-rush-to-cloud-computing-heres-one-question-not-enough-people-are-asking.

McKinsey & Company. 2013. "About Us." www.mckinsey.com/about_us.

McLuhan, Marshall. 1989. *The Global Village*. New York: Oxford University Press.

McMillan, Robert. 2013. "Cloud Computing Snafu Shares Private Data between Users." *Wired*. www.wired.com/wiredenterprise/2013/04/digitalocean.

Medina, Eden. 2011. *Cybernetic Revolutionaries: Technology and Politics in Allende's Chile.* Cambridge, MA: MIT Press.

Meehan, Chris. 2013. "Google's Project Loon Makes Cloud Computing a Reality with Solar-Power and Balloons." *Daily Fusion.* http://dailyfusion.net/2013/06 /googles-project-loon-makes-cloud-computing-a-reality-with-solar-power-and -balloons-12074.

Mell, Peter, and Timothy Grance. 2011. "The NIST Definition of Cloud Computing." National Institute of Standards and Technology, Information Technology Laboratory. www.csrc.nist.gov/publications/nistpubs/800-145/SP800-145.pdf.

Meyer, David. 2013. "Cisco's Gloomy Revenue Forecast Shows NSA Effect Starting to Hit Home." *Gigaom.* http://gigaom.com/2013/11/14/ciscos-gloomy -revenue-forecast-shows-nsa-effect-starting-to-hit/.

Miller, Claire Cain. 2011. "Amazon Cloud Failure Takes Down Web Sites." *New York Times.* http://bits.blogs.nytimes.com/2011/04/21/amazon-cloud -failure-takes-down-web-sites.

———. 2013. "Data Science: The Numbers of Our Lives." *New York Times.* www .nytimes.com/2013/04/14/education/edlife/universities-offer-courses-in-a -hot-new-field-data-science.html.

Miller, Claire Cain, and Quentin Hardy. 2013. "Google Elbows into the Cloud." *New York Times.* www.nytimes.com/2013/03/13/technology/google-takes -on-amazon-and-microsoft-for-cloud-computing-services.html.

Miller, Eden. 2002. "Designing Freedom, Regulating a Nation: Socialist Cybernetics in Allende's Chile." Working Paper #34, Program in Science, Technology, and Society, MIT, Cambridge, MA. http://web.mit.edu/sts/pubs/pdfs/MIT _STS_WorkingPaper_34_Miller.pdf.

Miller, Kathleen, and Chris Strohm. 2013. "IBM Wins Its Largest Cloud-Computing Contract." *Bloomberg.* www.bloomberg.com/news/2013-08-15/ibm-wins-its -largest-u-s-cloud-computing-contract.html.

Mills, Mark P. 2013. "The Cloud Begins with Coal: Big Data, Big Networks, Big Infrastructure, and Big Power." Digital Power Group. www.tech-pundit.com /wp-content/uploads/2013/07/Cloud_Begins_With_Coal.pdf.

Mims, Christopher. 2013. "Amazon Doesn't Reveal What It Makes on Cloud Computing, but Here's the Number, Anyway." *Quartz.* http://qz.com/78754/amazon -doesnt-reveal-what-it-makes-on-cloud-computing-but-heres-the-number -anyway.

Mishkin, Sarah. 2013. "Foxconn Admits Student Intern Labor Violations at China Plant." *Financial Times.* www.ft.com/intl/cms/s/0/88524304-319f-11e3 -817c-00144feab7de.html.

Mishkin, Sarah, Patti Waldmeir, and Katharin Hille. 2013. "Apple Supplier Faces Sanctions in China." *Financial Times.* www.ft.com/intl/cms/s/0/cafeb812 -7ce2-11e2-adb6-00144feabdc0.html.

Mitchell, David. 2004. *Cloud Atlas.* New York: Random House.

Moeller, Katy. 2013. "Taxes on Computing Irk Idaho Tech Businesses." *Idaho Statesman.* www.idahostatesman.com/2013/01/11/2408172/computing-tax -clouds-tech-economy.html.

Morozov, Evgeny. 2013a. "Open and Closed." *New York Times.* www.nytimes .com/2013/03/17/opinion/sunday/morozov-open-and-closed.html.

———. 2013b. *To Save Everything, Click Here: The Folly of Technological Solutionism.* New York: PublicAffairs.

Mosco, Vincent. 1982. *Pushbutton Fantasies: Videotex and Information Technology.* Norwood, NJ: Ablex.

———. 2004. *The Digital Sublime: Myth, Power, and Cyberspace.* Cambridge, MA: MIT Press.

———. 2009. *The Political Economy of Communication.* 2nd ed. London: Sage.

Mosco, Vincent, and Catherine McKercher. 2008. *The Laboring of Communication: Will Knowledge Workers of the World Unite?* Lanham, MD: Lexington Books.

Mosco, Vincent, Catherine McKercher, and Ursula Huws, eds. 2010. *Getting the Message: Communication and Global Value Chains.* London: Merlin.

Mosco, Vincent, and Elia Zureik. 1987. *Computers in the Workplace: Technological Change in the Telephone Industry.* Report for the Canadian Federal Department of Labour Technology Impact Research Fund.

Moses, Asher. 2012. "How the Internet Became a Closed Shop." *Sydney Morning Herald.* www.smh.com.au/technology/technology-news/how-the-internet -became-a-closed-shop-20121221-2brcp.html.

Moskowitz, Milton, and Robert Levering. 2013. "The 100 Best Companies to Work For." *Fortune,* February, 85–96.

Musil, Steven. 2012. "Foxconn Working Conditions Slammed by Workers' Rights Group." *CNET.* http://news.cnet.com/8301-13579_3-57444213-37/foxconn -working-conditions-slammed-by-workers-rights-group.

Nagel, David. 2013. "Cloud Computing to Make Up 35% of K–12 IT Budgets in 4 Years." *Journal.* http://thejournal.com/articles/2013/02/19/cloud-computing -to-make-up-35-of-k12-it-budgets-in-4-years.aspx.

National Institute of Standards and Technology (NIST). 2011. "US Government Cloud Computing Technology Roadmap: High Priority Requirements to Fur- ther USG Cloud Computing Adoption." www.nist.gov/itl/cloud/upload/SP _500_293_volumeI-2.pdf.

———. 2013. "NIST Cloud Computing Program." www.nist.gov/itl/cloud/.

National Science Foundation (NSF). 2012. "Report on Support for Cloud Comput- ing." www.nsf.gov/pubs/2012/nsf12040/nsf12040.pdf.

Naughton, John. 2013. "Digital Capitalism Produces Few Winners." *Guardian.* www.guardian.co.uk/technology/2013/feb/17/digital-capitalism-low-pay.

Neff, Gina. 2012. *Venture Labor.* Cambridge, MA: MIT Press.

Negroponte, Nicholas. 1995. *Being Digital.* New York: Knopf.

Nelson, D. Schwartz, and Charles Duhigg. 2013. "Apple's Web of Tax Shelters Saved It Billions, Panel Finds." *New York Times.* www.nytimes.com/2013

/05/21/business/apple-avoided-billions-in-taxes-congressional-panel-says
.html.

New York Times. 2013a. "Report: Deepening Ties between N.S.A. and Silicon Valley." http://bits.blogs.nytimes.com/2013/06/20/daily-report-the-deepening
-ties-between-the-n-s-a-and-silicon-valley.

———. 2013b. "Should Companies Tell Us When They Get Hacked?" www.nytimes
.com/roomfordebate/2013/02/21/should-companies-tell-us-when-they-get
-hacked.

Nextgov. 2013. "Pentagon Signs $5 Million Deal for Cyber Battleground." www
.nextgov.com/cybersecurity/2013/06/pentagon-signs-5-million-deal-cyber
-battleground/65594.

Noble, David. 1997. *The Religion of Technology: The Divinity of Man and the Spirit
of Invention.* New York: Knopf.

Novet, Jordan. 2013. "Long-Shot Distributed Data Center Project in Canada
Like SETI for Mobile." *Gigaom.* http://gigaom.com/2013/03/07/long
-shot-distributed-data-center-project-in-canada-like-seti-for-mobile.

Nye, David. 1990. *Electrifying America: Social Meanings of a New Technology,
1880–1940.* Cambridge, MA: MIT Press.

———. 1994. *American Technological Sublime.* Cambridge, MA: MIT Press.

O'Connor, Mark. 2013. "How to Regulate Cloud Computing." *Guardian.*
www.guardian.co.uk/media-network/media-network-blog/2013/mar/28
/regulation-cloud-computing-data-protection.

O'Connor, Sarah. 2013. "Amazon Unpacked." *Financial Times.* www.ft.com/intl
/cms/s/2/ed6a985c-70bd-11e2-85d0-00144feab49a.html.

O'Neill, Shane. 2011. "Forrester: Public Cloud Growth to Surge, Especially
SaaS." *CIO.* www.cio.com/article/680673/Forrester_Public_Cloud
_Growth_to_Surge_Especially_SaaS.

Ong, Josh. 2012. "Cloud Atlas: A Weather Forecast on the Chinese Cloud
Industry." *Next Web.* http://thenextweb.com/asia/2012/12/01/cloud-atlas
-the-state-of-the-chinese-cloud-industry.

Orenstein, Gary. 2010. "Selling the Infrastructure Cloud." *Gigaom.* http://gigaom
.com/2010/07/11/selling-the-infrastructure-cloud.

Osborne, Charlie. 2013. "Chinese Labor Group Alleges Worker Abuse by Apple
Supplier Pegatron." *ZDNet.* www.zdnet.com/chinese-labor-group-alleges
-worker-abuse-by-apple-supplier-pegatron-7000018660.

Page, Lewis. 2011. "DARPA Wants Weapons-Grade Military Cloud Computing."
Register. www.theregister.co.uk/2011/05/17/darpa_war_clouds.

Palmer, Maija. 2013a. "Cloud Computing Hinders Data Deletion." *Financial
Times.* www.ft.com/intl/cms/s/2/0e8aad72-7444-11e2-80a7-00144feabdc0
.html.

———. 2013b. "Data Mining Offers Rich Seam." *Financial Times.* www.ft.com/intl
/cms/s/2/61c4c378-60bd-11e2-a31a-00144feab49a.html.

Panattieri, Joe. 2012. "Top 100 Cloud Service Providers List 2012." *Talkin' Cloud*. http://talkincloud.com/%5Bprimary-term%5D/top-100-cloud-services-providers-list-2012-ranked-10-1.

Parkhill, Douglas F. 1966. *The Challenge of the Computer Utility*. Reading, MA: Addison-Wesley.

Parkman, Ralph. 1972. *The Cybernetic Society*. New York: Pergamon Press.

Parry, Marc. 2013. "'Big Data' Is Bunk, Obama Campaign's Tech Guru Tells University Leaders." *Chronicle of Higher Education*. http://chronicle.com/blogs/wiredcampus/big-data-is-bunk-obama-campaigns-tech-guru-tells-university-leaders/47885.

Parsons, John J. 2013. "The Unutterable Name." *Hebrew Names of God*. www.hebrew4christians.com/Names_of_G-d/YHVH/yhvh.html.

Pellow, David, and Lisa Sun-Hee Park. 2002. *The Silicon Valley of Dreams*. New York: New York University Press.

People's Daily Online. 2013. "Tencent to Build Chongqing Cloud Computing Center." http://english.peopledaily.com.cn/90778/8294842.html.

Perkins, Tara. 2013. "Should Data Centers Have a Canadian Address?" *Globe and Mail*. www.theglobeandmail.com/report-on-business/industry-news/property-report/should-data-centres-have-a-canadian-address/article13224735.

Perlin, Ross. 2011. *Intern Nation: How to Earn Nothing and Learn Little in the Brave New Economy*. New York: Verso.

Perlroth, Nicole, and Quentin Hardy. 2013. "Bank Hacking Was the Work of Iranians, Officials Say." *New York Times*. www.nytimes.com/2013/01/09/technology/online-banking-attacks-were-work-of-iran-us-officials-say.html.

Perlroth, Nicole, David E. Sanger, and Michael S. Schmidt. 2013. "As Hacking against U.S. Rises, Experts Try to Pin Down Motive." *New York Times*. www.nytimes.com/2013/03/04/us/us-weighs-risks-and-motives-of-hacking-by-china-or-iran.html.

Perrow, Charles. 1999. *Normal Accidents: Living with High-Risk Technologies*. Princeton, NJ: Princeton University Press.

Pew Research Center. 2013. *The State of the News Media: 2013*. Project for Excellence in Journalism. http://stateofthemedia.org.

Pilling, David. 2013. "America Cedes Moral High Ground on Cyber-Spying." *Financial Times*. www.ft.com/intl/cms/s/0/0a11deea-d831-11e2-9495-00144feab7de.html.

Poe, Emily. 2013. "Google's Bad Case of the Flu." *Fierce CIO*. www.fiercecio.com/story/googles-bad-case-flu/2013-02-15.

Pogue, David. 2013. "Photoshop's New Rental Program and the Outrage Factor." *New York Times*. http://pogue.blogs.nytimes.com/2013/07/05/photoshops-new-rental-program-and-the-outrage-factor.

Porat, Marc Uri. 1977. *The Information Economy: Definition and Measurement.* Office of Telecommunications Special Publication 77-12, May. Washington, DC: US Department of Commerce.

Powell, Rob. 2013. "Pacnet Has Big Plans for China." *Telecomasia.net.* www .telecomasia.net/content/pacnet-has-big-plans-china.

Pretor-Pinney, Gavin. 2011. *The Cloud Collectors Handbook.* London: Hodder.

Qian, Zhao. 2013. "China's Cloud Computing Chain Ready." *People's Daily Online.* http://english.peopledaily.com.cn/90778/8273069.html.

Qing, Liau Yun. 2013. "China's Cloud Deployment Dampened by Nascent Enterprise Demand." *ZDNet.* www.zdnet.com/cn/chinas-cloud-deployment-dampened -by-nascent-enterprise-demand-7000012662.

Quinn, Michelle. 2013. "Samsung's Lobbying Grows with Its Market Share." *Politico.* www.politico.com/story/2013/01/samsungs-lobbying-grows-with -its-market-share-86784.html.

Rachman, Gideon. 2013. "A Conspiracy of Reasonable People." *Financial Times.* www.ft.com/intl/cms/s/0/6e78755a-693d-11e2-b254-00144feab49a .html.

Ragland, Leigh Ann, Joseph McReynolds, Matthew Southerland, and James Mulvenon. 2013. *Red Cloud Rising: Cloud Computing in China.* Vienna, VA: Center for Intelligence Research and Analysis. http://origin.www .uscc.gov/sites/default/files/Research/Red%20Cloud%20Rising_Cloud %20Computing%20in%20China.pdf.

Raimondo, Justin. 2013. "The Great Cyber-Warfare Scam." Antiwar.com. http:// original.antiwar.com/justin/2013/02/19/the-great-cyber-warfare-scam.

Rampell, Catherine. 2010. "They Did Their Homework (800 Years of It)." *New York Times.* www.nytimes.com/2010/07/04/business/economy/04econ.html.

Rao, Leena. 2009. "McKinsey's Cloud Computing Report Is Partly Cloudy." *TechCrunch.* http://techcrunch.com/2009/04/16/mckinseys-cloud -computing-report-is-partly-cloudy.

———. 2010. "Google Spent $1.34 Million on Lobbying in Q2, Up 41 Percent from Last Year." *TechCrunch.* http://techcrunch.com/2010/07/21/google -spent-1-34-million-on-lobbying-in-q2-up-41-percent-from-last-year.

"The Reasons Why Amazon Mechanical Turk No Longer Accepts International Turkers." 2013. Tips for Requesters on Mechanical Turk. http://turkrequesters .blogspot.ca/2013/01/the-reasons-why-amazon-mechanical-turk.html.

Regalado, Antonio. 2011. "Who Coined 'Cloud Computing'?" *MIT Technology Review.* www.technologyreview.com/news/425970/who-coined-cloud-computing.

Reid, Stefan, and Holger Kisker. 2011. *Sizing the Cloud.* Cambridge, MA: Forrester.

Reinhart, Carmen M., and Kenneth S. Rogoff. 2010. "Growth in a Time of Debt." Working Paper 15639, National Bureau of Economic Research, Cambridge, MA. www.nber.org/papers/w15639.pdf.

Reuters. 2013a. "Huawei Springs Back with 33% Rise in Net Profit." *New York Times.* www.nytimes.com/2013/01/22/technology/huawei-springs-back-with-33-rise-in-net-profit.html.

———. 2013b. "Survey Details Data Theft Concerns for U.S. Firms in China." *New York Times.* www.nytimes.com/2013/03/30/business/global/survey-details-data-theft-concerns-for-us-firms-in-china.html.

Revken, Andrew C. 2012. "Exploring the Roots of an Emerging Planet-Spanning 'Mind.'" *New York Times.* http://dotearth.blogs.nytimes.com/2012/12/26/exploring-the-roots-of-an-emerging-planet-spanning-mind.

Ribeiro, John. 2013. "Microsoft's Azure Service Hit by Expired SSL Certificate." *PCWorld.* www.pcworld.idg.com.au/article/454609/microsoft_azure_service_hit_by_expired_ssl_certificate.

Rivlin, Gary. 2004. "The Tech Lobby, Calling Again." *New York Times.* www.nytimes.com/2004/07/25/business/the-tech-lobby-calling-again.html.

Robinson, Duncan. 2013. "Tech Trends Increase Cybercrime Threat." *Financial Times.* www.ft.com/intl/cms/s/0/806d7d72-7d16-11e2-adb6-00144feabdc0.html.

Roeder, Ethan. 2012. "I Am Not Big Brother." *New York Times.* www.nytimes.com/2012/12/06/opinion/i-am-not-big-brother.html.

Rogers, Mike, and C. A. Dutch Ruppersberger. 2012. "Investigative Report on the U.S. National Security Issues Posed by Chinese Telecommunications Companies Huawei and ZTE." US House of Representatives, Permanent Select Committee on Intelligence. http://intelligence.house.gov/sites/intelligence.house.gov/files/documents/Huawei-ZTE%20Investigative%20Report%20%28FINAL%29.pdf.

Romm, Tony. 2013a. "How Google Beat the Feds." *Politico.* www.politico.com/story/2013/01/how-google-beat-the-feds-85743.html.

———. 2013b. "Twitter's Hacker Problem." *Politico.* www.politico.com/story/2013/04/twitter-ap-hacking-problem-90510.html.

Roose, Kevin. 2013. "Up, Up, and Away!" *New York Magazine.* http://nymag.com/news/features/draper-university-silicon-valley-2013-8.

Ross, Christopher. 2012. "Keep Your Heads in the Cloud." *Corbus.* www.corbus.com/blog/2012/01/06/keep-your-heads-in-the-cloud/.

Ross, Duncan. 2012. "Turn Your Analytical Skills into a Public Good." *Causes.* www.causes.com/actions/1694321-turn-your-analytical-skills-into-a-public-good.

RTT News. 2013. "Is Your Private Life Safe under Cloud Computing?" www.rttnews.com/2044231/is-your-private-life-safe-under-cloud-computing.aspx.

Sachs, Jeffrey. 2013. "Professor Krugman and Crude Keynesianism." *Huffington Post Canada.* http://blogs.ft.com/the-a-list/2012/07/12/move-americas-economic-debate-out-of-its-time-warp.

Sadowski, Jathan. 2013. "Why Does Privacy Matter? One Scholar's Answer." *Atlantic.* www.theatlantic.com/technology/archive/2013/02/why-does-privacy-matter-one-scholars-answer/273521.

Sanger, David E., David Barboza, and Nicole Perlroth. 2013. "Chinese Army Is Seen as Tied to Hacking Attack against U.S." *New York Times*. www.nytimes.com/2013/02 /19/technology/chinas-army-is-seen-as-tied-to-hacking-against-us.html.

Sayare, Scott. 2012. "On the Farms of France, the Death of a Pixelated Workhorse." *New York Times*. www.nytimes.com/2012/06/28/world/europe/after-3 -decades-in-france-minitels-days-are-numbered.html.

Schiller. Dan. 1981. *Telematics and Government*. Norwood, NJ: Ablex.

———. 2014. *Digital Depression: The Crisis of Digital Capitalism*. Urbana: University of Illinois Press.

Schmidt, Eric, and Jared Cohen. 2013. *The New Digital Age: Reshaping the Future of People, Nations, Business*. New York: Knopf.

Schuman, Michael. 2013. "Marx's Revenge: How Class Struggle Is Shaping the World." *Time*. http://business.time.com/2013/03/25/marxs-revenge-how -class-struggle-is-shaping-the-world.

Schwarz, Ariel. 2013. "How Maps Can Change the World." *Fast Company*. www .fastcoexist.com/1681766/how-maps-can-change-the-world.

Schwarz, Matthew J. 2013. "Microsoft Hacked: Joins Apple, Facebook, Twitter." *InformationWeek Security*. www.informationweek.com/security/attacks /microsoft-hacked-joins apple-facebook-tw/240149323.

Scott, A. O. 2012. "Spielbergian, on a Budget." *New York Times*. www.nytimes .com/2012/12/30/movies/awardsseason/beasts-of-the-southern-wild-shares -something-with-lincoln.html.

Sengupta, Semini. 2013. "The Pentagon as Silicon Valley's Incubator." *New York Times*. www.nytimes.com/2013/08/23/technology/the-pentagon-as-start -up-incubator.html.

Shannon, Claude E., and Warren Weaver. 1949. *The Mathematical Theory of Communication*. Urbana: University of Illinois Press.

Shaw, Robert. 2013. "A Quick Guide for Cloud Companies That Don't Understand Marketing." *Cloud Tweaks*. www.cloudtweaks.com/2013/01/a-quick-guide -for-cloud-companies-that-dont-understand-marketing.

Sherr, Ian, and Don Clark. 2013. "H-P's New Servers Will Cut Power Use." *Wall Street Journal*. http://online.wsj.com/article/SB10001424127887324504704 578410643910775254.html.

Shields, Greg. 2013. "How to Beat a Cloud Skeptic: Four Steps towards Rationalizing the Great Cloud Debate." *InfoWorld*. http://resources.infoworld.com/ccd /show/200014814/006365700798971FWGC2RZTF220.

Silver, Nate. 2012. *The Signal and the Noise*. New York: Penguin.

Silverman, Gary. 2013. "Digital Intelligence and Dumb Terrorists." *Financial Times*. www.ft.com/intl/cms/s/0/800d3268-d8d4-11e2-84fa-00144feab7de .html.

Silverman, Rachel Emma. 2013. "Tracking Sensors Invade the Workplace." *Wall Street Journal*. http://online.wsj.com/article/SB10001424127887324034804 578344303429080678.html.

Singer, Natasha. 2012. "A Vault for Taking Charge of Your Online Life." *New York Times.* www.nytimes.com/2012/12/09/business/company-envisions-vaults -for-personal-data.html.

———. 2013. "When Your Data Wanders in Places You've Never Been." *New York Times.* www.nytimes.com/2013/04/28/technology/personal-data-takes-a-winding -path-into-marketers-hands.html.

Singh, Gurjeet. 2013. "The Big Data World Is Operating at 1 Percent." *Gigaom.* http://gigaom.com/2013/03/10/the-big-data-world-is-operating-at-1-percent.

SmartData Collective. 2013. "Cloud Computing Use Increases among Supply Chains." http://smartdatacollective.com/onlinetech/99516/cloud-computing -use-increases-among-supply-chains.

Smith, Eve. 2013. "Aristophanes' Cloudcuckooland to Terry Pratchett's Discworld: Comedy as Social Conscience." *Comedy Studies* 4, no. 1: 23–33.

Smith, Zadie. 2012. "Some Notes on Attunement." *New Yorker*, December 17, 30–35.

Solman, Paul. 2013. "Web Oils the Wheels of Progress." *Financial Times.* www.ft .com/intl/cms/s/0/002d4e10-ad8d-11e2-82b8-00144feabdc0.html.

Solnit, Rebecca. 2010. *A Paradise Built in Hell: The Extraordinary Communities That Arise in Disaster.* New York: Penguin.

Soto, Onell R. 2011. "Big Desert Solar Farm Means Big Factory in S.D." *U-T San Diego.* www.utsandiego.com/news/2011/mar/10/big-desert-solar-farm -means-big-factory-in-san-die.

Sprint. 2013. "iPhone 5 'I Am Unlimited: Picture Perfect' Commercial." YouTube. www.youtube.com/watch?v=C9qxjBlL3ko.

Spufford, Francis. 2010. *Red Plenty.* London: Faber and Faber.

Stapleton, Jay. 2013. "Cloud Computing Trend Raises Ethical Issues." *Connecticut Law Tribune.* www.ctlawtribune.com/PubArticleCT.jsp ?id =1202609066339&Cloud_Computing_Trend_Raises_Ethical_Issues_ &slreturn=20130608132308.

Steadman, Ian. 2013. "Big Data and the Death of the Theorist." *Wired.* www.wired .co.uk/news/archive/2013-01-25/big-data-end-of-theory.

Steel, Emily. 2012a. "Data Scientists Take Bite Out of Mad Men." *Financial Times.* www.ft.com/intl/cms/s/2/db8d250e-4279-11e2-979e-00144feabdc0 .html.

———. 2012b. "TV Companies in Digital Ad Fightback." *Financial Times.* www .ft.com/intl/cms/s/0/bd47e5fc-4bb6-11e2-b821-00144feab49a.html.

Stewart, James B. 2013. "Looking for a Lesson in Google's Perks." *New York Times.* www.nytimes.com/2013/03/16/business/at-google-a-place-to-work-and-play .html.

Stoller, Jonathan. 2012. "Why Cold Canada Is Becoming a Hot Spot for Data Cen-tres." *Globe and Mail.* www.theglobeandmail.com/report-on-business/economy /canada-competes/why-cold-canada-is-becoming-a-hot-spot-for-data-centres /article6598555.

Streitfeld, David. 2013. "As Competition Wanes, Amazon Cuts Back Discounts." *New York Times.* www.nytimes.com/2013/07/05/business/as-competition -wanes-amazon-cuts-back-its-discounts.html.

Sunyer, John. 2013. "Big Data Meets the Bard." *Financial Times.* www.ft.com/intl /cms/s/2/fb67c556-d36e-11e2-b3ff-00144feab7de.html.

Sutter, John D. 2011. "iCloud: Revolution or the Next MobileMe?" *CNN Tech.* www .cnn.com/2011/TECH/web/06/07/icloud.reaction/index.html.

Swinhoe, Dan. 2013. "Green IT." *IDG Connect.* www.idgconnect.com/blog -abstract/743/dan-swinhoe-asia-green-it-asia.

Szoldra, Paul. 2013. "Google: If You Use Gmail, You 'Have No Expectation of Privacy.'" *Business Insider Australia.* www.businessinsider.com.au/gmail -privacy-google-court-brief-2013-8.

Takahashi, Dean. 2013. "It's Crowded in Here: CES Attendance Tops 150,000." *VB.* http://venturebeat.com/2013/01/12/its-crowded-in-here -ces-attendance-tops-150000.

Talbot, Chris. 2013. "Cloud Outages: Power Loss Blamed as Main Cause." *Talkin' Cloud.* http://talkincloud.com/cloud-computing-research/cloud-outages -power-loss-blamed-main-cause.

Talib, Nasim. 2012. *Antifragile: Things That Gain from Disorder.* New York: Random House.

Tanaka, Edward Tessen. 2012. "The NSA and Military Cloud Computing: Just Painting a Cyber Bullseye for Attackers?" *Pateixia.* www.patexia.com/feed /the-nsa-and-military-cloud-computing-just-painting-a-cyber-bullseye-for -attackers-2401.

Tang, Han. 2013. "China's Young Workers Fight Back at Foxconn." *Labor Notes.* www.labornotes.org/2013/08/china%E2%80%99s-young -workers-fight-back-foxconn.

Taylor, Paul. 2013a. "Cloud Computing Industry Could Lose Up to $35 Bn on NSA Disclosures." *Financial Times.* www.ft.com/intl/cms/s/0/9f02b396 -fdf0-11e2-a5b1-00144feabdc0.html.

———. 2013b. "Hesse Puts Sprint Back among Frontrunners." *Financial Times.* www.ft.com/intl/cms/s/0/0fe039f4-56b1-11e2-aad0-00144feab49a.html.

Teilhard de Chardin, Pierre. 1961. *The Phenomenon of Man.* New York: Harper Torchbooks.

Tett, Gillian. 2013. "Break a Wall of Silence on Cyber Attacks." *Financial Times.* www.ft.com/intl/cms/s/0/d5b2464e-6648-11e2-b967-00144feab49a.html.

Thibodeau, Patrick. 2013. "Cloud Computing's Big Debt to NASA." *Computerworld.* www.computerworld.com/s/article/9237439/Cloud_computing _s_big_debt_to_NASA.

Thiel, Tamiko. 2012. "'Clouding Green' @ Zero1 Biennial." Mission-Base. http:// mission-base.com/tamiko/AR/clouding-green.html.

Thomas, Daniel. 2013. "Baidu Nets France Telecom Browser Deal." *Financial Times*. www.ft.com/intl/cms/s/0/07812948-5d92-11e2-ba99-00144feab49a .html.

Tilahun, Gelila, Andrey Feuerverger, and Michael Gervers. 2012. "Dating Medieval English Charters." *Annals of Applied Statistics* 6, no. 4: 1615–1640.

Tunstall, Jeremy. 1986. *Communications Deregulation: The Unleashing of America's Communications Industry*. New York: Blackwell.

Turk, James. 2013. "Outsourcing to Google: A Bad Deal for York Academic Staff." Presentation to York University Academic Staff. Canadian Association of University Teachers. www.yufa.ca/wp-content/uploads/2013/02/2013.02 -Google-YUFA-final.pptx.

Tydeman, John, Hubert Lipinski, Richard P. Adler, Michael Nyhan, and Laurence Zwimpfer. 1982. *Teletext and Videotex in the United States*. New York: McGraw-Hill. www.ft.com/intl/cms/s/0/07812948-5d92-11e2-ba99-00144feab49a .html.

Udell, Jon. 2012. "Is It Time to Mandate Cloud Storage Preservation?" *Wired*. www .wired.com/insights/2013/01/guaranty-associations-cloud-storage.

U.S. National Endowment for the Humanities, Office of the Digital Humanities. 2013. "Digital Humanities Start-Up Grants." www.neh.gov/grants/odh/digital -humanities-start-grants.

U.S. Office of Science and Technology Policy. 2012. "Obama Administration Unveils 'Big Data' Initiative: Announces $200 Million in New R&D Investments." White House. www.whitehouse.gov/sites/default/files/microsites/ostp /big_data_press_release.pdf.

Vega, Tanzina. 2013. "Two Ad Giants Chasing Google in Merger Deal." *New York Times*. www.nytimes.com/2013/07/29/business/media/two-ad-giants-in -merger-deal-chasing-google.html.

Verizon Wireless. 2013. "Verizon Powerful Answers—'Suddenly: 60' Commercial." YouTube. https://www.youtube.com/watch?v=xpuoN6S3Efk.

Vina, Gonzalo, and Simon Kennedy. 2013. "Finance Chiefs Endorse Cuts as Reinhart-Rogoff Challenged." *Bloomberg*. www.bloomberg.com/news/2013 -04-19/finance-chiefs-endorse-cuts-as-reinhart-rogoff-challenged.html.

Wainewright, Phil. 2013. "Cloud Providers Working with Big Data." *ZDNet*. www .zdnet.com/cloud-providers-working-with-big-data-7000013521.

Waldrop, M. Mitchell. 2002. *The Dream Machine: J.C.R. Licklider and the Revolution That Made Computing Personal*. New York: Penguin.

Walker, Michael. 2013. "Data Science Is a Team Sport." *Data Science Central*. www .datasciencecentral.com/profiles/blogs/data-science-is-a-team-sport.

Wallsten, Peter, Jia Lin Yang, and Craig Timberg. 2013. "Facebook Flexes Political Muscle with Immigration Bill." *Washington Post*. www.washingtonpost.com /business/economy/facebook-flexes-political-muscle-with-carve-out-in -immigration-bill/2013/04/16/138f718e-a5e7-11e2-8302-3c7e0ea97057 _story.html.

"The Warhol: Silver Clouds." 2010. www.warhol.org/uploadedFiles/Warhol_Site /Warhol/Content/Exhibitions_Programs/Exhibitions/EX_20100903_TE _SilverClouds.pdf.

Warren, Tom. 2010. "Microsoft Shows Off Its 'Cloud Power' with New Advertising Campaign." *WinRumors*. www.winrumors.com/microsoft-shows-off -its-cloud-power-with-new-advertising-campaign.

Waters, Richard. 2012. "Oracle Takes to Cloud with Buying Spree." *Financial Times*. www.ft.com/intl/cms/s/0/73a7facc-5043-11e2-805c-00144feab49a.html.

———. 2013a. "Big Intelligence to Tackle Cyberthreats." *Financial Times*. www.ft .com/intl/cms/s/0/87ed6bc8-8105-11e2-9fae-00144feabdc0.html.

———. 2013b. "Google Search Proves to Be New Word in Stock Market Prediction." *Financial Times*. www.ft.com/intl/cms/s/0/e5d959b8-acf2-11e2-b27f -00144feabdc0.html.

———. 2013c. "IBM Looks beyond the IT Department for Fresh Growth." *Financial Times*. www.ft.com/intl/cms/s/0/9ecf5a64-d8cf-11e2-a6cf-00144feab7de .html.

———. 2013d. "Inside Business: Cloud Hangs over Old Guard of Business Software." *Financial Times*. www.ft.com/intl/cms/s/0/33099ad8-b7e6-11e2 -bd62-00144feabdc0.html.

Wegener, Al. 2013. "Big Data Plumbing Problems Hinder Cloud Computing." *Electronic Design*. http://electronicdesign.com/communications/big-data -plumbing-problems-hinder-cloud-computing.

Weisinger, Dick. 2013. "Cloud Computing: Skills Gap Threatens Technology Boom?" *Formtex Blog*. www.formtek.com/blog/?p=3541.

Whittaker, Zack. 2012. "Samsung Hikes Apple Chip Prices by 20 Percent." *ZDNet*. www.zdnet.com/samsung-hikes-apple-chip-prices-by-20-percent-report -7000007254.

Wiener, Norbert. 1948. *Cybernetics; or, Control and Communication in the Animal and the Beast*. New York: Wiley.

———. 1950. *The Human Use of Human Beings*. Boston: Houghton Mifflin.

Wiles, Will. 2012. "Before Fruit Ninja, Cybernetics." *New York Times*. www.nytimes .com/2012/11/30/opinion/the-no-10-dashboard-and-cybernetics.html.

Wilhelm, Alex. 2012. "Microsoft's Cloud Vision." *Next Web*. http://thenextweb .com/microsoft/2012/12/13/microsofts-cloud-vision-how-azure-is-the -linchpin-to-the-firms-new-devices-and-services-corporate-strategy.

Wilson, James, and Barney Jopson. 2013. "Amazon Hit by Old World Strike Action." *Financial Times*. www.ft.com/intl/cms/s/0/e4d3bdde-bc82-11e2 -9519-00144feab7de.html.

Wilson, Karin. 2012. "Avoid Failure When Marketing Cloud Computing." *Cloud Computing Journal*. http://cloudcomputing.sys-con.com/node/2307497.

Wilson, Valerie Plame, and Joe Wilson. 2013. "The NSA's Metastasised Intelligence-Industrial Complex Is Ripe for Abuse." *Guardian*. www.guardian.co.uk /commentisfree/2013/jun/23/nsa-intelligence-industrial-complex-abuse.

Wingfield, Nick, and Melissa Eddy. 2013. "In Germany, Union Culture Clashes with Amazon's Labor Practices." *New York Times.* www.nytimes.com/2013/08/05/business/workers-of-amazon-divergent.html.

Winner, Langdon. 2004. "Resistance Is Futile: The Posthuman Condition and Its Advocates." In *Is Human Nature Obsolete?* edited by Harold Bailie and Timothy Casey, 385–411. Cambridge, MA: MIT Press.

Winslow, George. 2013. "The Measurement Mess." *Broadcasting and Cable.* www.broadcastingcable.com/article/494609-The_Measurement_Mess.php.

Wise, Bill. 2013. "Big Data's Usability Problem." *All Things D.* http://allthingsd.com/20130423/big-datas-usability-problem.

Wojtakiak, Mark. 2012. "Tag Archives: Deloitte Cloud Computing Forecast Change." *Storage Effect.* http://storageeffect.media.seagate.com/tag/deloitte-cloud-computing-forecast-change.

Wolf, Gary. 2010. "The Data-Driven Life." *New York Times.* www.nytimes.com/2010/05/02/magazine/02self-measurement-t.html.

Wolonick, Josh. 2012. "Are Apple and Google in Race for North Carolina's 'Black Gold'?" *Minyanville.* www.minyanville.com/sectors/technology/articles/Are-Apple-and-Google-in-Race/12/7/2012/id/46453.

Woodall, Angela. 2013. "Amazon Files Court Complaint over CIA Cloud Contract." *CRN.* www.crn.com/news/cloud/240158953/amazon-files-court-complaint-over-cia-cloud-contract.htm.

World Economic Forum. 2013. "The World Economic Forum Leadership Team." www.weforum.org/content/leadership-team.

Wortham, Jenna. 2013. "Cisco Plans to Cut 4,000 Jobs as It Posts Profit Gain." *New York Times.* www.nytimes.com/2013/08/15/technology/cisco-plans-to-cut-4000-jobs-as-it-posts-profit-gain.html.

Wyatt, Edward, and Claire Cain Miller. 2013. "Tech Giants Issue Call for Limits on Government Surveillance of Users." *New York Times.* www.nytimes.com/2013/12/09/technology/tech-giants-issue-call-for-limits-on-government-surveillance-of-users.html.

Yafang, Sun. 2012. "Foreword." In *The Global Information Technology Report 2012,* edited by Soumitra Dutta and Beñat Bilbao-Osorio, ix–x. Geneva: World Economic Forum.

Yang, Lin. 2013. "Foxconn Tries to Move Past the iPhone." *New York Times.* www.nytimes.com/2013/05/07/business/global/foxconn-tries-to-move-beyond-apples-shadow.html.

Zhu, Julie. 2013. "Lanfang: China's Cloud Computing Hub." *Financial Times.* http://blogs.ft.com/beyond-brics/2013/05/15/langfang-chinas-cloud-computing-hub.

INDEX

About the Author

Vincent Mosco (PhD, Harvard University) is Professor Emeritus of Sociology at Queen's University, where he held the Canada Research Chair in Communication and Society. Dr. Mosco is the author of numerous books and articles on the media and information technology, including *The Political Economy of Communication* and *The Digital Sublime: Myth, Power, and Cyberspace.*

34 95

Received

FEB 23 16

Mission College Library